Three artful creations of nature and man, all products of the pearl-bearing mollusk. The bird was carved from mother-of-pearl from an abolone shell by the Mexican silversmiths, Los Castillos of Taxco. The pearls, clasped by a diamond around its neck, were probably brought up by divers from the Persian Gulf; they were once owned by the Duchess of Sutherland, lady-in-waiting to Queen Alexandra of England in 1900, but were sold to an American in 1916 for $750,000; they are still being worn but are now worth only about one-tenth that price. The triple-strand necklace, clasped by a star, is of cultured pearls about 8 mm in size, grown in Japan about seven years ago and sold for $1,000 then. Notice the slightly greater iridescence of the natural pearls and the more nearly perfect shape of the cultured ones.

Color Photograph by Dominick Pasquerella; pearl collection made by the author.

The Book of
PEARLS

Their History and Romance
from Antiquity to Modern Times

JOAN YOUNGER DICKINSON

BONANZA BOOKS · NEW YORK

These are my pearls:

Beverly,

Theresa,

Rosalind,

and Diana

Contents

Introduction

No jewel has captured the human imagination as vividly as has the pearl. It is the most feminine and therefore the most sympathetic of all jewels. The soft glow of the pearl's luster and the translucency of its skin complement the beauty of the wearer. Although intrinsically merely a small bead, nature has endowed it with such fabulously beautiful qualities that throughout history the pearl has been worn not only by crowned heads but by appreciative women the world over.

Internationally, the pearl is so sought out that today, wherever planes fly, pearls fly with them. The huge markets in America and Europe find their counterparts in India and Hong Kong, and wherever there is a jewelry store, however modest, women will be buying—and wearing—pearls and pearl necklaces.

The discovery of a method of producing cultured pearls has revolutionized the pearling industry, at the same time furnishing a livelihood for literally thousands of workers in Japan and creating a new worldwide trade. We can be equally grateful for the courage of the South Sea diver and the devoted toil of the Japanese farmer that has given us these beautiful, mysterious pearls. Thanks must also be given to the skilled jewel merchants and designers everywhere who have provided the women of the world with new and often startling pieces of pearl jewelry.

I have spent my lifetime with pearls: as a merchant, a purchaser, and, more recently, a producer at Turtlehead Bay, in Australia. Even after such a lifelong attachment to pearls, I find that this book on pearls by Joan Dickinson excites me tremendously. Obviously she has thoroughly researched every aspect of the history of pearling and the growth of the great pearl industry. What has resulted is an authentic and highly colorful story of the pearl. The many illustrations in the book splendidly show the amazing wealth of variety the pearl possesses as well as the creative art of jewelers of all periods. The historical pearl pieces shown here are mostly of very great value; the more modern pieces are more modest, in keeping with the aim of the pearl industry today to provide beautiful gems at all prices.

I heartily recommend this book to all those who love beautiful jewelry, and especially to the connoisseur and those who deal in pearls.

JOHN M. JERWOOD

Tokyo, Japan
March 1968

The bone of the gods turned into pearls, that, animated dwells in the waters.

This do I fasten upon thee unto life, luster, strength, longevity, unto a life lasting a hundred autumns.

May the amulet of the pearl protect thee!

Hymn sung when the Hindus indoctrinated young Brahmin disciples and gave them pearl and pearl shell amulets.

1

The Role of the Pearl in the Shell Cult of Antiquity

The growth of civilization followed the lines of distribution of pearl beds, gold-fields . . .
W. J. PERRY, *The Growth of Civilization,* London, 1924

*T*hirty-five hundred years before the birth of Christ, and possibly more, when the men of western Europe were clad in the skins of animals and housed in caves and nests of leaves, there were civilized people of the East who knew and prized the beauty and charm of the pearl. Indeed, it was to them the most precious of the gifts of the gods, a shining, tranquil symbol of the moon—of life-giving unity, of radiant harmony and immortal perfection.

The other substances which we think of now as equally or more precious—gold, diamonds, iron, and more recently their synthetics—came into use later as symbols of divine grace and/or worldly power. In the beginning, before gold had been polished and diamonds cut, among the people who lived by the sea, the pearl was the central object in a great cult of worship, the cult of the shells.

Echoes of this cult come whispering down to us on the winds of time and tradition; the pearl is still valued as a symbol of chastity, modesty, tranquillity, and a gem of natural beauty. We can now control its development, copy its round radiance and sport it, or something like it, in profusion but only the careless or reckless take it for granted—it is still to all thoughtful men something extraordinary, a gift of mystery and complexity.

It is not surprising then that in the beginning the pearl provoked great awe. To a degree all natural things did. The first great religion was a simple worship of the major forces of nature—the earth, water, fire, and air—and the powers that controlled them, the moon and the sun. The central point was the marriage between the sky and the earth; this was where the action took place, and the action was creation, not only of man, but of trees, fish, animals, fruits and grains, and their spirits.

The first deity worshipped is believed to have been the moon, the special ruler of the sea and the rain and the menses of women, the earth mother. The waxing and waning of the moon—and the "face" within it—were early a recognizable touchstone to the passage of time. A child was a few moons old—an old man had seen countless moons. The tides that buffeted the beaches and tossed up shells, fish, and stones were under the moon's power, and by watching the moon in its phases, the tides could be calculated. As the air cooled the night and the moon rose, the rains came; clearly they too were under control of the moon, as was sleep, knitting up the raveled sleeve of care, and so it was inevitable that the moon-god became the god who brought the rains—did not the frog croak to it for water?—and thus fertility. Inland, when it was discovered that the earth could be cultivated and grains could be made to grow, perhaps the sun became a great god first. But along the sea where the kelp and the fish provided all the nourishment man needed, where the sea presented him with shells and stones prepolished for his shelter and his tools, and the heavens lay open to his sight as a guide, the moon was the greater god, the stars were the moon-god's court, and the things in the waters were the god's manifestations.

By what right of science do we say this was so? The cult of the shells is difficult to study. Its relics are more fragile than those of the earth, not only because water is destructive as well as productive but because shells themselves return to dust before gold and diamonds do. Coastlines have changed, rivers have shifted, whole towns have sunk into the sea, whole harbors silted over even in our time.

In the millennia before Christ, there were many mysteries which may never be unlocked, but there is enough tangible evidence of moon-worship, the cult of the shells, and the eminence of the pearl to give proof of its certain existence in some ancient early cities, and enough links to suggest to the intuitive the meaning and power it held in many other places.

It probably began in the east, but came to us through the Red Sea, that slit of water that connects the Mediterranean with the Arabian Sea and thus also connects the Atlantic and Pacific oceans, Europe and Asia and America. Although the Red Sea—so called because of the color of its algae and its coral reefs—is difficult to navigate because of its swirling, salty waters and has few coves because of its volcanic origin, it has served men since the most ancient times as a waterway for the trading of goods, ideas, and beliefs. Until the Suez Canal was built by the British in the last century, it was controlled by the Egyptians; in the time of which we are now speaking, the third millennium before Christ, it was the great link between the ancient civilizations of the Greek islands of Minos and Crete, Egypt itself, Sumer and Assyria, and southern India. We are used to thinking of civilization as having begun with agriculture because, we declare, it was agriculture that first permitted men to stop hunting for food like other animals and settle down to a social and political life, but we tend to forget that fishing, and particularly group fishing, provided the same kind of base for the men who lived by the sea and the rivers. From the beginnings of man there must have been societies of fishermen. Certainly early men used the water as a god-given pathway of civilization, sailing out on logs tied together with grasses, or tree trunks hollowed out by knives of flint, or burned out by fire, and guided by the stars and the wind. Even before the time of the pyramids—roughly 3000 B.C.—the Red Sea boats were capable of carrying huge numbers of people and cargoes of stone. They are pictured in the old Sumerian records, simple in design—canoe or raft in type—but in ornament extraordinarily handsome, stained and painted to look alive, some with great eyes on the sides of their prows and scales on their sterns. It was thought that possibly such paintings (forerunners of the later figure-heads) would press life upon the ship; to further advance this belief the painted eyes were often stuck with cowrie shells or brightly colored stones.

Great skill and faith were demanded of the ancient skippers of these ships; they learned geometry the better to plot their courses by the stars—the Dog Star Sirius, ever constant, was a favorite guide; they cast oil upon the waters to smooth them, they blew conch trumpets to ward off demons, and they hijacked slaves to row, punt, and raise their clumsy canvas sails. They also needed courage and daring; unless we can believe—and I can't —that identical practices, similar beliefs, related hierarchies of gods, modes of worship, and general know-how sprang up independently in widely separated groups of men in far-flung parts of the world, we have to grant that these early skippers linked them together; that ships braved great distances and somehow succeeded in conquering great oceans, the Pacific and the Atlantic, millennia before the European explorers were written into Western histories.

The fish-god of Vishnu was believed to have brought the Word to the Hindus from the depths of the sea where it had been hidden in a shell, like a pearl, by the Deity.

TRUMPET-SHELLS.

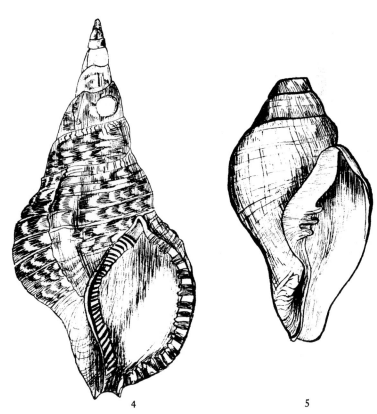

(1) *Murex trunculus*, L. $\frac{1}{2}$.
(2) *Purpura hæmastoma.* Lam. $\frac{1}{2}$.
(3) *Murex branderis*, L. $\frac{1}{2}$ (after Reeve).
(4) *Triton tritonis*, L. $\frac{1}{8}$, showing blow-hole on side of spire.
(5) *Turbinella pyrum*, L. (the Chank), $\frac{1}{2}$, showing blow-hole at apex of spire.

(From drawings by Mrs. Wilfrid Jackson.)

Five sacred conch shells; the one in the center top produced the royal purple dye; the large one, bottom left, was the Triton shell blown (see hole) to ward off evil spirits or call the gods. The one at bottom right is the Indian chank which was also a trumpet shell.

Is this hard to believe? It is little more than a century ago that we still thought the splendors of the Nile, of Tyre and Babylon, were but an exaggerated dream; modern study has proved them real. Since the first finds of the curious, we have come upon the ruins and graves of the civilizations of India and rebuilt the ancient glories of the Central American peoples. Moreover, as the hieroglyphics have been deciphered and the paintings on pottery and observatories read, we have had to face the fact that history does not, after all, show us man moving forward inexorably and delightfully toward better and better modes of social organization and culture of which we moderns are the peak, but instead, that man has had great cultural and technological ups and downs, successes and failures. Many of the ancients knew how to count, write, read, and philosophize. They ritualized marriage, studied medicine, performed operations, irrigated their lands, cremated their dead, and though their machines were few (so far as we know), they created buildings and gardens as magnificent as any known today. Their art was sensitive and revelatory, their jewelry, clothing, and cosmetics had meaning as well as use, and their great theocratic governments were wise in the ways of peace as well as in war.

There were probably two worlds then, in the beginning of man's time; the world of the inland peoples, sometimes isolated from one another, sometimes connected by river valleys, and the world of the seafarers, certainly connected by the seas to one another, and in some places connected by river to the inland people. It is hard to date them; inland China was reportedly civilized when England was sheep-grazing land; certainly southern India was, so were Sumeria, Assyria, and Egypt. Since we know the pyramids were built about 3000 B.C., this is the date usually chosen as the beginning of man's civilization. But new finds and new studies suggest there were older cultures; written history in Sumeria goes back to 4000 B.C., and the myths of the Dravidians of southern India predate these records and show connections between the two countries.

The pottery, paintings, friezes, and early religious epics have revealed to us much of what we know about this period called ancient history, and, sometimes, prehistory. Because these artifacts are man-made, they hold a particular significance. But before the alphabet, arithmetic, and even language were written on baked clay or papyrus, there were natural objects that were used as symbols of belief and value, and as a means of communication, recording, and trading. They were things like sticks, birch bark, stones, fire, and shells, and the most important of these to the sea peoples of the very ancient times, the people who shared a worldwide diffusion of culture thousands of years ago, were shells, and especially certain shells.

In this early one-world of seafarers and fishermen, three shells and three shell products stand out as symbols in the great religion of the elements: the cowrie, the snail, and the conch chank; the shellfish purple, the pearl shell, and the pearl.

This importance was distinct from their food content or their beauty, although it may be related animistically to their shape. To us, the pearl is the most important of these, but we shall review the others first, in part because their stories have charm but chiefly because understanding of them is vital to the role the pearl played.

The smallest and most widely used shell was the cowrie shell, a strange slitted shell with a sturdy, varicolored exterior. Cowries—some say because of their resemblance to the female pudenda—were thought to have the power of creating life, and were thus a special shell of women, worn on girdles, and given as dowries to aid in fertility. But they were not confined to the women's world; they were also pasted on ships (as we noted earlier), to bring them life, stuck in the eyes of mummies, and buried in graves with the dead, perhaps to nourish the eyes of the spirit, perhaps to resuscitate the body into new life. Inevitably, as life-givers, they had value; before gold was found, cowries were money, good-luck charms, amulets to ward off the evil eye, and tokens in games of chance. Rates of value were drawn up, storage places built, and the shells were sought across the seas "far and wide and often at great peril." They are still in use as money in isolated places today.

The snail shell was equally esteemed as a parent of life but its different characteristics gave it a separate role. It was only vaguely thought of as a female parent; it was too fragile to be used as money, or even to be worn, but since its spiral was more easily portrayed than the curves of the cowrie, it seems to have been used as a symbol of a cowrie. Rare is the frieze of a temple to the moon or rain god without it; even today it can be seen on those pillars of government which are derived architecturally from the Ionians of Greece. Is it perhaps also a part of our alphabet? The hieroglyphics of the ancient Babylonians suggest their alphabet was set first in the sand with fish bones; is it too fanciful to think that the C the Egyptians used early in the predynastic period, the spiral C which stood first for 100, and which we use for cent, century, percent, and like words, was a snail shell?

The third shell of importance was the conch shell, known in India as the chank. Like the cowrie and the snail, it too was seen as a bringer of life, but not of worldly life, but spiritual, symbol-life—the Word—the Sacred Law. Perhaps this was due to its shape; it looks somewhat like a mouth. Perhaps it was because, when held to the ear, the voice of the sea

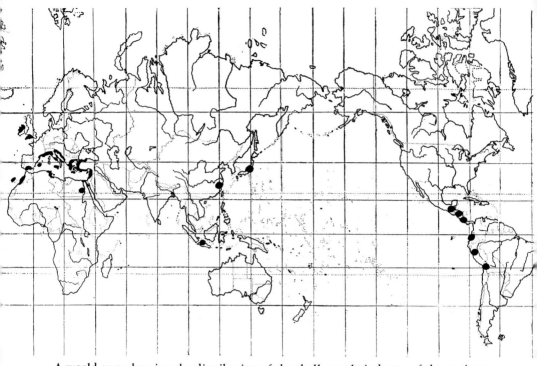

A world map showing the distribution of the shell purple industry of the ancient period; this dye, made from juice from shellfish, produced the royal purple color that early royalty wore to indicate their divine origins.

A map showing the distribution of pearls and pearl shell in early history. The round dots indicate freshwater pearls; the black dots, marine pearls. The maps were drawn at the University of Manchester in England.

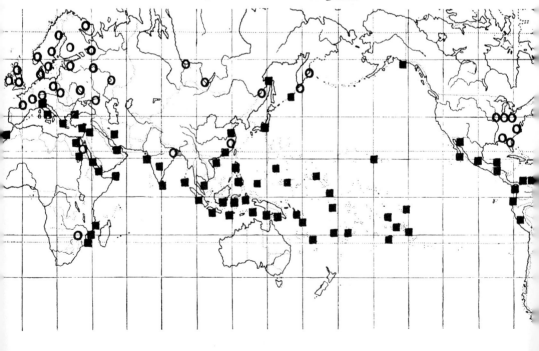

god murmured through it. For whatever reason, it was held to be the mouthpiece of the gods, and thus the dispenser of knowledge and guidance.

As a sacred object the conch served chiefly as a trumpet to enlarge the god's voice, and it was blown to still the waves, chase off demons, or summon worshippers. We know it best as the shell-trumpet of Triton, the assistant to Neptune, god of the sea in the Homeric legends, but it was also used in India, in Tibet and China, in Egypt, and among the prehistoric Zapotecs and Mayans of the Central Americas in similar rites. In some parts of India it is still used to call the worshippers of Vishnu to the temple; in Crete it is used today by shepherds as we might use a siren, to call for help; it was still employed as a call for rain in Mexico when the Spanish conquered the Aztecs in 1515. In the earliest of the written legends of ancient India, the conch was the place where The Word was kept by the great Deity. Vishnu in his first incarnation was a fish which dove into the sea to rescue it, even as Moses, the earthling, climbed a mountain to get the Ten Commandments from God on tablets of stone.

Did the natural perforations of the abalone conch first suggest to human man that his tongue and his ear should be pierced the better to receive the god's voice? The great archaeological scholar of England, Sir Elliot Smith, thought it highly likely, noting that the earliest earrings are of this shell's nacre, mother-of-pearl. Earrings may have begun as a yearning for an omnipresent connection—a sacred pipeline—with the gods, or the motivation may have been more mystical, reflecting a desire to be like the god-shell. In early ceremonies in Minos, India, and Mexico, when the priests of the moon or rain gods wished to make sacrifices to propitiate the gods, shell trumpets were blown and the people pierced their ears and their tongues until the blood ran. "This linking together of ear piercing and the use of shell-trumpets is of considerable significance," wrote J. Wilfrid Jackson, the Manchester (England) Museum authority, in his book on the ancient use of shells the world over.

The shell product which to my mind is final proof that early man navigated the oceans of the world is the juice of the shell known as the murex. In its natural state this juice is cream-colored; mixed with salt and boiled, it slowly becomes a dye of rich red-purple—the royal purple not only of the earliest times but of the present. Is it possible that early men could have found this juice, worked out a method of making it turn purple, and viewed the result as sacred, separately around the world? Surely these early peoples communicated with one another, and most probably they traded; near the great Phoenician cities of Tyre and Sidon enormous collections of crushed and broken dye-bearing shells have been found. Tyre, legend has it, was

famous for its dye and for the bad smell of its chief industry. The Phoenicians, however, were only traders, and even where the shell was not found
in nature, the purple dye was used, and research reveals that this occurred
both where the Phoenicians established branch factories, so to speak, on
other shores, and where they didn't. The process was expensive; it took 200
to 300 pounds of shellfish juice to dye 50 pounds of wool, as well as three
to five days of steeping. The rewards, however, were great, for its value
was high. To be without it was to be a peasant or a slave. The dyestuff was
used for the clothing of kings, and when defeated or when humbling themselves they were forced to "rend the purple," that is, to sacrifice their
claim to divine sanction. As late as the Roman period, the purple cloth
brought a thousand dinars a pound, a price comparable to $300 today.

How did this value become established? In some mysterious way the
purple linked the gods and man through the sea serpent, the masculine
symbol of creativeness and fertility, in early legends in India. In the early
paintings this serpent is red-purple. In modern times we have viewed this
symbol as phallic; it is the precursor of the serpent who brought worldli-
ness, and with it, sin, to the Garden of Eden, but in the earlier legends, the
power of creating life with which it was bestowed was honored and even
worshipped. Was it because the ancients believed that only the gods
granted this power? It is possible to read our own legend of creation this
way—that it was the assumption on Adam's part that man could decide for
himself when or when not to procreate that was sinful, that the evil of
disobedience was not the action itself, but the use of it in times not of God's
choosing, that it was rape (not sexual congress) that was evil.

The wearing and displaying of the purple has signified wealth and
power for centuries, and it is still found in context. There are modern
echoes of it in the robes of Queen Elizabeth II of England and the wall
hangings of palaces, cathedrals, and opera houses.

But even when the cult of the shells was the great medium of belief
and knowledge, the shellfish purple was no more important than the two
naturally beautiful shell products, mother-of-pearl and pearl. Indeed, the
pearl was the most important, for while the stories of it are similar to that
of the shellfish purple, they suggest that the pearl has always been renowned for a characteristic unique among gems: it came from the Creator-
God to the sea worshippers in shining, tranquil perfection and unity
out of the shell of the humblest of God's creatures. It suggested that
there was always a prayer of life even in the wildest ocean, that in the low-
liest and most battered of living things some protective hand worked to
keep beauty and integrity alive. The pearl was believed to be guarded in

the watery depths by dragons, or sea dogs, but capable of appearing in the most unlikely places, in a frog's forehead, for instance. It was at once new life and the promise of life everlasting. It was at once male and female like the oyster that cradled it. The serpent-dragon purple was a symbol of masculine fertility; the cowrie and snail shells, of female fertility. The pearl which they guarded between them was something akin to man's life, given by the Creator-God, truly royal, truly sacred. When perfect—round, flawless, and of great luster—it was itself sometimes worshipped, but as a prime gift *from* the gods, it was, like life itself, worthy to be the finest gift *to* the gods. Among the ancients who believed in the cult of the shells, none gave the sea pearl second place. It was the symbol of symbols: It was the moon-substance.

I like to think it was the Dravidians of southern India who were the first men to know pearls, even as they were the first to know diamonds, and that it was they who introduced them into the Red Sea civilizations. We do not know a great deal about these men; we know more about the northern Hindus than we do of these men of Tamil land, cut off as they were from the north by mountains and forest. But we do know that the Hindus, to whom the Greeks and the Arabs owed such a cultural debt, in turn owed a debt to the Dravidians. When the northern culture was still in its early stages, southern India, which together with Ceylon and Malaya, made up Tamil land, was a major power. A single huge cemetery—114 acres—testifies to the ancient position of the Dravidian capital port of Korkai and to its thriving, prosperous populace of seafarers and fishermen who traded their catch of pearls, cowries, and chanks from the Gulf of Manaar with the peoples of Sumeria and Egypt at least 3,000 years before Christ and possibly more. It is a queer cemetery, raising almost as many questions as it answers; it consists of row upon row of pottery jugs filled with ashes, surrounded by huge stones, and laid down at a time when other civilizations were burying (rather than cremating) their dead. Moreover, here and there among the ancient megaliths and the pottery have been found bronze bowls and plates. How did they get there? India had no Bronze Age; it went from stone to iron and to iron processes not unlike our steel-making. The bronze relics suggest that the Phoenicians were once here, but when and why we can only guess. Some argue they may have founded this great old pearl fishery, even as later they founded Carthage, but other scholars suggest that perhaps, instead, they and the Jews to whom they were related, came from here. If they did, then our culture, our monotheism, our symbols, and our skills had their shadowy origins here in Tamil land.

There is evidence for this in the writings of the Greek historians. Herodotus wrote that the Phoenicians had told him they were twenty-eight centuries old and came from beyond the Persian Gulf. Clearchus of Soli stated flatly that the Jews were descended from the philosophers of India and that Aristotle had told him of his great debt to them. Megasthenes, the Greek who lived in India in the third century before Christ, wrote: "All the opinions expressed by the ancients about nature are found with the philosophers foreign to Greece, with the Brahmins of India, and in Syria with those who are called Jews." The Brahmins, in turn, were known to have learned from the wise men of Tamil land; their philosophy predated that of the Hindus, and the luxury, refinement, and riches of the great capital of Korkai astonished and influenced the Brahmins when they came to study there early in their history.

There is other evidence concerning the Phoenician-Jewish relationship in the work of the modern scholar Immanuel Velikovsky, the student of ancient history who correlated the existence of the volcanoes, the earthquakes, and the plagues of the Bible with Egyptian histories. His controversial work (because of his redating) on the ancient period before Christ sheds a different light not only on the chronology of the exodus of the Jews from Egypt but also on their origins and their tribal ties with the Phoenicians. Whoever the men of Tamil land were, the shells of the sea and the pearls they produced were very early beloved objects of both symbolic value and worldly reward, bringing not only awe-filled delight but education to the people who knew them. Wars were fought for them, and prayers were said for them, gods were worshipped and devils were imagined. In the early days, Ceylon, Malaya, and Madras were all part of Tamil land, as was the Deccan plateau to the north. Ceylon and Malaya became known for spices and precious woods, Madras for cottons and the purple, the Deccan plateau for gold and diamonds. Korkai alone lived by pearls and the conch chank. But it was Korkai that was the city most renowned for its learning and riches. Even if it were not the place where knowledge of the great Creator-God first developed, it would appear that it was here that the cult of shells began.

Opposite

Krishna—the incarnation on earth of the god Vishnu—wore pearls into battle to ensure himself long life. Here he is seen dancing on a snake—symbolizing evil—he has just subdued in a river. The girls on right (also in pearls) are part of the snake's kingdom; they are begging for mercy. *Courtesy, The Metropolitan Museum of Art, Rogers Fund, 1927.*

Pearl fishing in the Red Sea was done by slaves at nightfall; the pharaohs of Egypt and their wives wore pearls for religious reasons, although they worshipped the sun god, or gold.

Persian Gulf pearl diver; the knife was used to rip the pearl oysters from the rocks they adhered to; the framework was a lowering device necessary because of the depth of the beds.

A VIEW of the PEARL-FISHERY.

This is probably a romanticized view of a pearl fishery in Ceylon; note the children of the slaves, the one woman (in the tent), the piles of oyster shells, and the arrogant manner of the fishery owners.

We can see from the early Dravidian legend of creation—a legend as splendid in its way as our own legend of the garden of paradise—how closely the pearl was associated with the heart, with love, gentleness, and compassion. It is told in that legend that in the beginning the great deity created the four elements—air, fire, earth, and water—and in their joy of life each gave a gift to the god. The air gave a rainbow to halo his head, the fire, a meteor to light his way, the earth a ruby to shine from his forehead, and water a pearl to soothe his heart. Similarly, in the later Hindu legends, the pearl was associated with Krishna the Adorable, the eighth incarnation of the great god Vishnu, who discovered it when he drew it from the depths of the sea as a gift for his daughter on her wedding day.

One poem from the great classic period of Tamil land, about 1000 to 800 B.C., illustrates the great spiritual reaches of this civilization and its kinship with our own. While the Egyptians were still preoccupied with idolatry, before the rise of Socrates and Plato, before the birth of Christ, the men of Tamil land were concerned with a religion based on love.

> Loveless natures, cold and hard
> Live for self alone
> Hearts where love abides regard
> Self as scarce their own.

> Where the body hath a soul
> Love has gone before
> Where no love infills the whole
> Dust it is, no more.

What has this to do with the pearl? It is possible that, as generally assumed, the pearl may have been known in Sumeria and Assyria as early as it was in Tamil land but, if so, it is curious that Sumerian legends do not concern themselves with its meaning. The pearl fisheries of the Persian Gulf, where the Tigris and Euphrates rivers empty, are of great antiquity indeed, but when they began remains a mystery, for no archaeological research has been done at the fishing sites. It is possible they were not worked in the very beginning; the oyster beds are not as readily accessible here as they are in the Gulf of Manaar, and research has revealed that in the early centuries these great people were occupied with building a series of dams, locks, and canals to hold back the powerful river water to protect themselves from floods. Ancient coins show the Sumerians were trading with the Dravidians at least as early as 3000 B.C. and that their earliest religion was at one with the great worldwide religion of the period, the worship of the gods of the elements. Was this communicated to them from India? We know the Sumerians had a sort of calendar and kept excellent commercial and historic records on clay tablets which are still readable but it may be significant that no legend of creation has been found, only a legend that the sea god brought them their primary knowledge, that is, The Word, even as Vishnu the sea god brought it to the Hindus.

There is evidence that the cowrie, mother-of-pearl shell, and the shell purple were valued here, and there is one painting, from early Babylon, that shows priests wearing strings of pearls around their necks. They were probably prayer beads. Some scholars hold that the lack of pearl relics is due to the moist saltpeter soil of the area, which might have caused any buried pearls to decay. Mother-of-pearl is used in the friezes, and one inscription suggests that pearls were valued—and it is a notation of import: A line on the obelisk at Nineveh states that the kings of Chaldea brought gold, precious stones, and pearls in tribute. It is quite possible that pearls were both sacred and rare here in early times. Were they taboo? It is thought that the island of Dilmun where the pearls came from was the Paradise island of the Babylonians.

The Egyptian civilization has been shown to have been clearly influenced by, if not born of, the Sumerian and Assyrian civilizations, although the Egyptian development was, in time, far more glorious and its kingdom of the gods far more complexly organized.

The most striking fact about the Egyptian civilization is, of course, its intense preoccupation with immortality. Egypt's worldly achievements were many but they seem to have sprung from a strong faith in the possibility of life everlasting and a great yearning to achieve it. The all but incredible pyramids tell us this, and so do the mysterious processes of mummification and the elaborate death rituals. In this effort, as in many, the sun god, Ra, was seen as more important than the moon god, the earth more important than the sea. Possibly this emphasis was derived from the Sumerians, for the Sumerians also thought highly of the sun god; possibly it was an inevitable outcome of Egypt's geographical position and the importance placed on agriculture. In any event, belief in the sun god as all-powerful brought different jewels into prominence. The Sumerians (who had silver mines but had to import gold) used silver for their jewelry and worked it with dedication and skill; the Egyptians, who had to import both, preferred gold.

Both are, of course, earth metals, although both can be seen to have heavenly connections since both are, when polished, shiny. Indeed, gold was reputed to be gilded personally by the sunny hand of Ra.

More pearls appear in Egyptian history than in Sumerian and Assyrian, however. Did they carry meaning? The gold breastplates of the pharaohs and their families were studded with pearls. Was this mere ornament? I would think this was a garment both practically and mystically protective. It would appear to me that it is related to another piece of wearing apparel which the archaeologists have pedantically dubbed "the pectoral pendant." This consists of a chunk of mother-of-pearl bored at each end and then strung around the neck on leather or hemp. Unlike the breastplate, it could have no practical use as armor; it must have had mystical

This pearl necklace of a Persian princess of about the fourth century B.C. was found in the ruins of the Winter Palace at Shushan (or Susa) by archaeologists in 1901 and is now in the Louvre Museum in Paris. It consists of 72 pearls strung intricately with gold and is a fine example of the ancient Eastern use of pearls and gold as mystic symbols or prayer beads.

significance, and if so, the coincidence of pearl in each suggests that pearl was the protector of life. These pearl-shell pectoral pendants have been found all over the world in ancient graves and burial grounds and are even among the relics of the North American Indians.

Mother-of-pearl was also prized in Egypt. It has been found studding the friezes of religious and government buildings and cut into chunks and strung as necklaces with carnelians. The carnelian is a desert stone; its connection with mother-of-pearl suggests a prayer for water upon the sands, life in the desert, a prayer to the moon as rain-bringer.

Was it the women of ancient Sumer and Egypt who kept the images of the moon god and the pearl alive? We can find indications of this in the fertility dances and rituals that took place when the moon was full and, more subtly, in feminine cosmetics. For instance, in the tomb of Queen Bhab of Sumer, a gilded shell and a gold spoon in a gold carrying case were found buried beside her. Although male scholars refer to this find as a "vanity" case, it is likely that just as poetry began as prayers, and jewelry as religious amulets, cosmetics began as symbols of religious devotion. Certainly the powder the Queen put in her gilded dish was ground-up shell and the whiteness she desired was that of the pearl and the moon. It must be more than a coincidence that the eye pencil and paint that the Egyptain women used fell in the same symbolic category, for the black kohl used to outline the eyes was made of ground-up small pearls from the Red Sea, moistened with olive oil. There is no ancient painting of an Egyptian princess without this dark etching of the eyes with pearl dust. Surely there is some connection between this and the placing of pearls and shells on the closed eyelids of the dead, as was often done in places where the moon was worshipped.

It is also held by Velikovsky that the Queen of Sheba who visited Solomon was most probably Queen Hatsheput of Egypt, who made a pilgrimage to an unnamed king of great repute. In the records of her voyage it says that the prize gifts she took to her king consisted of "precious woods and pearls."

You can read the love story of Solomon and his queen and the gifts these two great ones exchanged in the terse words of the Bible, in II Chronicles 9, I Kings 10 (where only "precious stones" are mentioned) and, if you think Hatsheput may be Solomon's love, you can compare it with her story on the frieze of her magnificent temple at Thebes. Her gifts were so many, so rich, and so beautiful that it was declared that "never was seen the like since the world was"—that in short, all the gifts were "marvels."

During the horrors of the Egyptian plagues, the volcanoes and the earthquakes and the deaths, the Jews vowed to place wisdom—God's wisdom—above all riches, and they sought God in their ancestral Holy Land. Once there, they continued worshipping the one God of wisdom, but feeling both chosen by God and blessed with peace under King Solomon the Wise, they began again to value riches, and their luxuries became renowned. Queen Hatsheput of Egypt was also a peace-loving ruler of wisdom and of great riches, and although she was a worshipper of Ra, she felt impelled by inner voices to visit a great king and to revere his Creator-God. The name of that king was not recorded but, like the meeting related by Solomon, it was a splendid meeting. From the inscriptions on her temple we know she came back full of reverence; from Solomon we have the Song of Songs, those great lyric poems that reveal the heights of his love for an unnamed woman of greatness.

The gifts Hatsheput exchanged with her king are listed in pictures on the beautiful temple of Deir el Bahari—literally The Most Splendid of Splendors—interwoven with a commentary on her response to them. She was enchanted by the rare trees, the perfumes and incenses, the strange animals and slaves, and the rich gems, and she took them all to be signs that her king's wisdom and blessedness were greater than her own, and that his God was the true God. The list of these "marvels" is remarkably like those listed by the Bible of Solomon's love-idyll.

Her conversion is stated in the inscribed verses and further emphasized (in my mind) by the marked change in her appearance when she returned. She went bearing pearls and wearing kohl dust on her eyelids; she returned with her face "shining like the stars" because it was "gilded with electrum." Electrum was the alloy of gold and silver which the Jews and the Phoenicians considered precious; did she paint her face with it as an amulet or as a dramatic display of the belief that all gods were as one, that the sun god and the moon god were united in the one God the Father?

It is possible, but not provable. The religious reforms that Hatsheput initiated in her new-found wisdom and the era of good feeling between Egypt and Jerusalem that she encouraged during the latter part of her reign did not survive her death. Her successor, and some say he was the offspring of her mysterious royal lover, stormed the Holy Land and carried Solomon's treasures back to Karnak and dedicated them to the sun god's idol, Amon. The full story is yet to be told in detail; biblical scholars do not accept these theories. The symbols of pearl and electrum played a role in Hatsheput's conversion, but we only conjecture what role Solomon's attitudes played in this.

Seeking more exact evidence of the cult of the shells in this period of changing systems of belief, we turn now to Persia, and the influence this once-great country had on the Mediterranean cultures and, through them, on our own. Pearl scholars do not agree on a great many things, but one thing they all note is that soon after the Persian conquest in the fourth century B.C. of Greece, Egypt, and Mesopotamia, pearls came into conspicuous popularity in these countries, and when the Romans in turn conquered the Persian citadel of Alexandria in 48 B.C., pearl-wearing became a veritable frenzy.

Most historians, however, have treated this sudden upsurge in the pearl's popularity as if the pearl was just super-booty, an Oriental luxury with no more meaning than a fine roll of silk or a carved dagger. I think this is an oversight, due in part to the fact that we can find no references to pearls in the extant fragments of ancient Persian literature, and in part to careless study of the few pieces of early Persian pearl jewelry the archaeologists have found.

In order really to scrutinize these pieces through Persian eyes, it is first necessary to understand sympathetically the connections between the ancient Persian religion and the ancient religion of India.

The early great Persian religion of Zarathustra was closer to the monotheism of the East than to the polytheism and idolatry then current in Greece and Egypt. Stated briefly, the prophet Zarathustra knew only one god, the great creator God of Light, Knowledge, and Love, Mazda. The gods of the elements, which Mazda created, were his helpers and a part of his being —his eyes, his breath, his inner fire. His enemy was the devil. For centuries Zarathustra and his laws were honored and the laws of the one god were followed. But because Zarathustra also preached freedom of choice—that is, that each individual was free to choose between the God of Light and the Devil of Darkness—the releases from duty began in time to outrun the controls. By the time of the conquest, religious regulations were in disarray; barbaric practices were rampant and, what is most important in this study, the power and privileges of the priest-elite were thoroughly undermined. In terms of such objects of worship as pearls and the rituals of which they were a part, this meant that no amulets, no symbols, were sacred to the priests or the kings but were allowed to all men and, surprisingly, in view of what happened to women in Persia later, all women.

This democratization did not necessarily mean, however, that these symbols lost their religious character. It is probable that they didn't; they kept it at least in part. But it is not easy to see that they did in the diffusion and confusion, in the multiplicity of deviance from the sacred rituals. Only when the Persian pearl jewelry is examined empathetically, with an eye to its role in the belief system of this ancient period, is it apparent that the ancient cult of the shells still had its followers.

Of course, whenever such democratization of formerly controlled objects takes place, there is inevitably a certain change in the power of the original meanings. The cross worn around the neck of a child, for instance, does not evoke the same awe as that same symbol does in the hands of the Pope. But this does not mean that the child's cross has lost its religious meaning and become a secular object; it is still a sacred symbol to the believer regardless of how universally it is handled. Only a nonbeliever would look upon the child's cross as merely an ornament.

Our first question, then, about the ancient pearl jewelry of Persia is: Are there any hints in its arrangement or appearance that link it with the early cult of shells and the religious tradition of which this was a part?

Let us look at a prize example with this question in mind. This is the pearl neckpiece of an Achaemenid princess found (in 1901) in a bronze sarcophagus in a tomb of the winter palace of the kings of Persia at Shushan, or as it is now called, Susa. This piece of jewelry is the oldest and finest of all pearl pieces found anywhere; it dates from at least the fourth century B.C. and possibly earlier. To archaeologists, its charm has suggested decoration; the gold in it, value. But the arrangement of the beads suggests to me that it is part of the ancient cult of the shells.

For this piece of jewelry consists of three strings of seventy-two pearls, each string being divided by round gold discs into nine equal sections. Other pearls were also found in the tomb but were not a part of the necklace, which, it is clear, is built around the number three, a prime number, indivisible, and to the Persians (as it is in the Christian Trinity) symbolically sacred. There are the three strands and nine (or three sets of three) sections of pearls; and ten sets of three gold disc dividers; the total number of pearls on each strand is seventy-two, two numbers which add up to nine; and the final total, 216, also includes numbers adding up to nine.

Can this be happenstance, or just the number of pearls that happened to be around the winter palace? It seems unlikely. The ancients believed that all numbers were either male or female, that those which were divisible into two (even numbers) were female (that is, could give birth), and those not divisible by two—the odd numbers—were male, and had only the power of fertility. Three was a male number held in particular esteem because it also was the number of parts of the male phallus, in ancient and not so ancient religions an important object of worship as a fertility symbol.

Far from being just a fine necklace, then, this pattern of numbers in pearl and gold suggests this was a string of prayer beads dedicated to both the sun god (through the gold) and the moon god (through the pearls) in a plea for fertility and vitality, not only in this world, but in the next.

Moreover, it was linked to Hindu ritual. In the Atharva Veda, the sacred history compiled at about the same time in India, there is a string of pearl shell and pearl beads which was fastened upon the youths who passed the tests to become Brahminical disciples. The ritual was accompanied by a hymn. I quote from it briefly:

> Born in the heavens, born in the sea, brought on from the river,
> this shell, born of gold, is our life-prolonging amulet.

The amulet born from the sea, a sun, born from Vritra [a cloud] shall on all sides protect us from the missiles of the gods and the Asuras.

Thou art one of the golden substances, thou art born from Soma [the moon] Thou art sightly on the chariot, thou art brilliant on the quiver. (May it prolong our lives!)

The bone of the gods turned into pearl; that, animated, dwells in the waters. That do I fasten upon thee into life, luster, strength, longevity, unto a life lasting a hundred autumns. May the amulet of the pearl protect thee!

The ancient epic of India, the Ramayama, reveals this was a necklace of twenty-seven (three times three times three) pearls.

Other relics that underline the sacred use of pearls along the Persian Gulf, as derived from India, are the coins showing the ancient kings of Persia wearing a single pearl hanging from the right ear and the paintings showing women wearing a ring through the left nostril with three pearls strung from it—a Hindu symbol indicating that the wearer was noble and properly married in the eyes of God.

As well as the sacred three-pearl arrangement for fertility and the prayer beads for long life and protection, there was another arrangement of pearls adopted by the Persians from Eastern tradition. This was the royal arrangement symbolizing descent from the gods; it consisted of two bands of pearls set on a broad piece of ribbon and worn around the head. We can only guess that in the old nature religion this might have been a moon-inspired halo; by the time we see it in the head wreaths of the kings of Persia its origins apparently were taken for granted.

To find suggestions that the Persian wearing of pearls had a mystical meaning does not prove that the Greek and Roman frenzy for the pearl also had symbolic overtones. We must look at how the Greeks and the Romans themselves handled the pearl for this link. The evidence is clear that in both these nations the pearl had traditional meanings, even as did the shellfish purple.

When Homer, for instance, sang his great ballad-histories of the ancient days of Greece, he thought it important to describe the pearls displayed by Hera, or Juno, Queen of the Heavens and the special goddess of women and women's fertility.

> . . . In three bright drops
> Her glittering gems suspended from her ears.

That is the couplet in the Iliad, Book XIV. In the Odyssey, Book XVIII, he repeated the description:

> . . . Earrings bright
> With triple drops that cast a trembling light.

Another link is Aphrodite, the renowned Greek goddess of beauty, who was first thought of as the personification of the pearl. The earliest legends said that she sprang from the foam of the sea (like a pearl) and this remained the literal translation of her name, although she was later held to be the daughter of Zeus. In Roman mythology, she is known to us as Venus, and it is interesting to see that after the Punic Wars and the capture of the Persian treasures, a great temple studded with pearls was dedicated to this fabled goddess of beauty, who was later portrayed stepping from her shell by Botticelli.

As the use of pearls became widespread, some hysteria entered into and debased the old meanings, even as the old religion was being debased. Toward the close of the millennium, shortly before the appearance of Christ, it was reported that pearls were being strewn on the floors of temples like so many rose petals. "It is not sufficient for the women to wear pearls, but they must trample and walk over them," Pliny wrote. The historian Martial mocked a woman who he said "hugged and kissed" her pearls and loved them more dearly than she did her two sons. The puritanical Seneca was appalled at the three-pearl earring and viewed it as largely inspired by greed rather than religion. "Pearls offer themselves to my view," he wrote. "Simply one for each ear? No! The lobes of our ladies have attained a special capacity for supporting a great number. Two pearls alongside each other, with a third suspended from above, now form a single earring. The crazy fools seem to think that their husbands are not sufficiently tormented unless they wear the value of an inheritance in each ear!" Julius Caesar gave a single pearl to his mistress Servilia, the mother of Brutus, and the historian Suetonius said it cost him six million sestertia and was: "The spoils of nations in an ear, changed to the treasures of a shell."

The most famous pearls of the period were reportedly worth ten times as much, however—these were the earrings Cleopatra wore to the celebrated banquet with Mark Antony. The story goes that Cleopatra wagered publicly that she could give Antony a dinner more costly than any banquet in history. It was a proud boast of a proud queen, and Antony agreed to test its truth. When the banquet table was laid before him, however, there was nothing on the golden plates placed before Cleopatra and himself, and only vinegar wine in the glasses. Then Cleopatra removed from her right ear her pearl earring, and dropping it into the wine glass, pulverized it, and drank the solution, after which she presented Antony with the pearl from her left ear for his delight. But he did not drink it. Instead, with the encouragement of an arbiter, he agreed that Cleopatra had won her wager—that she had presented him with a banquet more costly than any the world had ever known.

What is meaningful about this story? On the surface, not much. But perhaps it has suffered in the telling of it. Let us look a little deeper. First, it should be noticed that in that time two great matching pearls were equal in cost not to the sum of the price of each but to twice as much, or the square of the cost of each. When Cleopatra drank down *her* pearl, then, she destroyed the great value of the one she gave Mark Antony, and therefore he had no recourse but to surrender and grant her victory even though he received nothing whatsoever to eat.

Second, pearls historically meant something to the queens of Egypt; it was pearls that Queen Hatsheput took to her king when she sought his love; pearls were divine gifts, with special overtones of feminine purity and perfection. Scholars have long debated the literal truth of this old story, declaring repeatedly that no pearl of this size could be dissolved in either vinegar or wine and that it would take more than a few stirs to pulverize it into a powder easily drunk. But none have asked whether, this being true, the story was not meant to be taken literally but figuratively—and that the story of Cleopatra's costly pearl drink was a way of telling how, when Mark Antony arrived at the banquet table, he found his share was to be simply and purely Cleopatra herself. Did he reject her? Is that what the rejection of his pearl means? It is possible. Although he stayed on as her guest, in due course she was defeated, not victorious, in the war between them, and when Antony returned to Rome, she killed herself by holding a poisonous serpent to her breast, an act which also has symbolic overtones.

Certainly Antony could have been counted upon to get symbolic shell and serpent messages. Just as pearls meant more than just feminine ornaments to Egyptian queens, pearls were far more than ordinary ornaments to Roman emperors.

The early kings of Rome had been content with laurel wreaths but, in the triumphal procession that followed Pompey's conquests, no less than thirty-three crowns with double circlets of pearls, which had long been the Persian symbol for royal or divine birth, were displayed. When Julius Caesar became emperor, he claimed descent from the gods and was crowned with the pearl diadem. The men who came after him, like their women, often displayed the pearl with a lavish carelessness, but never permitted it to be worn by the lower classes. Caligula, the monster emperor who mocked everything and tormented many, made his horse a consul and, in the ceremony, draped a pearl necklace around his brow; Nero, who tortured Romans as well as Christians, not only had his crown of pearls but a throne and a scepter studded with pearls. The ambassador from the Jews, Philo, noted their association with the royal purple: "The couches upon which the Romans recline at their repasts . . . are splendid with purple coverings interwoven with gold and pearls," he wrote.

Doubtless Philo was interested but was he impressed? Since the sacking of Jerusalem by the Egyptians, the Jews had had few jewels of any kind and had returned again to the traditional source of their strength, their love of wisdom, and the compiling of their ancient history. In general they scorned the old cults and the old idols.

Authorities differ as to whether the Old Testament includes pearls in the category of precious gems. The Talmud, the Jewish book of laws, however, frequently mentions pearls as something rare, beautiful, and costly, though never as holy: The coats God made for Adam and Eve were "as beautiful as pearls"—manna from heaven was "as white as a pearl." There was a "pearl that has no price."

One ancient rabbinical story suggests that to the early Patriarchs pearls had a special connection with beloved women. It is the story of how, when Abraham was entering Egypt, he hid his wife Sarah in a chest so that foreign eyes would not look upon and covet her beauty. As he came to the customs men, however, he was stopped and asked what he carried in his chest. He evaded answering by saying that he would pay customs for clothes, gold, the finest silk, and even for pearls. When the customs officers found that they could name nothing of greater value than pearls to assess him for, they demanded he open his box and reveal what treasure of even greater value he carried. And so, the story goes, the chest was opened and the land "was illumined with the luster of Sarah's beauty."

Opposite
Rembrandt's vision of an Old Testament Jewish bride—the man showing his possessiveness through his embrace, the woman signifying submission by placing her left hand on his right. Her pearls symbolized her chastity and purity; it is possible that her hand covers his wedding ring. *Courtesy, Rijksmuseum, Amsterdam.*

Abraham was more than just another patriarch; he was God's chosen father of the Jewish people, blessed in his old age with a son, Isaac. In the Bible, this was God's reward for virtue. Abraham was God's agent; his descendants were God's chosen people. But Abraham already had a son by Sarah's maid when God told Abraham Sarah would have a son. Why was Sarah among the chosen? The mythic overtones in this story—the placing of her value above pearls, or perfection, and the declaration that her "luster illumined the land"—suggest quite subtly that Sarah, the mother of Isaac, was to be seen as something akin to a goddess. That Abraham held some belief in the pearl as life-giver is legendary; he was said to wear a pearl amulet on his forehead.

We do not know when the Old Testament and the rabbinical histories were written but their content indicates it was after the exodus from Egypt. It was between these two events that the Greek-Roman-Persian wars took place. Although Jerusalem was not directly involved, undoubtedly the conflict had many consequences for the Jews, including threats to their stern, monotheistic attitudes and beliefs. The major message Christ brought was love. The major new symbol the Christians introduced was the cross, but in the development of the new religion of Christianity there was a distinct carryover of feeling toward the pearl from the oriental mystique.

This can be seen even in the teachings of Christ. Here the mundane value, that is, the worldly costliness, of the pearl symbolizes spiritual perfection. For instance, in the parables as revealed in Matthew 13 : 45–46, Christ straightforwardly compares the kingdom of heaven to supreme treasure: "The kingdom of Heaven is like unto a merchant man, seeking goodly pearls: who when he had found one pearl of great price, went and sold all he had, and bought it."

In the Sermon on the Mount, the allusion is similar. (Matthew 7 : 6) "Give not that which is holy unto the dogs, neither cast ye your pearls before swine, less they trample them. . . ." In other words, recognize that which is of value and appreciate it.

The book of Revelation, however, suggests that the followers of Christ felt some necessity to place the old sacred symbols and particularly the pearl—which was in that period the most precious of all gems—in a new mystical context. In chapter 21, John describes his vision of the kingdom of heaven and in so doing incorporates many of the old symbols sacred to the religion of nature in the wall that bounded the heavenly holy city. "All manner of precious stones" appear in this wall, as does gold, but pearl is reserved (verse 21) for the twelve gates: "And the twelve gates were twelve

Cleopatra dissolving the pearl
at her famous banquet with Mark Antony.

pearls." The pearls, however, were not there as objects of worship for the moon god or the gold for the sun god—"and the city had no need of the sun, neither of the moon, to shine in it: for the glory of God did lighten it"—but rather as an aspect of God's glorious light.

This mystical approach at once to God's heaven and to oriental sacred symbols is underlined by the repeated use of the numbers twelve and seven. Here again the old numbers are not rejected but incorporated into new numbers and then elevated. Twelve, for instance, is three times four, while seven is a prime number, indivisible, composed of three plus four. Three is the old prime number; four indicates the new four points of the cross and

of God's world. The wall had twelve foundations, twelve gates, twelve
angels with twelve tablets on which were written the names of the Twelve
Tribes of Israel. The city within lay foursquare, twelve thousand furlongs
wide, broad, and high, and was based on twelve foundations in which were
inscribed the names of the Twelve Apostles. "And the twelve gates were
twelve pearls."

This revelation of heaven and the incorporation of the pearl into
Christianity marks the end of the early period of nature-worship in our culture, and the beginning of the monotheistic man-centered period known as
the Medieval. Gone were the sun god and the moon god, but for centuries
thereafter the pearl still held a strange, unworldly power and was employed
in almost as many mystical and magical adventures and misadventures as
it was when the ancients held it to be a major object of love and worship.
It is to those events that we will now turn for the pearl's later history.

2

Pearl as Magic, Medicine, and Royal Marvel

And lo, you are lord (says an Eastern scroll) of heaven and earth, lord whole and sole, Through the power in a pearl.
ROBERT BROWNING (1812–1889),
"A Pearl, a Girl"

*I*t is not possible to trace the role of the pearl in religion, magic, and ornament in the years of the Middle Ages in the actual way in which they intertwined, separated, or ran parallel. Just as we must sort out the skeins of wool muddled together in a knitting bag before we can work with them, so must we sort out the aspects of the pearl to recognize its importance. First, then, for its religious role: When the capital of the Roman empire moved to Constantinople in the fourth century after Christ's birth, many of the treasures of Rome moved with it to join the great wealth of the East. Constantine, its first Christian emperor, had wished to rename the old city (for a millennium called Byzantium) Nova Roma, or New Rome, but even in his lifetime, it was called by his name instead. He was a forceful man, and a man who, for all his Western education, clung to the great symbolic value of certain jewels and metals. Until this time the Roman emperors had worn their pearl crowns only at festivals. Constantine at all times wore the traditional Persian regalia: in court, the gold circlet banded by a diadem of pearls on velvet, and in battle, a helmet of gilded iron, topped with a sleeve of pearls and other precious stones.

31

As the Christian church grew in strength, it commanded what the historian Gibbon called "the wealth of nations": booty from the infidels, gifts from the believers, and the inherited wealth of the pagan rulers and their temples. For the next ten millennia all European wealth was to be concentrated in churchly hands, and from the start those who aspired to either the ownership or the working of great jewels and precious metals first had to secure the approval and blessing of church rulers.

It is a schoolboy's joke that this period was called the Dark Ages "because it had so many knights in it," but scholars agree that knowledge of what actually went on between the third and the thirteenth centuries is pretty cloudy. This is also true in the world of pearls. Many ancient writings were destroyed in the countless wars, counterwars, and local battles, and a great many art objects and pieces of jewelry were burned, smashed, broken up for cash, or carried off as secret, hoarded wealth or magic. Pearls, of course, suffered easily—while a gold ring could be cut off with a finger without hurting the ring, pearls scattered and were trampled when a necklace was seized or a bracelet grabbed. We can surmise that pearls were in the early centuries still the preferred jewel, as Pliny had stated in his Natural History in A.D. 77, because of their use in royal regalia and especially the crown. The long-lived Justinian, ruler of Constantinople from A.D. 527 to 565, the golden age of this great city on the Bosphorus, certainly honored pearls; he can be seen in the famous mosaic at San Vitale in Ravenna with his head totally covered with a pearl- and jewel-embroidered cap, while beside him, his beautiful but stern wife Theodora displays a tiara encircled by three rows of pearls and dripping strings of pearls almost to her waist.

Coins from the period suggest that there may even have been more pearls in use in Constantinople in this period than there had been in Rome at its most extravagant and profligate. Men, women, and even churches displayed them. Justinian built the great domed church of St. Sophia of many-colored marble, inlaid the interior with great gold plates, lined the aisles with silver rails, lit the nave with forty silver chandeliers, and studded the pulpit with thousands of pearls. The historian of the age, Procopius, detailed the awe this glory struck in all Christendom: "the soul lifting itself to the sky, realizes that here, God is close by. . . ." As a building, St. Sophia was the great achievement of Byzantine workmanship—built grandly on a huge scale, but finished as tenderly as a small piece of jewelry. Justinian's empire paid heavily for his vanity and the Christians' high living, however; it was usually feast or famine. During his reign of thirty-eight years, twenty-five gorgeous churches were built but three large-scale wars were fought, and

Theodora, wife of the Emperor Justinian, portrayed in her royal pearl cap in a mosaic at San Vitale at Ravenna, Italy.

upon his death the treasury, once the richest in the world, was found to be empty. Of his regalia, only his crown and his great marble throne, the top of which was covered with a cloth so thickly covered with pearls, rubies, and diamonds that it "shone like the sky bedecked with a multitude of stars," were left. Other rulers were not so lucky with their regalia and their wars. King Perezes (also chronicled by Procopius) "in the very moment of falling into the pit into which he had been trapped by the feigned retreat of the Huns, tore from his right ear his great pearl, the glory of his realm, and cast it before himself into the abyss, there to be eternally lost amidst the hideous chaos of crushed men and horses."

For centuries, all major work in precious metals and jewels was done in Constantinople and elsewhere by men trained in that great capital of skill and luxury. Dagobert of France, for instance, who vied with the Eastern emperors in magnificence, sent his talented monk-jeweler Elgius to be trained there and when he returned with proofs of his new skills, raised him to a bishopric. As Saint Eloi, he became the patron saint of goldsmiths. Minor work like embroidery could be learned elsewhere; it was clearly considered one of the distaff arts of a lady as well as one of the bread-and-butter chores of a jeweler on the Via Margherita in Rome. Mallory's tales of King Arthur, for instance, praise Elaine, the fair maid of Astolat, for her gift of a "reed sleeve embroidered with grete perlys" which doubtless he wore over a bronze helmet made by his serf metalworkers.

Pearls in Britain, as in Sweden, Gaul, and Hungary, came from the rivers. These river pearls—known as margaritas—were not as lustrous as the orients (sea pearls). When the kings and queens of these lands wanted something really precious—gold, say, instead of bronze or a real ruby instead of red spinel or an orient—they sent to Constantinople. Although none of them liked to consider themselves inferior to the Roman emperors, the fact is that they were hard pressed to keep up with them, and not until the eighth century—with Pepin of France—did the gold circlet with pearls come into fashion among European royalty as the one and only true crown. The farther the distance from the royal city, the lesser the jewels. In 936, for instance, the English chronicler William of Malmesbury wrote that the jewels Hugh Capet of France brought from Constantinople for the hand of King Athelstan's daughter were so stunning that "the more steadfastly any person endeavored to gaze so much the more he was dazzled and had to avert his eyes." A custom of having only one superior crown on state occasions thus grew up in Europe: a rich one was made for the coronation, when the Pope placed the crown on the new king's head, but after a war or two had plucked out a pearl or sent the gold circlet into hock, a lesser, imitation crown was worn on state occasions. A few kings followed the old pagan practice of being buried in full regalia, and procured death crowns: Charlemagne, for example, was embalmed by Egyptian methods in a sitting position and lowered into his grave on a gold and ivory throne made in Constantinople with his golden sword and shield beside him. But Charlemagne was the first of the great kings of western Europe to be crowned by the Pope, and as a coemperor of the Holy Roman Empire, he had to surround himself with all sorts of special equipment fresh to Frankish eyes—gold buckles for his shoes, a pearl diadem for his helmet, and a great golden desk etched with a map of the universe. Whether these things were to Charlemagne's personal taste we do not know but we can guess that they were by the fact that even his private possessions, his books, were illuminated and were bound in enameled leather studded with pearls and

CHARLEMAGNE.

Charlemagne of France copied the East in his regalia but never could afford really great pearls.

semiprecious gems. An artist-monk might spend his whole lifetime on the task of illuminating capital letters with gold and entwining them with vines or small animals, while another grew old working on bindings.

In the tenth century, when all work except that of the church slowed to a standstill because of the great, paralyzing fear that the end of the world would come with the millennium of Christ's birth, these ornamented books were in great demand as sacrifices and were laid on the altars of the great churches by the hundreds. Panic and penitence stimulated even the wealthy to barter their personal ornaments for these gifts, and the demand for them raised pearls—still symbols of modesty and humility—to an even higher level of value as sacrifice.

When the world did not end, a feeling of confidence and a new burst of energy swept through Europe, and slowly the Dark Ages gave way to the period known as the Renaissance—the Rebirth. It was between the eleventh and the fifteenth centuries that the spirit of inquiry developed; the dogma of the church was questioned, scientific experiment began, and individual enterprise began to replace the corporate effort of the Church. It is strange to look at the great sweeps of history using the activities of one meaningful object—in this case the pearl—as a focal point and see how the attitudes toward it, the uses it was put to, and the values it had were all part of the great events that knitted together the ancient past, the teeming present, and the then invisible future.

In the years between the millennium of Christ's birth and the fifteenth century, which is generally considered the end of the Medieval period and the beginning of the modern period, the role of the pearl in the Western world took on a new aspect. On the one hand, it continued to be an object of religious symbolism discussed by such impressive theologians as St. Augustine; on the other hand, it entered a new sphere and became an integral part first of magic (the precursor of science) and finally a part of science itself.

It is easy to think of magic as an offspring of religion, but that is not precise, for magic is more of a protest. Religious ritual depends always on a belief in a supernatural force which is either symbolized in the ritualistic objects in a contrived manner or revealed through acts not otherwise understandable. In our age it is customary to debunk the miracles of the past; where we have evidence of priestly lies or access to knowledge of pathological conditions, this may be justified. But unquestionably great beliefs compel and re-create (by redefining) events, personages, and natural objects. As example: the Pope can be seen as a man like any other man, subject to whim, error, and mundane mortality, or, with faith, he can be considered as God's special voice and His presence on earth, and his words can be taken as commands. Faith—belief—makes the difference in the two views. Both the believer and nonbeliever accept the acts of the Pope as religious, however, for his rituals are dependent for their effect on his established claim to supernatural powers. The magicians who practiced alchemy (a precursor of chemistry, mineralogy, much modern medicine, some physics, biology, and psychology) were, on the other hand, not accepted as religious: They attempted to wrest away the power of the supernatural and make it man's. It was the desire of these alchemists to create life, turn mundane stones into gold, unlock the secrets of the soul or spirit, and because these were powers which the Church relegated solely to God, it was necessary for them to work in secret. Secrecy is always sinister; when the work held secret involves matters of life and death, it becomes even more suspect. But it is only because we know so little about the work of the alchemists that they have become, historically, a category for ridicule, a collective title for a group engaged in hocus-pocus. In fact, they were the intellectual bridge between the sages of churchly faith and the present-day sages of scientific faith, who in their own way are the greatest magicians the world has yet seen, as well as the priests of the new order.

This digression into the question of what was magic and what was religion needs one more dimension in the case of the pearl. The pearl achieved its original role of valuable gem because of its primary religious symbolism as life-giver, and its early acceptance as an article of ornament was born of this aided by its natural perfection. But as the "eye of the be-holder" changed its perspective from the worship of the natural to the worship of the supernatural, and as man took on the obligation to conquer nature in the name of the superior power, the attractiveness of the pearl changed its character. Lip service—as indicated by the biblical revelation of heaven—still was paid in the West to its once-sacred position, but only in backward communities, or where pantheism continued in force, such as in the Far East, was the pearl still revered. In short, as Nature herself became viewed simply as utilitarian to man, the pearl became viewed either as ornament or utility.

In early Constantinople, use of the pearl was largely religious. So was its use in the first crowns and royal apparel of western Europe. But long before Constantinople, wise men had reckoned with the secular powers of pearls and other gems. This we know from Solomon, who was said in Arabic histories to have sorted out their different roles in a single paragraph. "Diverse are the virtues of gems," he wrote. "Some give favor in the eyes of gods. Some protect against fire. Others make people beloved. Others give

Byzantine metalwork was the best in the world in the centuries after the fall of Rome. This is a piece from the sixth to seventh centuries. *Courtesy, The Metropolitan Museum of Art, gift of J. Pierpont Morgan, 1917.*

Byzantine bracelets of gold and pearls of the sixth century. *Courtesy, The Metropolitan Musum of Art, gift of J. Pierpont Morgan, 1917.*

wisdom. Some render men invisible. Others repel lightning. Some baffle poisons. Some protect and augment treasures, and others cause that husbands should love their wives."

Only the first sentence in this paragraph is religious in meaning. The rest suggest alchemy. It is a pity Solomon was not more specific as to the individual powers of each jewel, but undoubtedly they were so well known to his audience he considered it unnecessary. From other writings of his time and from earlier writings we can make a good guess as to which role the pearl played. It was, as we have seen, one of those which gave favor in the sight of God—indeed, in the dialogue of jewels, the wearing of it showed humility to the Deity, the life-force, and in so doing indicated God-given power over worldly affairs. But the pearl also belongs in the category of jewels that "make men beloved." How was it able to do this? Possibly when it was powdered and drunk; there were those who believed it held aphrodisiacal powers. But chiefly because it allegedly soothed the heart, rendering it pliable, calm, relaxed, and easy because of its promise of long life. It had been the gift of the sea to the great creative Deity of the ancient religion of India on these terms. Psychologically it made sense that it should now

A breastplate owned by Constantine IX about A.D. 1000; the cross was believed to be made of some wood from the true cross of Christ.

be a love-giving power among men; the modest, the sweet, and the merciful are more easily loved than are those who, wearing diamonds, claim insuperable strength. Was the pearl also reckoned among those jewels that give wisdom? Perhaps the mother-of-pearl—as shell—was. Certainly the pearl was not expected to repel poison—that was electrum, which sizzled and changed color when it came into contact with arsenic. Nor did it repel fire; pearls were always among the precious-inflammable; they burn easily. It is possible that pearls were thought to be able to augment treasures—as we have said earlier, a matching pearl doubled the value of each, and a perfect pearl, a "paragon," was the supreme treasure. Some fanciful writers also thought two pearls could beget a third, and a few mixed up the pearl's lustrous radiance with the brilliant flashiness of the carbuncle (the ruby and the emerald) whose perfection of crystallization in due course led us to the laser beam.

It is surprising, however, that Solomon did not list pearls as food or medicine. It was held in the East by the early Taoists that pearls steeped in malt, honeycomb, pumice stone, and serpent's gall until the stuff became taffy were a food so nourishing that nothing else need be eaten for long life, even for immortality. This was not, however, a legend accepted in the West; perhaps Western trial-and-error tactics precluded it. Certainly Pliny pooh-poohed pearls as food, although as "fish bones" he did not rule them out as medicinal.

But, even as the East sought immortality, the West sought long life, and in the long span of Western man's experiments there have been few things which have not been tossed down the throat in hopes that it might perk up the spirit, settle the stomach, remove the headache, heal the injury, or cure the disease. Gems and herbs were preferred but rusty nails were not banned (they do provide a little iron, after all), and for some centuries pearls were considered a top-ranking tonic for a variety of the ills of the flesh. Albertus Magnus, the thirteenth-century German monk—and note how close this comes to the early religious legends—listed pearls as particularly good for "mental diseases, affections of the heart (also known as love-sickness) and in hemorrhage and dysentery." In the thirteenth century, Alfonso the Learned of Castile and León further stressed their use by physicians in heart cases, advising them for "palpitations of the heart, and for those who are sad and timid, and in every sickness which is caused by melancholia because the pearl purifies the blood, clears it, and removes all its impurities." Mostly, he said, pearls should be powdered and swallowed in herbal mixtures but in some cases of melancholia, it was enough that they were "daubed on the eyes, because they clear up the sight wonderfully, strengthen the nerves, and dry up the moisture which enters the eye." He claimed as his source for this advice the books of Aristotle, who had then come back into vogue (via St. Thomas Aquinas) as a Christian thinker, but who also was a student of Eastern philosophy and thought.

Can these practices be said to be precursors of science? It is quite possible that pearls, which are alkaline and to some degree calcium, might be useful medically as soothing heart and stomach settlers, especially when they were coupled with the right herbs. No research that I can find has either proved or disproved that pearl dust or pearl water is good for the eyes. More likely they are only what Herodotus of Greece called so much early medicine—"silly nonsense," born of a muddling of old myths. Certainly we can have little faith in Pope Adrian's medicine chest—an amulet of a sun-baked toad and oriental pearls which he carried at all times. Pliny certainly was disgusted with the way the old pagan myths lingered on: He said that Britain cultivated magic with such enthusiasm and so many rites that "it might be thought they had taught it to the Persians themselves."

Pliny didn't know it all by any means, however. Indeed his Natural History has been called a storehouse of error. The theory that held together religion, magic, and/or pre-science (that is, magic that was successful pragmatically) was that the universe was ordered through the four humors which emanated from the four elements of fire, water, air, and earth, and that therefore there was a relationship between the waters of the sea and the fluids of the body, the stones of the earth, the stars in the sky and gallstones and kidney stones, etc. This is not as silly as it sounds or as the uses it was put to: Scientists have shown, for instance, that the moisture of space, blood plasma of man, and seawater are indeed so like as to be almost the same substance. But this does not mean that seawater transfusions would function long in the arteries of man. Nor because seawater, tears, and sweat are all salty does it mean that dew is the tears of God, or that, as Pliny held, "pearls are made from the dewe of heaven which dewe the shellfysk margherita receyveth in certain times of the year."

The writer Anselmus de Boot attempted to straighten out some of the confusion between the myths and the actually useful practices of pre-science. Some properties, he wrote, came from form and matter—for instance, the magnetic attractions of some metals were inherent in the metals; other properties, however, came from celestial influences. The first properties were self-evident—that is, they could be shown to exist scientifically by experiment. The other properties, however, required "profound thought" by way of proof. De Boot worked in the early part of the seventeenth century in the royal court of Emperor Rudolph II of Hapsburg and included in his book a recipe for *aqua perlata* which he said was "most excellent for restoring the strength and almost for resuscitating the dead." It is a complicated recipe but it sounds quite tasty. The pearls are first dissolved in vinegar, lemon juice, or in spirits of vitriol or sulfur. Fresh lemon juice is then added and the whole mixture sweetened with sugar. Now: "If there be four ounces of this solution, add an ounce each of rosewater, of tincture of strawberries, or borage flowers and of balm and two ounces of cinnamon water." And then—"Shake well before using." Along with this familiar warning, a charming bedside manner is indicated by the closing words, "Nothing more excellent can be had." A footnote of caution to the pharmacist is equally modern: De Boot declared that his recipe was far superior to "ordinary *aqua perlata*" but that it must be made carefully: "Cover the glass carefully while the pearls are dissolving, lest the essence should escape."

Analyzing this drink from a modern scientific point of view, it can be seen why it might well be recommended for "pestilential and pernicious fevers"—it contains considerable Vitamin C in the juices as well as a touch of calcium from the pearl. No wonder even the English scientist Francis Bacon believed in the efficacy of *aqua perlata* and drew up a simpler recipe —he dissolved one pearl in "the juice of a very sour and very fresh lemon."

But let us not pass over De Boot's division of gems into two categories —what worked and what required "profound thought"—too hastily. It was a reflection of widespread skepticism toward established religious and mystic beliefs. In the four centuries between Albertus Magnus and his heart remedies and De Boot with his pearl water, observation and experiment had proven that planets, including the sun, did *not* revolve around the earth (Galileo and Bruno) and that the earth *did* revolve around the sun along with the planets (Copernicus). Astronomy thus ended the myths that many stones carried forward from the planets an influence on the earth's activities, even as studying the stars in a primitive way had generated these myths in the first place. De Boot elaborated on this when he cast out from medicine all planetary stones—plus amulets and inscribed stones—but he had not the greatness of mind to push on with his observations and discover *why* some gem medicines like *aqua perlata* were efficacious when the simple swallowing of a pearl was not. Just as the alchemists lacked both the material and intellectual tools to transmute the baser metals into gold, as has since been done through nuclear fission, De Boot lacked the tools to discover what it was in his famous elixir that worked and what didn't.

Perhaps, too, he was indulging in psychological medicine for the sake of his royal patient. Despite pre-science, the myths of the pearl continued in great force. Part of this was due to the enormous respect the pearl then held as *pure*—that is, occurring naturally in perfection, harmony, and beauty, or as George Frederick Kunz, the great gemologist of the early part of the late nineteenth century declared: "The pearl owes nothing to man. It is absolutely a gift of nature on which man cannot improve."

As well as this natural fact of the pearl as beauty, there were Judeo-Christian statements which legitimized the pearl as a symbol of purity, harmony, and humility. Indeed, St. Augustine, noting that the pearl was not among the gems which in the Bible signified the Twelve Apostles, declared that the pearl was reserved in this manner by God for Jesus Christ himself. As religious, the pearl's name was also a holy name and Margarita was popular for baby daughters of the pious and for beatified saints in the languages of all Christian countries—in Italian, Margherita and Rita; in French, Marguerite and Margot; in German, Margarethe, Gretchen, and Gretel; in English, Margaret, Marjorie, Madge, Margie, but, unlike Mary, was also used by Jews. A few names for men derived from it also survive: Gareth and Garrett from Margherita. Two patron saints were even rechristened as "pearls": St. Margaret Aethling of Scotland, and Margeret, "the pearl of Bohemia," beloved of the Danes. Both this name and the pearl itself ripple universally through lyric poetry even today. These religioromantic views of the pearl's symbolism were a link between its seemingly actual potency in medicine and its psychological potency, and De Boot would have been a poor physician to dismiss it too suddenly. Perhaps he knew this intuitively, perhaps he sensed the psychosomatic relationship, taking his cue from Francis Bacon who preceded him by a few decades. Writing in his massive encyclopedia of science, Bacon listed gem recipes along with the statement that "precious stones may work by consent upon the spirits of men to comfort and exhilarate them." This was no idle remark on his part; he followed it with strong warnings to physicians that they should not betray this faith by using fake stones in medicine, but should use only the true and the real.

Moreover, alchemists' experiments had little effect on the internal use of pearls and other gems in medicine until medicine itself provided cures and preventives that really worked. Even Robert Boyle's early seventeenth-century experiments with *why* stones and pearls were healthful came to naught; he asked such questions as whether transparent gems had mineral waters in them and whether opaque ones contained earth, but while experiment now began to triumph over tradition, its victory was unconvincing until close study of the body's functioning began to show us what nourishment it needed to function properly. Boyle did manage to discredit one elaborate nonsense-medicine, however, within his own lifetime: the popular Gascoigne powder, named for a then-famous physician. This concoction consisted of white amber, powdered hartshorn pearl, the eye of a crab, the black tips of a crab's claw, and red coral. Boyle suggested that ordinary chalk and salt of wormwood contained the same elements and were much cheaper. Not until the eighteenth century, however, did the great college of medicine at Edinburgh shift from the use of stones and pearls in medicine to less mythic ingredients, and only in the recent past has it been proven just how these ingredients work as vitamins or enzymes or catalysts in what is now called chemotherapy but was long called nutrition.

In concentrating on pearls in religion, magic, and medicine, we have swept through several centuries without noting the changing use of pearls in ornament and social status. It is interesting that the pearl was the favorite ornament of both rich and Western poor during this period. Although inevitably the pearls of the rich were larger, rounder, and more lustrous than those of the poor, many of whom fished for their ornaments themselves in the streams of their own neighborhoods, only royalty had really great pearls. Great pearls came only from the Orient, and in Europe only the merchants traveling to Persia and India knew what a fabulous display great pearls in great numbers could make.

For, after the decline of the Roman Empire and the loss of Constantinople to the infidels, the rulers of India and Persia regained control of the Persian Gulf pearls and of the shipping channels that brought pearls from Tamil land—then called Malabar and Ceylon. Because they were not the traders the Romans had been either by temperament or desire, the Easterners' supply of pearls to the West slowed, and the Orient began to accumulate vast numbers, while the Europeans fell back on river pearls. Stories of the splendor in which the Far Eastern rulers garbed themselves were current in Europe, but not really believed, and so astounding were some of the early medieval accounts that they were for centuries taken as fiction rather than fact.

The most famous of the reporters, Marco Polo (1254?–1324), the real-life merchant of Venice, was not even published in his own country but in France, and his maps, sought after by navigators (Christopher Columbus carried one, annotated in the Venetian's own hand), were "corrected" so many times in reproduction that it is a wonder anyone got anywhere using them. It is surprising to us now how accurate he was; he was a keen observer. But his friends called him Marco Millioni half in jest, and half in respect for the jewels sewn into the ragged garments he wore when he arrived home.

Because Polo was not himself a writer, he dictated the book (while spending a year in a Genoa prison because of a naval defeat) and only the first part is in the first person. It is a marvelous story of adventure even today, and it provided the chief picture at this time of not only central Asia and the great ruler Genghis Khan, but also of certain parts of Siberia and Africa, with some vague references to Japan. Many are his descriptions of pearls but the most elaborate is of that of the King of Malabar who wore a great "rosary" of 104 pearls and rubies around his neck and on his ankles and toes pearl bracelets and rings: "The whole," said Marco Polo, "worth more than a city's ransom. And 'tis no wonder he has great store of such gear for they are found in his kingdom. No one is permitted to remove therefrom a pearl weighing more than half a *saggio*. The king desires to reserve all such to himself, and so the quantity he has is almost incredible."

The pearls of Malabar (or Tamil land) come from the shell known as *Margaritifera vulgaris,* or the lingah shell, and are known as the most fertile pearl-bearing shells of the world. They were native to this area and to the Persian Gulf and have migrated (or been imported) into the Red Sea waters, and are found today off Australia. To control their breeding

The pearl oyster of Ceylon, the *Margaritifera vulgaris,* or common pearl oyster, known to the ancients and found also in the Red Sea and the Persian Gulf.

IN HAC TABVLA FOL. INSERENDA SIGNIFICANTVR 4 PISCATIONVM MODI MARGARITARVM.

Primus Perimudensium Retibus piscandi modus.

secunda Indorum per Piscem margaritas piscandi ratio.

Tertius Ormutianorum Vrinatorum piscandi modus.

Quartus scottorum in Fluuiis piscandi modus.

An old print showing four ways of fishing for pearl oysters in the seventeenth century.

places in the thirteenth century was to have a corner on the pearl market of the world; the King of Malabar literally could have smothered in them had he desired.

The most romantic stories of the luxury in the East are, however, in the *Arabian Nights,* or as it is often called, *The Thousand and One Nights.* Although not published in Europe until the late eighteenth century, it was gathered together by a French archaeologist from the legends and bedtime stories of India dating back to around the tenth century. Looked down on by the learned men of the East in the same way scholars today look down upon popular fiction, it astonished and captured Europe with its suspense, its rich, exotic quality, and its imaginativeness. Westerners researching its history today suggest that many of the tales, while full of magic, reflect more or less accurately living conditions in India, Persia, and Turkey—especially Bagdad—between the tenth and fifteenth centuries.

There are other sources that reveal to us how prevalent was splendor, and how beloved pearls were in the East. In the ninth century when the Caliph Almunum of Bagdad was being married, the road entering the city was said to have been laid with cloth of gold, and his bride was carried down it wearing a headdress of one thousand pearls, each one of which was of great value. In China, the great emperors were wrapped in shrouds ornamented with pearls and placed in a coffin of jade. The favorite rosaries in India contained 104 pearls; they did not, however, replace the ancient twenty-seven-pearl necklace which represented the twenty-seven divisions of the zodiac. How commonplace pearls were in India even to schoolboys is revealed by a simple algebraic problem of the ninth or tenth century. Instead of talking about apples or bushels of wheat it speaks of jewels: "Eight rubies, ten emeralds, and a hundred pearls were purchased for an equal amount and the sum of the prices of the three sorts of gems was three less than half a hundred. What then is the price of each?"

Russia of this period was more Eastern in its ways than Western. The report of one visiting art historian of the late Medieval period, a man from Burgundy named Margeret, has been quoted by historians as saying that the Russian treasury was then "full of all kinds of jewels, but principally pearls, for they are worn in Russia more than in the rest of Europe. I have seen fifty changes of raiment for the emperors around each of which there were jewels for a bordering, and the robes entirely bordered with pearls, some of a foot wide, some half a foot, some four inches. I have seen dozens of bed coverings embroidered with pearls."

Merchant travelers and sailors had some influence upon the use of pearls in western Europe, but it is quite clear that the Crusaders of the twelfth and thirteenth centuries had a great deal more. It was they who brought home from their Holy Wars as plunder great pearls, gold cups, rich shields, and precious jewels. Both men and women adorned themselves with these pearls in great numbers—sewing them on their clothes, cementing them in rings, stringing them in necklaces, anklets, and bracelets, and draping them in long cascades from their bonnets and hats. In every account of a festive occasion—a marriage, a brilliant tournament, the consecration of a bishop or the celebration of a battle, there is mention of pearls.

The great European lovers of pearls were led by the members of the ducal house of Burgundy, Philip the Bold (1342–1404), Philip the Good (1396–1467), and Charles the Bold (1433–1477). The latter was said to have owned a full suit and cape of cloth of gold garnished with pearls worth 200,000 golden florins which he wore to the Diet of Treves, accompanied by 5,000 horsemen. The wedding of George the Rich with the

Russian Boyar ladies of the seventeenth century wore as many pearls as any Eastern potentate. Their caps were symbols of their married state, for many were shaved as brides.

daughter of Casimir III of Poland in 1475 was said to appear to be "almost a sea of pearls"—Duke George wore a pearl brooch that cost 50,000 gold florins on his hat.

The diadem was by the thirteenth century on almost every major crown in Europe, even on the English crown, although pearls were less in use there than on the Continent. The British pearls were from Scotland and quite beautiful, but the early English kings, hard pressed to catch up with their fellow rivals in display, treated them as if they were little but cash. Edward III was the first of the British kings to pawn his crown, but his son carried on the tradition—as the Black Prince, he even pawned the French king's crown which he won at the Battle of Poitiers. He liked jewels and also bought many—one record shows he got 8,559 river pearls for £115 which he considered, and rightfully, a bargain. The symbolism of jewelry meant much to him; the court was still semibarbaric. When he was crowned he stated he wore bejeweled bracelets as a sign "of honesty, wisdom, and enclosure by God." The richly adorned stoles of the period, seen so often in portraits of kings, were also a sign of this same sort of embrace when tucked into bracelets.

Diamonds were not yet known in Europe in any great amounts, and pearls at this time were prized particularly for their "brilliance"—the soft inner glow which today we call luster. It is clear from records that the pearls of the rivers of Europe varied considerably in both luster and color but, sadly, once a river was known for its beautiful pearls its shells were exploited at such a rate that it was swiftly exhausted.

The most celebrated and long-lived of the pearl fisheries of France was in the Vologne River which arises in the Vosges Mountains on the Alsace frontier. As early as the fifteenth century, its pearls were sought after; it was fished successfully up and through the nineteenth century. In the sixteenth century it was believed that the best pearls were Vologne pearls first swallowed and then ejected by pigeons—a curious idea which is found nowhere else and may have been some merchant's sales talk. By the seventeenth century, the Duke of Lorraine was thoughtful enough to place guards around the old beds to protect the growing shells and repel exploitation. In 1826 the Empress Josephine bathed in the river at the Plombières spa and found the pearls so to her liking that she ordered some shells transplanted to the ponds at Malmaison—an experiment that failed. The fisheries were almost depleted by then and her act overpublicized the small, lingering crop; in two decades there were so few pearl-bearing mussels that not

The Pearl of the Palatinate (the palace where the Roman emperor stayed when in Germany) was probably set in the twelfth century. It is now in the Museumsbibliothek der Bayer, Schlosserverwaltung in Schleb Nymphenburg. Both the weight of the pearl and its black cap were renowned.

Pearls, as well as being used to show royal status, also were used religiously: this pendant portrays the Assumption of the Virgin. *Courtesy, The Metropolitan Museum of Art, the Michael Friedsam Collection, 1931.*

enough could be found to make a bracelet for another noble visitor, the Duchesse d'Angoulême.

The best-cared-for fisheries were in Germany; fishermen at the six-teenth-century mussel bed in the kingdom of Saxony recorded the size, shape, and condition of every pearl taken from the Elster River and its tributaries, but its output has never been large. Other German rivers—and especially those of the Oder River of Silesia—also produced pearls in small amounts in the late Medieval period. In Austria, tributaries of the "beautiful blue Danube" were fished very early; in Hungary, pearls have been found since "time immemorial" and can be seen on the earliest Magyar costumes. Sea gems were early found in the Baltic waters off Jutland in Denmark but only briefly; the pearl fisheries of Sweden have also been known for four or five centuries. Indeed it is legendary that there was never a Swedish river that did not produce at least one good crop of pearl-bearing mussels. In Russia, where the well-to-do wore masses of pearls on great headdresses and the peasants wore them on blouses and trousers, the provinces of Livonia and Estonia were especially noted for their silvery-gray pearls; but countless rivers produced regular crops.

Outside of Russia, Scottish pearls led all others in European renown in the Medieval period, but because they were deemed to be of less value than the orientals, there were laws passed on the Continent forbidding the use of both species in a single ornament. The monk Bede, writing in the eighth century, said Scottish pearls came in all colors—"red, purple, violet, and green" but mostly white. Marbodus, Bishop of Rennes and famed for his study of stones written about 1070, thought they were as good as orientals. Certainly they were much better than the small pearls found in English waters, and thus may have had something to do with the Scottish-English wars. The early British kings were jewel-poor; their inventories were rich in purchases but their relics were likely as not to be fakes, replicas of the originals which after the first crowning were pawned, dis-mantled for gifts, or simply lost in battle. When crowns fell on the battle-field they were returned without the jewels in them. Henry V, for instance, lost his crown to the French at Agincourt but when he got it back it was stripped of its "rubies" (probably garnets) and pearls.

While British royalty has never been known for its love of art, they certainly enjoyed displaying their jewels. The famous garter worn by the knights of the House of York boasted nine rubies, four diamonds, and seventy-five pearls set in gold. The Tudors outdid earlier kings in both show and extravagance, however; the crown Henry VIII wore once was so heavy that none of his offspring could wear it—a massive golden piece

A German piece, circa 1600, hung with Bavarian river pearls. *Courtesy, The Metropolitan Museum of Art, the Michael Friedsam Collection, 1931.*

A baroque freshwater pearl used to delineate a swan on a gold and pearl chain. *Courtesy, The Metropolitan Museum of Art, gift of J. Pierpont Morgan, 1917.*

A German pendant of the sixteenth century showing Christ bearing the Cross and the Agony in the Garden. *Courtesy, The Metropolitan Museum of Art, gift of J. Pierpont Morgan, 1917.*

studded with eight balas rubies, eight sapphires, five pointed diamonds, and nineteen pearls. Henry VIII amassed an enormous amount of wealth, of course, when he confiscated the monasteries and took over their lands and their treasures. He also encouraged gifts and forfeits, but he was profligate about giving jewels away. His tastes were somewhat influenced by his rivalry with the French King François I, another dandy. Henry's jewel designer was the painter Hans Holbein of Holland who had his own workshop in the palace and his own staff of jewel and metalworkers. Like the European kings of the sixteenth century, Henry VIII had robes, mantles, coats, hats, and even shoes adorned with pearls, and he set a fashion that most of his court slaved mightily to follow—when, that is, they were in his favor and not in the Tower wearing old rags.

The learned chancellor to Henry VIII, Sir Thomas More—"the man for all seasons"—did not cater to royal fashion, however, and punished his daughter-in-law for her liking for pearls. She had repeatedly asked him to buy her a brooch set with pearls, and after he had put her off a few times, he pretended to give in. Instead of pearls, however, he had some white peas set in silver and, handsomely boxed, presented the brooch, or billiment, to her. The story, as related by a chronicler of the period, concludes with the sentence: "When she, with great joy, lookt for her billiment, she found, far from her expectation, a billiment of peaze; and so she almost wept for verie griefe."

The chancellor's views on pearls in politics did not affect Henry VIII, and both of his daughters inherited his taste for display and some of his pearls. Elizabeth I, the red-haired Virgin Queen, was famous for her showy clothes—she wore great collars, enormous skirts, chunky diamonds and rubies and masses of pearls. It is probable that she sincerely liked pearls, for she wore them even in private. Her christening cup was studded with pearls; her chest set framed in them. But it is her portraits which reveal her as a glittering show-off. The first, at twenty, shows her in a black dress trimmed with a double row of pearls at the neck, sleeves, and hem; her lace ruffles are looped with pearls, her headdress is decorated with pearls, and in her ears she wears large pearl-tasseled earrings. A later portrait shows her with a great necklace of rubies and amethysts hung with large pear-shaped pearls—and now the backs of her gloves are stitched with pearls. At the end of her life she sat for her portrait dressed "to meet the angel of death" in her most splendid jewels and her great pearl necklaces. The final portrait was a death mask for, after her death, her love of jewels was further commemorated by a full-length wax-work effigy which lay for a long time in the Tudor chapel in Westminster Abbey. Around her head was a coronet of large spherical pearls; around her neck her long necklaces; in her ears, her pearl pendant earrings; across her skirt, her magnificent pearl stomacher, and on her shoes, pearl medallions. When the populace viewed this resplendent effigy sailing down the Thames, the historian Stow reported that there occurred "such a general sighing groning and weeping, as the like hath not been seene or knowne in the memory of man." Doubtless this mourning was for the loss of the Queen herself; the role her pearls played is suggested by the verse of a poet of the day:

> Fish wept their eyes of pearl quite out
> And swam blind after.

INO · ÆTATIS ·   SVÆ · XLIX

Henry VIII portrayed by his artist-jeweler, Holbein, in a few of his many
jewels. He vied for status with his contemporary François I of France, whose
jeweler was Cellini.

Jane Seymour, the only wife of Henry VIII who bore him a son; pearls were her reward. Painting by Hans Holbein. *Courtesy, Kunsthistorisches Museum, Vienna.*

Never has there been such a pearl lover in the Western world as Elizabeth. As Horace Walpole said of her later, she appeared "like an Indian idol, totally composed of pearls and necklaces. . . . A pale Roman nose, a head of hair loaded with crowns and powdered with diamonds, a vast ruff, a vaster farthingale, and a bushel of pearls are features by which everybody knows at once the picture of Elizabeth." More sharply, Francis Bacon wrote that her glitter increased with age because "she imagined that the people who are much influenced by externals would be diverted by the glitter of her jewels from noticing the decay of her personal attractions."

Many of her jewels were inherited; many were purchased and many were gifts. But one necklace at least was all but purloined—and that was the great necklace of her rival, the queen she had executed, the romantic, unfortunate Mary Queen of Scots.

These pearls were a gift to Mary upon her betrothal to the French dauphin François II in April, 1559, when Mary was only fifteen. They consisted of six ropes of twenty-five loose purplish oriental pearls—"the largest and finest ever seen." When Mary was imprisoned for conspiring to seize the throne of England from Elizabeth she tried to buy her freedom with these pearls but failed. She sent them to London for sale but while all the queens of Europe competed to purchase them—including Catherine de Medicis herself—Elizabeth connived to secure them at a bargain. She was pitiless—obviously both too jealous and fearful of Mary to leave her anything. Mary, too, loved ornament, for even her veils were embroidered with pearls. But she had a mere fifty dresses of elegance compared to Elizabeth's two thousand (which were kept for her in a separate clothing house), and when Mary died, she owned little more than the clothing she had on.

Did Queen Elizabeth's display of pearls suggest any pagan yearnings? It is unlikely; she was torn between the Catholic religion which she was compelled to renounce upon her twenty-first birthday and the Protestantism which she immediately espoused. But her ropes of pearls held an ancient significance: In the letter an Italian jeweler wrote about the great necklaces, for instance, he noted that the pearls were "still strung as paternosters"—that is, as rosaries. Elizabeth did not change their arrangement, but if she and other queens still turned to pearls as special mythic ways, we don't know. Catherine de Medicis wore two rows of pearls on her bonnet and had what has been described as a "quaint" necklace made in sections of two rows of four pearls, with a large pearl in the center. This arrangement might or might not signify some permutation of the number nine; she also wore a pearl and ornament bracelet not unlike a modern charm bracelet.

Mary Queen of Scots is seen here wearing the famous rope of pearls she was given by her mother-in-law, Catherine de Medicis.

Elizabeth I in the same rope of pearls—she "bought" them from the Scottish
Queen after Mary was imprisoned in the Tower.

In heraldic devices the number and arrangement of pearls had definite significance, but rarely can these be connected with ancient myth.

Many of Catherine's pearls were inherited or purchased in Florence but some came from François I, her father-in-law. François, the Prince of the Renaissance, was young, handsome, and chivalric when he came to the French throne in 1515. Few of his ancestors had as great a love of jewels as he. Charles V had acquired seven crowns for himself and nine for his queen, but little in the way of personal ornament; his successor, Louis XI, was very religious and preferred an old felt hat with a lead saint on it, and gave away what crown jewels he'd inherited to the Church. There was not much in the royal treasury when François was crowned but he adorned himself with jewels like a peacock. His celebrated meeting with Henry VIII of England on the Cloth of Gold was part of a gigantic political maneuver designed to show his power on the Continent; some sort of show was vital, since he had just been defeated by Spain at Pavia, but the occasion he used as an excuse was his marriage to Eleanor, the Dowager Queen of Portugal. Although the historians' attention has largely been focused on the splendor of the two rival kings, it is probable that Eleanor outdid them both; she had full use of all Portugal's jewels, and Portugal by then was trading directly with southern India by way of Goa and Madras, as well as sharing (at times through pirating) the new pearls being brought in by Spain from the New World of the Americas. Eleanor came into the French court literally weighed down with jewels, the finest of which was her great collar of three rows of pearls, punctuated with rubies and diamonds. How much Eleanor's wealth helped François to become a great jewel collector is unknown. It is the law of France that queens do not own any of the crowns and regalia they wear, but that their dowries and gifts do belong to them.

François was shrewd about jewels; it was he who began the inventories of the state treasury that continued through all the years of the monarchy, but at one point at least he appeared ashamed of his methods of collecting—he ordered all the records of his purchases burned. One was saved from the fire; it shows that in the year 1532 alone, he bought 132 different pieces of personal jewelry. Benvenuto Cellini's memoirs also gave a picture of François' vast collection; Cellini was rescued from prison in Italy by him and set up in a house and workshop near the Seine to handle his jewelry. By then, François had arranged a marriage between his son— later Henri IV—and Catherine de Medicis who was as great a jewel collector as François himself. She wore at her wedding not only the six ropes of pearls which later were the pride of Mary Queen of Scots, but also two great pearls of 92 and 96 grams, which François had given her (along with

François I of France wearing only a small portion of his many jewels. He had better pearls and gold than Henry VIII of England, who had bigger diamonds. Painting by Jean Clouet. *Courtesy of the Louvre, Paris.*

a diamond) as a betrothal present. After François' death, she and Henri marched into Paris, as had been the custom for more than a century, wearing their crowns—but Catherine's was so loaded with pearls, rubies, and emeralds that the procession was frequently halted so that she might take it off and rest her head. It is sad to note that while many of her jewels were a part of her dowry, her royal husband gave his mistress, Diane de Poitiers, the key to the royal closet where the jewels were kept, and Diane was more than once seen wearing the Queen's necklaces. This affronted the young prince, Catherine's son, and when he became King he passed a law that no royal mistress could ever wear the state jewels again, at least in public. It was this same prince, François II, who married Mary Queen of Scots—and who knows? Maybe the reason Catherine gave Mary her great ropes of pearls that were once her dearest possession was the fact that Diane had worn them. Mary was a winsome, lovely young girl, and she must have looked very beautiful at her wedding. Her robe was white Persian velvet, and around her neck was a carcanet of the pearls, threaded with diamonds for the occasion in three great loops. The prince was a weakling, however, and died young. Catherine took over the royal treasury as well as the state— this was the period of the terrible religious wars that wracked France—and ran both with fierce protectiveness.

None of the kings of France were the great lovers of pearls that Rudolph II, Emperor of the Holy Roman Empire, was, however. The same De Boot who concocted the Emperor's pearl water also kept track of his jewelry, and there was one piece he particularly admired that "weighed 30 carats and cost as many thousands in gold pieces." Rudolph was educated at the Spanish court and it was there that he got his taste for pearls, as well as an interest in astronomy, alchemy, and chemistry. Few rulers in Europe of the late sixteenth century were as intellectually advanced as Rudolph—he backed Kepler, the chemist, for instance—but he was unfortunately subject to terrible fits of depression and even before his death was forced to cede major portions of his kingdom to his brother Matthias.

Most of Rudolph's collection of pearls came from America and marked the beginning of a new era of pearl-wearing in Europe.

This new phase was more notable for the number of its pearls than for any significant change of attitude toward them. That change was to come later, with the domestication and cultivation of the pearl, once the most mysterious of natural objects. It is curious how accurately the use of pearls in Western society reflects the philosophical and religious attitudes of its people. We have seen how sacred an object it was in the great pantheistic-pagan religion of the ancient period, and how this attitude was slowly transformed during the age of faith in the Catholic Church from rosaries into necklaces—and how the pearl became ornament. With the rise of individual thought and art and its penetration into dogma during the period of the Renaissance and the Protestant revolution, pearls became different things to different men; like so many other things, they lost symbolic classification and became categorized by material content. The discovery of the New World, a deed born of the great social change, and the discovery of its new, almost untouched pearl beds, further democratized pearls, even as the New World itself did. It was not a revolutionary change in terms of pearls, but since it is our own, and since it has so often been neglected in our histories, it is well worth telling in detail.

An Italian artist's vision of how Rebecca was seduced by an offer of pearls when she went to the well. Painting by Giovanni Battista Piazzetta. *Courtesy, Pinacoteca di Brera, Milan.*

A contemporary picture of Pocahontas, the Indian princess who married John Rolfe, wearing a royal diadem around her hat.

3

The Forgotten Pearls
of the Americas

*Some asked how pearls did grow, and where
Then spoke I to my girl
To part her lips and show them there
The quarelets of pearls.*
ROBERT HERRICK (1591–1674),
"The Quarrie of Pearls"

*T*here is no question but that the Indians of both North and South America knew pearls, honored them, and used them both ritualistically and ornamentally. We know this not only from archaeological finds of relics but also from journals and reports. The early chronicles of Virginia, for instance, speak of Indians of both sexes wearing pearls; Captain John Smith described the women's pearls precisely; like the women in ancient India, Greece, and Egypt, the Indians wore three at a time hanging from pierced ears, but they further adorned them with bone carvings and pieces of shell. The men wore necklaces of pearls or, like the Egyptians, of mother-of-pearl, over the heart.

Tribute in the Powhatan tribe was often paid in pearls, and a necklace of pearls was used by Powhatan himself in the way the Tudor kings used signet rings: He gave it to the leader of the colonists, Sir Thomas Dale, and told him that any messenger sent out by the English to his tribe should wear it as proof of good faith. This tribe dried their dead chieftains and

stuffed them with sand, pearls, copper (which they valued highly), and
shell, and then dressed the mummy in elaborately embroidered vestments
of leather and pearl. It was customary for a great chief to store up his
treasures against the day of his death; Captain Smith described the temple
of Powhatan as having nearby a treasure-house, with a great amount of
pearls, skins, beads, and copper; no less than seven priests ruled over this
domain. The tribe of Powhatan was the most sophisticated in the country
at the time of the first European colonies; the whole tale of Pocahontas and
Captain John Smith is not mere romance but the story of a political alli-
ance between two governments, similar to the political alliances made by
marriage in other civilizations.

No other Indians in the North American continent that we know of
made such extensive use of pearls as the Virginia and Tennessee tribes but
relics were also found in the ceremonial mounds of the Ohio River Valley
and other Mississippi tributary valleys. The Mound Builders often cremated
their dead and thus scorched the pearls that adorned them, most of which
were not real pearls anyway but beads made of mother-of-pearl carefully
rounded and quite large—sometimes as big as 20 millimeters. It is curious
to note that when the beads were countable there were usually five neck-

Indian women in both North and South America wore pearls for both religious
values and status symbols. This is one of John White's illustrations (for de Bry's
Grands Voyages) of the Indians in Virginia.

laces worn at a time, each with thirty-three beads. Analyzing these in terms of the number rituals of the East, this suggests that these are either counting records of phases of the moon, or symbols of rank. Perhaps it is worth noting that, as a prime number, eleven held some interest to the Egyptians, and, through games of chance, to us. Three had universal symbolism, as we have seen.

The Mound Builders apparently ate the food of the mussels; massive heaps of unworked shells have been uncovered along most of the rivers of middle America and on the shores of some inland lakes in Alabama and Florida. The real pearls discovered in graves were bored either with heated copper wire or with flint drills. The former is apt to leave scorch marks; the latter, when used with a skilled hand, does a more delicate job. In mounds in the Little Miami Valley—where so many lovely pearls were found by Ohioans centuries later—more than 60,000 chalky, crumbling relics of bored pearls were found near the wrists, ankles, or mouths of the bodies of tribal leaders. In the nearby Scioto Valley, in the area between Chillicothe and Portsmouth, some 900 mounds were discovered which, like the Little Miami Valley mounds, yielded both pearls and pearl-studded bear's teeth in arrangements that suggested ritual use. There were also large round copper discs which chroniclers have said represented to the Indians the sun, the great ancestor, and god. It is possible that the use of pearls and copper suggests that secondary attention was in this manner paid to the moon; certainly most Indians heeded the moon as a guide to time and festivals. The ritualistic role of the bear's teeth was related religiously; the bear was held to be of great spiritual strength, and his tooth was a symbol of victory approved of by the god.

Pearls have also been found among the ritualistic relics of the great Indian tribes of Mexico and Peru. Their use by the Mayans of Yucatán is so remarkably like their use by the ancient civilizations of India that it seems impossible that they were not in communication with each other at some very early date. Along the west coast of Mexico where the Olmecs—known as the rubber men because of their early use of rubber—lived, the royal purple was also used. These South American pearls were sea pearls, and far finer than the freshwater pearls known to even the most sophisticated of the North American tribes. One tribe in North America, however, was way ahead of its time in one area at least—it made artificial pearls much like the imitation pearls today. The bead was of baked clay, and the lustrous surface was made up of layer upon layer of thin mica in careful imitation of the layers upon layers of nacre that constitute the real pearl.

The pearl relics of the North American Indians can be seen today in the Field Museum of Chicago, under whose auspices much of the archaeological work was done. The great and beautiful archaeological museum at Chapultepec in Mexico City contains a few Mayan pearl relics; there is in Mérida in the province of Yucatán another collection found in the Mayan sacred well at Uxmal, where many a noble young girl symbolically adorned, nourished, and purified, was sacrificed.

Although many are the questions still unanswered about Christopher Columbus, there is no doubt that he was the first European to discover there were pearls in the American waters, and that it was chiefly because of this discovery that he was jailed and dishonored.

It is curious how little we Americans know of Columbus. He is generally accepted as the discoverer of the continent but his lifework is rarely studied except in playful ways. He was much more than an ordinary adventurer; he was a man schooled in astronomy, mapmaking, and mathematics, and he had worked for some years as a trader and merchant of cloth before he became a navigator and hero. Moreover, when Queen Isabella pledged her jewels to him so that he might oufit his ships, he was already versed in discussing his project with kings; earlier he had persuaded King John of Portugal to his views on a westward sea route to India, but the King had betrayed him by secretly sending out a Portuguese expedition which failed to discover land. It took Columbus six years of maneuvering to get his audience with Isabella—Spain was at war with the Moors and only after the Queen's confessor vouched for him was he allowed to approach Isabella. Columbus knew the worth of his venture, however; he did not come begging. He asked for two ships, the rank of admiral, and royal letters of introduction to the rulers of Japan and Cathay, both of which he had read about in his favorite guidebook, the story of Marco Polo's voyages. Isabella agreed to his terms and finally, when he had difficulties gathering a crew, gave certain criminals indemnity if they would sail with him. Few shared his bold faith, however. It was only through the aid of two shipbuilding brothers, Martín Alonso Pinzón and Vicente Yáñez Pinzón, that he finally gathered three ships and eighty-eight men. The Pinzóns, with eighteen men each, skippered the *Pinta* and the *Niña;* Columbus ran the *Santa María* with fifty-two men. Together they set out from Spain on August 2, 1492.

They had been almost two months at sea when they beached at what Columbus called San Salvador but which today is thought to have been Watlings Island. Because Columbus—whose chief mistake was to overestimate the size of the Asian continent—though these Caribbean islands were off the shore of India, they were named the West Indies. After further

An artist's vision of Columbus' departure from Palos, Spain; his men returned ahead of him with pearls, and he was imprisoned for secrecy.

Christopher Columbus; he found both gold and pearls but never profited personally from them.

Marco Polo.

discoveries, a group of forty-four of the sailors was left behind at Santo Domingo to build a fort from the *Santa María,* which had been damaged, while Columbus himself sailed home triumphantly to Barcelona with gold, cotton, parrots, and some Indians he had brought with him for baptism. He was highly honored; he was made a grandee and given the title of Don, and was well outfitted for a return voyage. His second trip took him deep into the Caribbean but when he got to Santo Domingo, he found the colony of men he had left behind him dispersed and their fort burned. He tried again; he put his brother Diego in charge, and fettering those Indians that could be captured, opened up a gold mine with slave labor in the name of the Spanish Crown. It was hard work, and he was glad to be through with it and sail westward again but this too proved a drain on him. The tropical heat, the bad food, and some sort of an infection combined almost to kill him; for thirty-three nights he went without sleep and then fell so ill he could not think, move, or make decisions. He convalesced at the new city of Isabella where his brother Bartolomé was in charge; and it was from here that the first slaves were sent back to Spain and here that the first land grants were applied, the two far-reaching actions which in due course were to break the native Indians of the Spanish territories both in spirit and strength.

But that was later. Once again Columbus returned triumphantly to Spain, and this time a new fleet of eight ships was put at his disposal. In 1498 he set out with six of them, still seeking the continent of Asia. He had all but given up when he discovered South America—indeed, when he sighted the continent he thought its peninsulas were but more islands. It was at the mouth of the Orinoco River, however, in what today we call Venezuela, that he realized that this was indeed mainland when he saw the volume and current of the great river. Did he think it India or Japan? We only know he went ashore to claim it for his Queen, and discovered pearls. But although he reported finding the mainland, he did not report the pearls.

Was it because new treasures meant little to him? After all, he had already brought back huge amounts of gold, established colonies, and brought countless natives under Spanish rule. Or did he fail in his duty because he knew that he was no longer in good favor at home—that King Ferdinand, who had never thought as highly of him as had Isabella, was now plotting against him? Or did he fall in love with this peninsula and its islands and desire to make them his own, as foes later reported? Whatever happened, his story to the palace was a far different one from that told by his sailors. He wrote that he had sailed into the Gulf of Paria and that the natives "came to the ship in their canoes in countless numbers, many of them wearing pieces of gold on their breasts and some with brace-lets of pearls on their arms." Then he said he asked them where their pearl fishery was, and they gestured that it was overland across the peninsula to the north and west but he was too tired and worried to go see it.

It is of course possible that Columbus wrote the full truth. He was enormously worried about the men—including his brothers—whom he had left on the islands to rule over unhappy sailors and the restless natives in the fetid heat. He was also worried about himself, for his eyes were weak and he had difficulty seeing.

Historians, however, tell a different story of what happened, and it was this story that Ferdinand believed when he cast Columbus into jail. The story, culled from the sailors who came home after that third voyage with their pockets full of pearls, was written most fully in the mid-sixteenth century by Francisco López de Gómara. Gómara's purpose was to chronicle "the Indies" and it is almost with an apology that he gave full credit to Columbus for discovering pearls there. Gómara's account reported that on the third voyage, when Columbus reached the islands of Margarita and Cubagua in the Caribbean Sea off the northern coast of Venezuela, he sent out a boat from his ship to some fishermen there to ask them what they were diving for. The sailors went ashore with pieces of earthenware, and when they saw a woman with pearls around her neck, offered to exchange the plate for the pearls. The woman was delighted, and the sailor brought the pearls back to the ship. To "assure himself better" Gómara said Colum-bus then ordered others ashore with buttons, scissors, needles, and more earthenware plates and said that this time they came back with forty-eight ounces of rough pearls. "We are in the richest country in the world," Gó-mara reported Columbus saying at that point. "Let us give thanks to the Lord." It is possible he thought he had reached Japan; Marco Polo had de-scribed it as the land of pearls. The prayer over, Columbus then left the "Isle of Pearls" (Margarita) and beached his ships at Cubagua. The natives were fascinated by the foreigners, and he welcomed them aboard; then he and his sailors went ashore to meet their chieftain, who hospitably asked them to dinner and gave them all pearls as "sweetmeats." The sailors were so pleased that they wanted to stay but Columbus refused, saying he must go back to Santo Domingo to see how the colony was doing there.

Gómara declared that it was because Columbus did not write the King and Queen of Spain about the discovery of the pearl fishery that he was jailed. Gómara said Columbus' sailors on this trip were mostly from one town, the town of Palos in Spain, and that when they returned home they sold some of the pearls they had gathered and told stories about the rest. The news reached the court at Seville before any report from Columbus concerning pearls did and made Ferdinand so angry that he gave Pedro Alonso Niño permission to outfit a ship, hire Columbus' sailors, and set out for the Island of Pearls before Columbus had time to defend himself. Niño found the island fishery swiftly, and although he took no divers (there were none who knew how to fish for pearls in Spain), he returned with ninety-six pounds of rough pearls, some of which weighed as much as five or six carats each, and most of which were round and lustrous.

Columbus, meanwhile, argued in his letters that he had planned to go back to Venezuela and get the pearls for the Crown himself and indeed had asked the natives to collect them for him in the name of the Crown. But he was not believed; the sailors' story that he wanted the fisheries for himself was accepted instead. There was considerable hostility against Columbus in the court anyway; some of the former colonists hated him and spent a lot of their time in what amounted to picketing the palace, crying they had not had a fair share of the riches they had worked to bring home. Ferdinand welcomed their complaints because the colonies had not prospered as well as they should have in his eyes and had instead caused a lot of trouble; both the colonists and the natives were continually sick (it has long been suggested that it was the Spanish sailors who brought venereal disease to the New World) and unruly, and the Crown had to send out more and more soldiers to keep them working in the island gold mines. Isabella, meanwhile, had become disgusted with Columbus' promulgation of slavery; a pious Catholic, she had welcomed the first Indians sent to Spain and had them baptized and well cared for. When Columbus sent Indians home as slaves, she turned temporarily against him. And so Columbus, with no one at court to argue in his favor, was in June, 1500, seized by the new governor of the Hispaniola-Haiti colonies, General Francisco de Bobadilla, put in irons, and sent back to Spain. Friends offered to remove his manacles but Columbus refused; he said he wanted to wear them until the monarchs who had ordered them put on ordered them taken off. Finally he told his story personally at court, and by Christmastime that year they were off, and once more Columbus was honored; indeed, Queen Isabella was said to have been moved to tears by the story of his sufferings.

At that point Columbus could have retired with a comfortable fortune but he chose instead to make one more try at finding Asiatic civilization without going around Africa. Vasco da Gama had by now sailed around the Cape to claim the coastal towns of southern India for Portugal and had brought home not only gold and pearls but also diamonds. If there had been a sea route through the Isthmus of Panama, Columbus might have succeeded; as it was, his next voyage took him only as far as Honduras, after which he contracted a bad case of gout and slowly returned home to die.

Did he ever realize he had not found the great cornucopia that was Asia? Did he know that what he had found was a new land? Had he any idea of the great stretches to the north? New research is now being undertaken that may satisfactorily answer some of these questions. Meanwhile we must, even as Gómara had to, give Columbus credit for discovering pearls in the New World, even while we give his colleague, Pedro Alonso Niño, the credit for first merchandising them in Europe.

Niño did not stay long in the business, but within a year after his return, there were speculators galore plying between Haiti (where they built ships and got food supplies) and the Venezuelan islands of Margarita and Cubagua. By 1515 the first pearl settlement of Europeans in Latin America was in Cubagua, a thriving but unpleasant little village called New Cadiz, which, because of the barrenness of dry, desolate island, had to import its food and fresh water from either Margarita or the mainland. Its residents were merchants and their slave divers, plus some government people headed by Columbus' son Diego. Soon the merchants were so cruel to the native divers that the King and Queen of Spain became seriously worried. The slaves were purchased for about 150 ducats of gold and then literally worked to death. Six and seven at a time, they were sent out in boats at dawn in canoes from the beach at Cubagua and commanded to dive until nightfall, with nothing to munch on for strength except the oysters they pulled in from the sea. When they returned they were expected to carry their catch to their "lord," who then commanded them to open the shells. Most of them held pearls; all contained oysters, which were then served to the natives, *ad nauseam,* for supper.

Although maltreated, the divers were much admired for their skill and stamina, and great things were expected of them. On rough days, or when the catch was slim in the shallow waters, stones were tied around their legs to aid them to descend more rapidly to the sea bottom where the oyster beds lay; when they were ready to rise, they had to remove the stones themselves. Nothing was reported about how the divers carried the shells upward; it is probable that they used hemp baskets tied around their waists or necks. "But all this aptness and agility in swimming is not the thing that causes men most to marvel," wrote their historian (I have modernized his spelling); "but rather to consider how many of them can stand on the bottom of the water the space of one hour more or less." It was undoubtedly an apocryphal report. The divers were not superhuman. Although we have no record of how quickly the men died of the pressure, the cold, and the overwork, we know that the Church was so exercised by the inhumanity of the pearl merchants that they persuaded the Crown in 1515 to pass laws protecting the divers, and from these laws we get glimpses of what not only the slaves but the natives suffered. The new laws forbad winter work, curtailed the fishing day in water over 36 feet deep to four hours, and insisted the divers get good nourishment (including a half quart of wine daily), clothes to put on when they came out of the water, and hammocks to sleep in. But even these laws were not enough; a few years later a stringent law was passed decreeing the death penalty to anyone forcing a free Indian to dive for pearls. This was in 1506—the same year Columbus died. By then things must have been very bad indeed for the men who had only a few years before casually and happily treated their pearls like beloved toys.

But as the supply of divers dwindled, the pearls piled up. Soon they were being discovered all along the coast of Venezuela, and the shore was nicknamed "The Pearl Coast." By 1515 the beds there produced big crops of small gray pearls the size of peas, while to the southwest, oysters producing larger pearls were being fished.

These beds were discovered in 1513 by the explorer Balboa almost accidentally. He was still looking for a passage to India and, having crossed the Isthmus of Panama, had reached the Pacific, where he met an Indian

Shell of the pearl-bearing mollusk of Panama, *Margaritifera mazatlanica* on left; at right, the smaller shell of the *radiata*, from Venezuela.

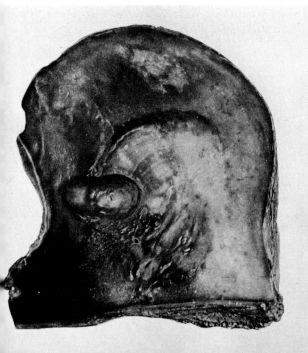

chief called Tomaco who was heavily decorated with pearls and who treated him with friendliness. Balboa conveyed to him admiration of his costume, and in return Tomaco led Balboa to some natives with canoe paddles studded with pearls who plunged into the Gulf of Panama to bring Balboa pearls for his own homespun shirt and pants. Balboa was charmed but Tomaco brushed aside his thanks and told him the gifts were nothing— that in the waters near the small island of Tararequi to the north there were pearls as big as a man's eye. Storms had been battering the area for some time, and Balboa was eager to return to his ship on the other side of the Isthmus, and so he personally did not get to Tararequi, but following his reports to Spain, other explorers did. There the pearls found were as large

Left
This old print of a pearl diver in Panama suggests the strength needed for the job; the knife is for fighting sharks as well as for cutting oysters from rocks.

Right
A sketch of pearl fishing in the Gulf of Panama, circa 1495; the vessels were both Spanish and Indian. Note the bartering of pearls for plate.

and lustrous as orients, although the waters were far more dangerous than those on the Venezuelan coast because they were infested with sharks.

Almost ten years later, discovery was made of still another important fishery, this time by Hernando Cortes, the conquistador who captured Mexico City. Cortes was given great numbers of pearls by Montezuma, the Olmec Indian chief who surrendered to him, and when he discovered the best of them came from western Mexico he set out for the coast. The chief bed he found was in the state of Sonora, on what was then called the Sea of Cortes and what is now called the Gulf of California. Later other explorers crossed the gulf to find an even larger fishery at La Paz on the lower (Baja) Californian peninsula.

As these discoveries came to the knowledge of the Spanish court, more and more adventurers went out to seek their fortune and more and more stories were told of the fabulous treasures awaiting the bold and the lucky on the shores and shoals of the New World. For decades America was known in Spain as the Land of Pearls. Even the North American coast was reported full of oyster and mussel beds. Although explorers who had their eyes peeled for them never found a single one on the shores of the northern continent, the hungry colonists of Raleigh's Roanoke Colony in Virginia were forced to invent a story about losing a ship of pearls in order to lighten the pressure they were under from England to find them.

How many American pearls were shipped to Spain during the sixteenth century is difficult to say; it is even more difficult to discover what happened to some of the really huge sea gems reportedly discovered.

The large bulk of the pearls taken to Spain was reckoned by the pound, or marc, and no records have been found describing the various sizes and types discovered. The Spanish never were data collectors in the way the Germans were; it is possible that there were great pearls that came in by the bagload and were dispersed along with quite ordinary ones. There was also a great deal of cheating at the source by the merchants, looting by sailors en route, and pirating on the seas by ships of other nations, so that many pearls did not go through Spanish customs at all.

A few great pearls stand out, however, and suggest the story of others. The most celebrated was La Peregrina—"The Incomparable" which was reportedly discovered in the Gulf of Panama in 1560 by a Negro slave, who was rewarded with his liberty and whose owner was given a grant of land and a title. When it was carried home to King Philip II of Spain by Don Diego de Temes, a Spanish grandee, the court jeweler reckoned it as priceless.

It arrived in 1554, the year of Philip's marriage to Mary Tudor, the daughter of Henry VIII, known to history as "Bloody Mary" because of her persecutions of the Protestants who had followed her father out of the Roman Catholic Church. Her marriage to Philip was not a popular one in either England or Spain nor was it a love match, but dutifully Philip presented her with The Incomparable —and dutifully she wore it around her neck on a chain. It weighed more than 200 grains and was pear-shaped. After Mary's death, it was believed taken by Philip back to Spain, and, probably by Mary's request, set in the crown of the Blessed Virgin at Guadalupe, a crown already famed for its great gems. Philip and Mary left no children; she was sickly all her life, and was eleven years his senior. In due course the pearl passed into the jewel boxes of the Spanish queens. In 1605, Margarita of Spain wore it around her neck at the celebration of a peace treaty between Spain and England; in 1700 it temporarily became one of a pair of royal earrings when another pearl almost its equal in size, shape, and luster was discovered in American waters. It remained, however, one of the most famous pearls in Europe and was instantly recognized no matter how it was worn. The witty, gossipy Duc de Saint-Simon of France, for instance, wrote that on a visit to Spain in the late eighteenth century, he saw it hanging on a clasp of diamonds in the folds of the King's hat— "perfectly shaped and bell-mouthed." When Joseph Bonaparte abdicated the Spanish throne in 1813, he took the pearl away with him and passed it on to his step-niece Hortense, who in turn left it to Louis Napoleon. When Louis went broke, he took it to England and asked his friend the Marquis of Abercorn to get him a trustworthy jeweler who might buy it, but the Marquis, upon seeing it, fell in love with it and bought it for his wife.

She was not so charmed. As her son, Lord Frederic Hamilton, wrote in his memoirs *Here, There and Everywhere* the pearl was to her "an unceasing source of anxiety" because it had never been bored and, since it was so heavy, was constantly falling from its setting. "Three times she lost it and three times she found it again," he wrote. "Once at a ball in Buckingham Palace, in putting her hand to her neck, she found the great pearl had gone. She was much distressed, knowing how upset my father would be. On going into supper she saw La Peregrina gleaming at her from the folds of the velvet train of the lady immediately in front of her. Again she lost it at Windsor Castle and it was found in the upholstery of a sofa. . . . When it came into my brother's possession after my father's death, he had La Peregrina bored, although it impaired its value, so that my sister-in-law was able to wear the great jewel as often as she wished without running the constant danger of losing it."

The great pearl is today still in the possession of the Abercorn family;

Princess Mary, the future Queen of England and future wife of Philip II of Spain, wore orients which were gifts of her father, Henry VIII. *Courtesy, Ashmolean Museum, Oxford.*

La Peregrina (at top) and the Azra Black pearl, pendant from a necklace. *From* A History of the Crown Jewels of Europe *by Lord Twining, published by B. T. Batsford, London.*

in 1913 it was polished and certified to weigh 203.84 grains.

La Peregrina was, as we have noted, pear-shaped. It is only in name that it is sometimes confused with another of the great pearls found in the sixteenth century, the shimmeringly lovely round pearl called La Pellegrina which was from India, and which was so long the prize pearl of the Zozima brothers of Moscow that it was sometimes called the Moscow pearl.

Another great Venezuelan pearl was the Charles II pearl, which was found almost a century after La Peregrina, and which then briefly became the other half of the earrings made of these two great pearls for the queens of Spain. It is generally thought that this great beauty was burned in the 1734 fire that consumed so much of the old palace at Madrid; Lord Twining of England, who has traced so many of the historic European crown jewels into the present, was unable to find any recent reports of it.

There were also some great pearls from Tararequi that became crown jewels and the most famous of these was the Huerfana—"The Orphan"— named because it was found not *in* an oyster, but loose in the sea bed. It was worn briefly by the daughter of the general who took Columbus home in irons, Isabel de Bobadilla, but was given by the general to another Isabel, the wife of Emperor Charles V of Spain. Where it is now is not known.

Another Tararequi pearl from the Gulf of Panama was reportedly 26 carats and was called the Oviedo, after the Spanish historian Gonzalo de Oviedo y Valdés who purchased it. He fell in love with the round, lustrous pearl but was shocked at the price he had to pay for it, recording it as "650 times its weight in pure gold."

The productiveness of the beds along the Venezuelan coast dwindled steadily as the divers were pushed to bring even the smallest of the oyster shells back to their "lords." When the divers could not satisfy them with their hands, improvised rakes and drags were used literally to sweep the ocean beds clean. As one historian wrote: "They have at times collected them all so that another could not be found, and have had to abandon their fishing for a considerable time to give the oysters a chance to lay their eggs and grow their pearls." But many overlords could not wait. By the end of the sixteenth century, the native divers were in a general state of revolt and hostility, partly because of the acts of cruelty and impatience of the Spaniards and partly because of the slimness of the take. Early in the seventeenth century, many of the pearl merchants became terrified and abandoned the pearl beds for mining projects in the interior or turned to making artificial pearls to offset the competition of some ingeniously crafted glass imitation pearls which were being produced in Venice.

In short, the pearl boom of Venezuela lasted two centuries; by the mid-seventeenth century it was completely over, and only a few insignificant pearls were being picked up in the region by passing tourists. Twice since then the beds have been revived: first in 1823 and again in 1900. In 1823 Rundell and Bridge, the London goldsmiths, obtained a ten-year monopoly of the fisheries from Colombia in return for which they promised Colombia one-fifth of the pearls secured. For six years, both prospered, then when Venezuela broke away from Colombia and demanded it get a cut too, the Londoners found it too expensive to operate there and slowly withdrew.

The beds had grown up again during their long rest, but the size of the pearls was no bigger than before.

Around 1900, the Venezuelan government began granting concessions to individuals to go pearl fishing in dredge-boats which rented for about three dollars an hour. A few Indians were around to dive naked in the old-fashioned oriental way, but not many, and comfortable, safe diving armor had not yet been developed for the Europeans. Even with erratic diving, however, reportedly about $350,000 worth of pearls annually were taken up between 1895 and 1900. They were admittedly small, most of them, but of good quality, and in color they ranged from white to bronze. Most were sold in Paris.

Today a few pearls are still being collected along this coast but they are of a poor color and are very small. None are exported; tourists often take a few home more as curiosities than as valuables. Today these relics of a great line cannot compete with cultured pearls as gems, either in appearance or in production costs, and so, with a new airplane base, the isle of Margarita is slowly becoming something of a minor tourist resort instead of a pearl kingdom. There is even a possibility that perhaps someday it will be discovered anew by a speculator in seaside resorts of beauty and charm, an explorer of the twentieth-century school.

The pearl beds of the Gulf of Panama lasted a great deal longer. Pearl fishing by slaves continued there until the middle part of the eighteenth century; and even during this late period every slaveholder included among his staff a few slaves so skilled in pearl diving that they were required to deliver a set number of pearls each day during the season. Only a few of the Gulf pearls were exported to Europe; most were sent by the owners to Lima, Peru, where the demand was great. As the century waned, the beds slowly became exhausted and the shells started becoming more valuable than their misshapen, tiny pearls, the last of this great line of beauties.

For unlike the Venezuelan oysters, the Panama mollusks had thick lustrous shells which were excellent for buttons, brooches, ornaments, and the like, and for some time after pearl production dwindled, mother-of-pearl supported the population. But yellow fever and sharks made the area very dangerous for Europeans, and as the number of slaves grew smaller, even mother-of-pearl fishing was not very profitable. In 1908, George Frederick Kunz reported that nude diving was still being practiced by a handful of natives of the Isla del Rey, at first under the auspices of Colombia, and later under the aegis of the newly formed Panama government, and while valuable pearls were rare, there were a few that brought as much as $2,000 in Paris—although the market in Lima disdained them.

The best-known pearl city to Americans during the late-eighteenth and early-nineteenth centuries was La Paz in the western part of Mexico on the peninsula known as Baja (Lower) California. Pearls from this coast varied greatly in color—a large percentage being black, some brown, and some an iridescent green. Most were small and irregular, but a few were found there of two and three hundred grains. When Cortes discovered the beds, they were already several centuries old, and despite the fact that the Spaniards had exploited them (and the natives) with a cruel greed, they lasted another three. In the mid-nineteenth century, after Mexico won its independence from Spain, England sent out expeditions primed to work the fisheries. Head-diving was by then in vogue—traditional divers merely jump—but it was impossible to use diving bells because the sea was too rough and the seabed too uneven. Native divers would not work for the foreigners more than three hours around noontime, and the foreigners themselves were untrained and unequipped for the art. For a few years a catch of some $8,000 in pearls a year was brought in, and then the beds were left again to the natives to work themselves. In 1857 the Mexican government divided the coast into four pearling areas and rotated the fishing so that three beds lay idle each year; fishing was good only in the morning before the wind came on, and the season was from May to September, when the waters grew too cold. As well as in cash, the divers were paid off in a portion of the catch, and in tobacco and tequilla. Most of the divers were Yaqui Indians who dove nude and well but who rejected diving suits and air pumps, and when these were allowed in from England and Australia, foreign divers put the simple Yaquis out of business. As well as pearls, there was beautiful mother-of-pearl, thick, glowing, and often peacock green in color. The mollusk here was technically a *margaritifera mazãtlanica,* but it was known as the *concha de perla fina* to the Mexicans and as a conk to the English and Americans. The species liked shallow waters and was firmly affixed to the bottom rocks or the stone corals and had to be yanked off. In the northern part of the gulf, near the mouth of the Colorado River, there was another mollusk known as *concha negra* or black conk with a thin, convex shell without commercial value but famous for producing great pearls.

La Paz, today a sleepy little fishing village with a small airport but no road into it from the north worthy of the name, was, around 1900, an animated city of 5,000 who lived, breathed, and even—when ill—ate, pearls. Armored diving was habitual then, and it was held that a diver could stay fifteen fathoms under for a half hour without danger, and at six or eight fathoms could work for two or three hours. Rheumatism, deafness, and nervous breakdowns were frequent among the divers, however, although sudden death from sharks diminished as the armor grew thicker and the diving helmets harder. There was some nude diving in the shallow waters during the warm summer months.

To take care of the aging and infirm divers, the companies separated the tasks of diving and shell opening and put the weaker, older men on receiving vessels beside the catch armed with knives to open the oysters. Most worked all day long for only a few seed pearls, but some squeezed out large beauties from the oyster flesh. One of these reportedly went for $14,000 wholesale, because of its pinkish-white color, and another brought more than $10,000 for its flawless pear shape and weight of 96 grains. As early as 1859, a great 400-grain pearl netted its finder an award of $90 and was given to the Queen of Spain. In due course many were donated to the local missions to adorn the heads and bosoms of saints; today some of the finest pearls in the world can be seen in exhibitions of those old mission ornaments; in 1940, however, an epidemic wrecked the pearl beds.

The mother-of-pearl industry of Baja California is not yet dead, however. Quite recently the silversmiths of Taxco and Mexico City began to work the shell with the same sort of superb skill used in the past for silver and gold. The result has been a collection of *objets d'art* of charm and beauty; small hinged fishes and large birds gleam with that many-colored iridescence which is one of the great delights of the abalone pearl from this area. Some are carved from a single shell; others are layered in slices curved as fins, feathers, or pointed as hairs. Where possible the natural markings of the pearl are used as a part of the sculpture: a black dot for an eye, perhaps, or a striped bit for the markings of a fish. I have a bird I particularly admire, crafted by Castille of silversmith fame, of a peacock-green radiance. It is about eight inches long, and almost as high; its twiggy legs and toes are of metal but otherwise it is a single abalone shell.

Some day La Paz may come back as a center of activity. It is only a few hundred miles northwest of Mazatlán, the newest of the Mexican seaside resorts, although it is separated from both it and its famous sister resort, Acapulco, by water. Meanwhile, however, relics of La Paz's great prosperity still stand in the fine colonial buildings, the giant warehouses, and the wide streets. Fishermen are still the chief residents but their catch is food; the great pearls of Latin America are found now in jewel boxes and museums.

The sixteenth-century pearls from America had to compete in Europe with the pearls being brought back from Asia in slowly increasing quantities. The period of discovery and exploration of which Columbus was a part also opened up new routes to India and in due course a way station at the Cape of Good Hope. Some pearls came out of the ports of Goa and Madras,

Silver-gray pearls from Baja California set with diamonds in a display piece for the Pan-American Exposition, 1901. La Paz was then at its height as a pearl center.

The Rana of Dholphur about 1900. His pearl regalia gave him the nickname "Prince of Pearls."

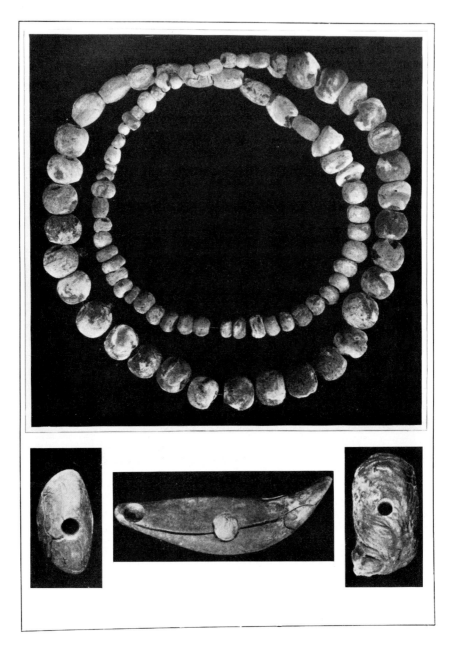

This relic from the Indian burial mounds in Ross County, Ohio, near the Scioto River, gives us more than a hint of the size and shape of the pearls once found there and worn by the chieftains. Other pearls, dulled by time and worn by acid, were found in the mouths of the dead, a burial custom like that of ancient India.

which were Portuguese; these were the lustrous pearls of ancient Tamil land fame, now being taken in the shoals off the coast of Ceylon. There were also pearls to be found in the Japanese waters, and although these fisheries were not developed, the Dutch brought some of the pearls back to Europe.

Jean Baptiste Tavernier, the dauntless French jewel merchant of the seventeenth century, who preferred overland routes to the east after one unpleasant experience at the Cape of Good Hope, differentiated among the pearls of the world: the pearls of Manaar Straits of Ceylon, he said, were the whitest and roundest, the pearls from the Persian Gulf were yellowish, the pearls from Japan were white but baroque in shape, and only in American waters were found colored pearls (like the pink conch pearls of the Gulf) and jet-black pearls. He believed that it was both the method of handling the pearls and the kind of waters they grew in that changed their color. The Orientals, to whom he sold pearls while buying diamonds, would look only at pure white pearls; the Japanese, he said, were not interested in jewels and cared nothing for their pearls.

Tavernier's lengthy and engaging account of his travels as a jewel trader is usually read by people interested in diamonds; it was he who supplied Louis XIV with his great collection of stones, including the beautiful blue diamond that became the Hope, and which is now in the Smithsonian. With him, diamonds, which had long been coveted by kings, came into direct competition with pearls as part of the expected regalia.

In Tavernier's time, the mid-seventeenth century, Goa on the southern coast of India was still the great jewel market of the Eastern Hemisphere, but it was fast losing ground to Golconda, where the diamonds from the mines of the great moguls of India were traded. Aurangzeb, who ran India with a fierce Mohammedan passion and who surrounded himself with an enormous show of jewels, had secured most of his treasury from his father, whom he imprisoned, and his brothers, all of whom he killed to secure the throne. He did not personally care for jewels himself, and although his chief throne (of eleven) was the famed peacock throne adorned with a wealth of diamonds, he possessed only one jewel which he had purchased himself—a large, perhaps 70-carat, flawless oval pearl. It was suspended from the neck of a peacock made of precious stones which stood on the top of the great Mogul's throne. There were several other huge pearls which had been part of his booty in the family struggle for power. One was a perfect olive-shaped pearl which Aurangzeb wore in a chain of emeralds and rubies around his neck; another he had left unbored and unmounted because it was held to be the most perfectly round pearl in the

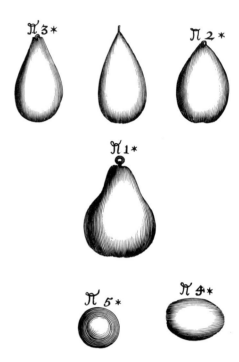

The great jewel merchant Tavernier called these the five greatest pearls in the world in 1660—all of them orients except the one at top left (No. 3) which was from Columbus' Isle of Pearls, Margarita, in Venezuela. The center pearl hung from the neck of a peacock which surmounted the throne of the great Indian Mogul Aurangzeb of India.

world. According to Tavernier, he hoped some day to find a match for this beautiful pearl so that he could mount them both in earrings: "Each would have been placed between two rubies or two emeralds, in conformity with the custom of the country, there being no one," Tavernier wrote, "whether small or great, who, in proportion to his means, does not carry in each ear a pearl set between two colored stones."

Tavernier admired Aurangzeb's relatively small round stone for its perfect form, but he admired a pearl-shaped pearl of the King of Persia even more; it weighed 70 carats, and he declared it to be the "largest and most perfect pearl ever discovered." Both kings owned massive quantities of smaller pearls, of course; Tavernier described almost with awe the costly canopy about Aurangzeb's great throne. It was supported by twelve columns literally ringed with beautiful rows of pearls which were "round and of fair water." The designer of this throne was the same architect who helped plan the delicately beautiful Taj Mahal, Austin de Bordeaux, a Frenchman titled by Aurangzeb's father, Shah Jehan, "Jewel Handed," a fair title for a man who may well have been the greatest of all the many jewel workers in history.

Were the American pearls as beautiful as the orientals? Tavernier did not even bother to voyage to America to look for pearls; he was interested only in pure white pearls, and these were likely to be either Persian or Indian in source, not American. At one point he attempted to sell twelve jet-black pearls from American sources but failed; Europe, he maintained, like the Orient, wanted only white pearls.

Tavernier was shrewd, however; if he had been Spanish, he might have taken another approach to the new pearls; as a Frenchman who would have to pay taxes to a foreign state, he felt that American pearls could not be as profitable to him even if they were as beautiful. In due course Tavernier earned a baronetcy for his aid to the French Crown in bringing to his beauty-loving king the greatest diamonds yet seen in Europe. It was another merchant who brought in the twenty-seven-carat round pearl of the French Crown called La Reine des Perles (The Queen of Pearls). This orient was stolen in 1791 when the treasure-house *(Garde-Meuble)* was ransacked by revolutionaries and was taken to Russia, where it became known as the Zozima pearl.

Pearls from the Orient and pearls from the rivers of Europe were so prevalent in the jewel boxes of Europe by the sixteenth century, however, that only the new, very great purchases and the pearls from America caused any excitement. The inventories of royalty include countless numbers of pearls, some in earrings, others in necklaces, many worn as buttons, and some sewn into royal garments. They were too fragile to make bracelets, and only rarely used for rings; here the diamond was a delightful change from the emerald and ruby, the ancient amber and cameo. We will discuss some of the ways in which pearls were worn by the new kings and queens of the world—the American millionaires of the nineteenth century —as well as how pearls were finally rediscovered in the rivers of North America in the next chapter.

This painting of the Viscountess Maynard by Sir Joshua Reynolds shows how eighteenth-century aristocracy wore their pearls with taste and dignity. *Courtesy, The Metropolitan Museum of Art, Fletcher Fund, 1945.*

4

Pearl Status, Splendor, and Sport in the Modern Period

> *Errors, like straws, upon the surface flow;*
> *He who would search for pearls must dive*
> *below.*
>
> JOHN DRYDEN (1631–1700),
> *Prologues and Epilogues: Pro-*
> *logue, All For Love*

*W*hen Queen Isabella of Spain died, she left behind her a will that has been generally interpreted to be one of history's finest love letters. When read closely, however, with a knowledge of both the role jewels played in history and the role Isabella herself played, more can be found in it than royal romance.

"I beseech the king, my lord," Isabella wrote, "that he will accept all my jewels, or such as he shall select, so that seeing them, he may be reminded of the singular love I always bore him while living and that I am now waiting for him in a better world; by which remembrance he may be encouraged to live the more justly and holily in this."

Certainly there was love in this, her last testament. But there is also in it a transfer of power. One lock of her hair could have carried the same remembrance of her "singular love"—the whole casket of her jewels would not be necessary for such a purpose. A lock of her hair, however, would not have carried the full thrust she wished to deliver. All her jewels were

93

necessary for that. It had been her jewels which had launched Columbus—and her secret action. King Ferdinand had played no role either in the conferences Isabella held with her priest or in the actual pawning of the jewels themselves to raise money for Columbus' explorations.

Secret action was permissible because these were not the crown jewels which she pledged, they were her own jewels, gifts from Ferdinand and others, as well as private possessions she had brought to the marriage. Still, were she quite the submissive creature this will suggests superficially, she would have discussed pledging them with Ferdinand; after all, had they been lost, the royal family as a whole would have suffered, for their children too would have lost something. Was the King angry when he found out? History does not say. We can only guess that he would have been at least annoyed if he found them missing *before* Columbus' success—and that even if he knew about the transaction only after it proved successful, he might have been irked enough to suggest that she not run such risks again. Certainly he was not as well disposed toward Columbus as she was; it was he who gave the order to arrest Columbus when rumors of the new pearl bed were reported—and it was she who wept when Columbus told his story in court. It is unlikely, however, that he could really argue with her about Columbus; the man proved himself one of Spain's greatest benefactors. But the jewels doubtless were a touchy subject, particularly since Spain was continually in need of money for its many wars. There is also a hint of reproof in Isabella's words. Having used her jewels as she alone saw fit while she was living, she passed them on with the suggestion that he could profit by her successes. That is, that he be "encouraged" by them to act more "justly" and "holily" than he might without memories of her actions.

Is this a crass interpretation? I think not. We of the modern world find it difficult to understand the great role jewels once played in the state affairs of Europe. They were far more than ornaments and love souvenirs; they were status symbols and collateral of an importance we can only imagine.

There are several reasons for this argument and they are worth pursuing. The Industrial Revolution changed Western attitudes toward what constitutes wealth; today those things which are useful industrially have the greatest value. Diamonds, for instance, retain value even when poor because of their industrial uses—they are cutting edges of precision and strength.

Opposite
Queen Isabella of Spain, as seen in a detail of the picture "Virgin and Child with Isabella the Catholic" by Fernardo Gallego. *Courtesy, Colegiate de Santa Maria la Mayor, Toro, Spain.*

Secondly, most of the royal jewels we see today are weak relics of the past. Very few pieces of great value have survived; in time of war-disaster need, the gold was melted down, stones pledged, sold, given to the church; a change of ownership meant diamonds were cut and recut, pearls threaded and rethreaded, earrings separated, sets of matching jewels (parures) broken up. Royal inventories are helpful but even they are incomplete (no dowries, no personal purchases), and besides, who but jewel scholars peruse them? Even economic historians, bred in today's tradition of thinking of jewels chiefly as ornament, tend to ignore them.

There is also the fact that many of the old jewels carried values that varied greatly during different periods. A balas ruby, prized in Europe until the eighteenth century, was discovered to be nothing more than a spinel, a pretty, fairly hard stone, when the great rubies of the East were examined by scientists. Without microscopes, X-ray machines, and other precision instruments, the value of jewels was determined by merchants or artisans. Weight was important but, in general, value was what a buyer could pay, or how fine one piece was in comparison with another. When François I of France and Henry VIII of England were competing for power, they used jewels in this manner. Both kept their own artist-designers—Cellini and Holbein. Meetings were arranged that were great contests of show: each night a different costume, a different display. The number of troops each paraded was also important, provided, of course, that they, too, were expensively arrayed, handsome, and healthy. Wars were fought for jewels; kings were elevated and dethroned by their handling of them; cities were ransacked, and power alliances manipulated through marriages were often purchases demanding large transfers of jewels.

Great jewels in the past not only symbolized great power, but in actuality were great power. The power of Pitt's great diamond lasted for generations; it was the foundation stone in the great family's political fortune. And it was a diamond necklace that contributed to the downfall of Marie Antoinette and her hapless husband; had not it been reported that even while hungry mobs besieged Versailles begging for bread, she dickered for jewels, both she and Louis XVI might have been exiled rather than executed.

In contrast, today Onassis of Greece is one of the world's great jewel lovers but it is his fleet of ships that brings him what power he has. England's great royal diamonds are among the world's great jewels but even in this hour of economic stress, they are no longer helpful to her even as articles to be pawned. The two mightiest nations of the world—the United States and Russia—measure their power by their gross national

The Virgin Mary and St. John mourning before the crucifix set in rock crystal
and adorned with pearls by a Spanish goldsmith. Fifteenth century. *Courtesy,
The Metropolitan Museum of Art, gift of J. Pierpont Morgan, 1917.*

product and their industrial ability to gear for war, not by the jewels—or even the gold—they have.

Pearls had their greatest value in ancient times when they were of religious and magical value. They took second place to diamonds about the time of Christ but remained prizes of great worth. When the East was opened up and diamonds became more available, the gap between the two widened; pearls also suffered from competition with emeralds and rubies.

At the time of which we speak, however, the beginning of the modern period, fine pearls were not only beloved—especially by queens—but enormously valuable still as status and power, and it is this thrust which is revealed in Isabella's will.

Isabella's favorite jewel was the collar that Ferdinand gave her as an engagement present but which was pledged so often that she rarely wore it. It consisted of eight large oriental pearls separated by seven large balas rubies. After the discovery of the American pearls, she had another collar made which was heavier and fancier—it included twenty big rubies, which were strung with sixty large pearls, thirty small ones, and fifty very

small ones on three ribbons of silk. There had never been any crown jewels
in Spain before her time; swords had been the only regalia passed along
from king to king. Did she—who was able to make war with the best of
them—secretly dream of a day when pearls would replace swords? Certainly she loved them, but she bought them as prizes, not ornaments. When
the large American pearls started coming, the most notable—such as the
Peregrina—became part of the Spanish crown jewels. Some are now in
private hands; some belong to the Spanish royal family in exile—but many
of the old ones vanished into the market at the time of the Spanish
armada's defeat, and others were ruined or lost when fire swept the royal

A Medusa portrait hung with a large pearl made by an Italian jeweler circa 1550, and (*opposite*) a pendant of similar design but of Diana and in cameo by a Frenchman, two centuries later. *Courtesy, The Metropolitan Museum of Art, gift of J. Pierpont Morgan, 1917.*

Spanish pendant of the seventeenth century with the Virgin of the Immaculate Conception, gold with enamel and pearls. *Courtesy, the Hispanic Society of America, New York.*

palace in Madrid in 1734. Alas, the heirs of Isabella didn't manage the kingdom's wealth or her jewels with the "justness" she had practiced.

In two centuries Spain's great moment in history was over, and it was Britain's turn. Spain, like France, Italy, and Scandinavia, could not both exploit her new finds and hold her trade routes at the same time—and so by 1750, Britain, who had worried little about discoveries but a lot about its brash, bold navy, had pirated Europe out of most of her colonies. It was a time of great ferment. As well as wars between nations, there were clashes between the Protestants and the Catholics, between the philosophical ideas of Rousseau with his "natural man" and the traditional belief in the nobility of the aristocrat, between individualism and hierarchy, and between populaces and their rulers. In 1759, one commentator of the midcentury tells us, the bells of London literally rang out day after day in celebration of sea victories against France, Scandinavia, Italy, and Spain. The English called it a "year of miracles," and when, in 1760, George III took the throne, he commanded (theoretically at least) vast areas of North America—including the former French and Spanish colonies in Canada and Florida—and large chunks of Africa and India.

With the collapse of Spain, jewel-display as power was almost over.

Although Britain had the wealth and the power of her Industrial Revolution, her people did not feel as self-assured as might have been expected of such new power. Instead they deferred to European culture in the same way in which America was later to defer to English culture. No young eighteenth-century English boy was considered educated without the grand tour of Italy and France; no bachelor's apartment was complete without its Continental touches, its mirrored walls and mother-of-pearl frames. The fashion plates of the day were masculine rather than feminine; the macaronis of the late eighteenth century were veterans of the grand tour who sported their gold-headed canes, watches, and ruffled pearl-studded shirts with an affected foppish chic, both in England and America. In the early nineteenth century they were superseded by Beau Brummell, the misunderstood dandy of Bath and London, whose far-reaching contribution to elegance was based on an impeccable cleanliness. His king was the fat, foolish George IV who built the ornate Pavilion at Brighton. When the Beau was in royal favor—they quarreled during the Regency—he had a restraining influence on Georgian dress, art, and architecture. His taste was admirable, and he deserves far greater credit for it than history has given him, but, perhaps because he could not afford really great ones, his jewels were more likely to be set in snuffboxes than worn.

By the late eighteenth century the Georges of Hanover were played out as England's rulers and so were the Bourbon kings of France. Only in Germany and Russia was regal power what it had been in preceding centuries. In short, western Europe was ripe not only for colonial revolt but for a Napoleon, and it got him. But Napoleon—unlike Disraeli later—was bent not only on achieving regal power but also on the kingly way of life.

Even as he plotted for war, he planned for peace—for a future hegemony run by his own heirs, supported by a vast treasure. His heirs failed but his treasure rebuilt the state. Some of the Bourbons' enormous collection of jewels had been stolen in the robbery of the treasury (the *Garde-Meuble*) in 1791 but many Napoleon recovered. He also made his own purchases, spending more than a million dollars, but unlike Louis XIV, who bought the greatest diamonds in Europe, Napoleon bought pearls. Even his first gift to Josephine was a necklace of 300 pearls which she wore with a diadem of bejeweled laurel leaves—his favorite crown because it recalled the Roman emperors.

Theirs was a love match which might have lasted until death had she given him an heir, and had it not been for his great need for political alliances as he was pressed harder and harder by the blockade of ships England threw around the Continent. Shortly before their fifteenth wedding anniversary Napoleon divorced Josephine (allowing her to keep her pearls) and married the Hapsburg princess, Marie Louise. The following year she became pregnant, and again Napoleon celebrated with pearls, giving her a necklace, earrings, and brooch of 408 huge pearls and several diamonds.

When—a mere four years later—the allied armies of England, Prussia, Spain, and Italy besieged Paris, young Marie Louise fled, wearing all of her great baubles, in the belief that no matter what happened, no one would dare harm her personally. She was right; although brigands ransacked her carriage, no one laid a finger on her. Napoleon, by now in Elba, was furious at her theft of the French crown jewels (as he called them) and sent her a message that she must return them immediately. Her father backed Napoleon up, but Marie Louise had her own views. She returned to Napoleon only the great pearl necklace he had given her before the birth of his son, saying to the messenger: "Hand this to him, but say nothing." Her message rested in the pearls themselves; even as Isabella believed her jewels carried certain memories, so did Marie Louise. Her intent was to remind Napoleon that, deposed though she might be as his Empress, she was still the mother of his heir. Napoleon got the message. He answered that she and his son belonged at Elba with him and made no more pleas for the jewels. Not until their son was lost to them both, a political toy of the Italians, did the Austrians return the "crown jewels" to the Bourbons.

And the celebrated pearl necklace? Napoleon returned it to the treasury too, but the pearls, like the Emperor, had suffered greatly from tragedy, and for a long time after they were said to be accursed, that the old legends that pearls were the tears of the gods was still true. From time to time a royal princess took out a strand or a brooch but for the better part of the next thirty years the necklace lay in a vault in the state treasury. Not until Napoleon III married Eugénie—known as Empress Eugénie and famed for her beauty and charm—were they worn again en masse in all their glory as the unfortunate Marie Louise had worn them. But even while she put them on for the great ceremony at Notre-Dame, Eugénie was warned by her maids of the sorrow they forecast. She wore them anyhow, and since her life was in the main a tragic one, the legend grew in strength. The English poet John Milton expressed it two centuries earlier in writing about the pearls of the Marchioness of Winchester:

> And those pearls of dew she wears
> Prove to be presaging tears . . .

Did Eugénie herself consider her pearl parure especially cursed? When

The Imperial Austrian Crown was ordered made by Rudolph II in 1604; Rudolph thought so highly of pearls as both medicine and magic that he not only wore them, he ate them.

she, too, had to flee Paris, she left it behind in the state treasury, taking with her only her personal jewelry—some hundred pieces—which she used to reward the Philadelphia dentist, Dr. Samuel Evans, who had hidden her in her carriage and driven her from the city. Those pieces reside now in another vault, this time a bank.

The great pearls, meanwhile, stayed only a few decades in the vaults

One of the many elaborate jewels of the eighteenth-century French which in due course found its way to America. This necklace was said to contain 126,000 seed pearls.

of the newly created French Republic. When Napoleon III left, the jewelers moved from the Palais Royal to the Place Vendôme, where still they congregate today. It was understood from the start that, with the exception of a few literally priceless stones like the great diamond known as the Regent, which went to the Louvre, the crown jewels would be inventoried and put on sale. For thirty-seven years, as the republics changed presidents, the sale was postponed and postponed but finally, on May 12, 1887, it took place at the Pavillon de Flore, a part of the Tuileries.

It was not the first time royal jewels had been on sale—kings and queens had been bartering their jewels since time began. But this was a peak point in the history of the declining power of jewels because it was public; never before had any and all merchants and agents who wished to been permitted to participate in a great dispersal of royal valuables.

Where did the jewels go? We shall try to trace as many of the pearls as we can but there were literally thousands of offerings.

Probably the most important purchases were made by the two great English jewelers, Rundell and Bridge, and Edwin Streeter. Both kept quite quiet about their dealings that day and later, but some of their purchases were recognizable—although the most notable were not seen publicly again until 1902 when Alexandra, the beautiful Danish-born wife of Edward VII, wore them to their coronation.

In the interim, as they had for so long, they lay in a royal vault, but this time it was Victoria's vault. Victoria already had great pearls at the time of the sale, many of which had come to her at eighteen when she was crowned Queen of England. For a time the pearls that Elizabeth had bought after her victory over the Spanish and which she wore in her famous Armada portrait went out of the family, along with the pearls she had won from Mary Queen of Scots. Some had been sold on the Continent when the Tudors went broke; others had been handed down through the princesses. However, with the coming of the Hanovers to the throne—the many Georges of North Germany—the lost jewels began coming back, and Victoria made a deliberate search to find those that were still missing. She did well. In the great Winterhalter portrait we see her in all her bejeweled glory. The pearls Pope Clement VII gave to Catherine de Medicis—who gave them to Mary Queen of Scots, who was compelled to sell them to Elizabeth—are again around a Queen of England's neck. Temporary display, however, was enough for Victoria; having bought them, worn them, and had them painted recognizably upon her, England's old jewels were returned to the vault.

Small, plump, and strong-willed, Victoria was sentimental about her personal ornaments. Her favorite pieces were rings: She wore so many that she had trouble wearing gloves. She had her children's milk teeth united in a bracelet which she wore almost as often as a three-strand bracelet of pearls which had been her mother's. She received a short double strand of pearls at her coronation, and she liked that for dressy occasions; with it she wore small pearl earrings. After the British triumphs in India when she was longing to be called Empress although Parliament forbade it and her sensible Prince Consort Albert cautioned against it, she dressed herself again in a gaudy array of loot and had herself painted again, and then again put most of it away, condescending to wear only pearl earrings framed in small diamonds as a sort of reminder of what was in the safe and the mines.

Victoria in short was an enormous influence on jewel history because (unlike Eugénie) she downgraded it and let Britain's industrial might speak instead. As many—or more—women copied her dowdiness and fussiness as copied Eugénie's great dresses from Worth or her magnificent way with pearls. Simple and orderly and compulsively possessive, Victoria literally threw nothing away, and when she died every dress she had owned in her sixty-four years as queen was still in her wardrobe, shrouded, numbered, and catalogued, ready to be put on again whenever desired.

Her jewels were in a similar state. After her husband died, she grew even more sentimental about keepsakes, but she preferred little statues and miniatures to jewels as reminders. As the years passed, her rooms became cluttered with small idols of the Prince Consort and of dear, but dead, friends. Particularly appalling was her custom of having a cardboard picture of Albert beside her when she slept; even when she traveled, the servants carried it along and pasted it to the headboard of her bed.

But as the Queen grew older, some of her jewels were taken out of the vaults for her children's marriages and for parties. Alexandra, the wife of her eldest, Edward, Prince of Wales, had access to many, for she needed them; the Prince was thrust into the social world both by the rigid demands of his mother that the palace be kept in mourning and the long length of her life after she was widowed. Edward's was a gay and frivolous life, rather like a court in exile, where he was waiting not for the ax to fall on his head, but the crown. Edward and his wife sought popularity and won it. Alexandra, as one duchess put it, "whose very breasts and arms seemed designed for a fabulous display of glittering jewels," dazzled the British with her exquisite dress, proud carriage, and smiling face. Edward was equally splendid to look upon, his tailoring impeccable, his cravat tied just so, his collars crisp and high, and the tails of his coat as graceful as any dandy's. On grand occasions Alexandra's jewels were always displayed. With her diamond trellis necklace she wore the old pearls in a single rope that looped below her waist and was caught with a brooch.

When finally her prince—by then sixty-one—was crowned King Edward VII in June, 1902, Alexandra wore a fortune in pearls, only a portion of which had been among the crown jewels at the time Victoria came to the throne. She was literally yoked in them. As well as a dog collar of small pearls that circled her throat four times, she wore seven rows of large pearls which were graduated from 24 inches to 30 in length. Beneath these, so to speak, were her diamonds: a choker of three rows and two chains; and below, like a stomacher, was a huge brooch set with diamonds and hung with large pear-shaped pearls. They had been purchased with diamonds and gold—the hard-won booty of Victoria's triumphs in India and South Africa —and the pear-shaped drops were recognizably Napoleon's. Did their tragic history influence her? To Alexandra and to her husband, pearls must still have held some of the portents that had made them the symbol of divine rights of rulership in the Orient. At the coronation Edward decreed that none but the royal family could wear crowns with pearls on them; that all crowns of the lesser nobility must be adorned only with silver beads.

But it is no news that royalty buys royal jewels; the reason why the French sale of crown jewels was a watershed in jewel-power was that for the first time the new kings—the American millionaires—came into possession of great historic jewels.

Before we arrive at this moment of American triumph, however, let us review the history of American jewel-wearing, and go back to the days of New England's founding when, for a time, no jewelry at all was worn.

Laws limiting the wearing of jewels have been customary since the beginning of time; after all, symbols carry no message if they are not restricted to meaningful uses. The Puritans disdained jewels not so much as jewels but as symbols of the pagan religion that fortified the monarchy, or rule by inherited divine right. All symbols of the monarchy were distasteful to them. In the Massachusetts Bay Colony, they even passed laws against the wearing of silk by the "lower classes," and in their early years in England they had felt so violently about what they called "pagan symbols" that at one meeting all Puritan wives were called upon to throw their wedding rings into the fire. (Who combed the ashes for the molten gold is not recorded.)

In America, the Puritan influence on feminine ornament was offset by the customs of other pioneer groups: In New York, the Dutch were far less

Queen Alexandra of England, widow of Edward VII, in 1912 in a walking
suit, the shawl collar elaborately embroidered in seed pearls.

concerned about such serious matters and delighted with whatever jewels
they could get. In New England, the first jewelers—as we know them
today—were silversmiths who made useful objects like cups and plates
(Paul Revere, son of a French goldsmith, is a leading example). In New
York, however, there was a variety of jewelry in the shops along The
Broadway to Boston even before 1700, and as Nieu Amsterdam developed
near the southern tip of Manhattan Island where the Battery of cannon
stood, there was many a jeweler's display to be admired by a girl wending
down Maiden Lane to the river with a load of washing on her back, or
often enough, with a load of washing on her lover's arm. Dutch girls liked

chip earrings of diamonds or beads of pearl below their crisp white caps, and pearl buttons on their shirtwaists. And their men often wore even more jewels than they did; as in England, it was the males who glittered with knee buckles, shoe buckles, watches, and gold-headed canes.

For some, indeed, pearls retained something of the old royal feeling. George Washington, for instance, wore no crown, but he did wear a pearl and gold ring that bore in the center a lock of his hair set in glass framed in red, white, and blue enamel in a circle of thirteen pearls. After it was decided he was not to be king but simply President, he wore it only rarely, but when one of his favorite officers, Lieutenant Richard Somers, was dispatched to fight the Algerian pirates at Tripoli, he gave it to him. It was no help as a regal talisman; Somers lost his life.

How it happened that neither the New England colonies, which were friendly with the Indians, nor the New York and Philadelphia colonies, which first traded with and then fought them, never became aware that there were pearls in the local river mussels is not known. Possibly there were not many at that time. The Indian's wampum was shell from pearl-bearing clams, not the pearls themselves, and although pearls were found later in the same beds the Indians had once fished, it is possible that in the late eighteenth and early nineteenth centuries the beds were exhausted. In any event, the pearls worn along the east coast were imported and came in from Paris; this was also true in New Orleans, although a few came up from the South American pearl markets in Lima, Peru, and La Paz, Mexico.

While there were not nearly as many jewels in the early colonies as there were in Europe during the same period, there was considerably more luxury than is generally thought. George Washington, for instance, most of whose own fortune was in land, became a multimillionaire when he married the rich widow, Martha Custis. As sea captains, the New Englanders made —and lost—many a fortune in china, silk, rum, sugar, and slaves. Few of the Virginians brought any money with them from Europe when they immigrated, but many made great fortunes here as the country prospered and their crops of cotton and tobacco became a part of world trade. Furs and lumber were other important sources of wealth; so too, by the mid-nineteenth century, was gold, as well as other metals. Land rapidly became valuable, especially as new cities such as Washington sprang up; indeed at about the time that Dolley Madison was holding her famous soirees at the White House with her head swathed in jeweled turbans not unlike those of the Indian rajahs, the daughter of a real-estate man was considered the city's richest heiress. By midcentury, because of the new British triumphs in India, diamonds were the status gem, but every woman who was well dressed during this period had at least one string of fairly good pearls with earrings to match. Anything more elaborate was not considered quite nice, for pearls were still thought of as attributes of royalty as well as expensive.

President Van Buren's pearl story is indicative. He was given two large pearls and a necklace by the Imam of Muscat. As a nonroyal chief of state of a great democracy, the President did not think it seemly that he should keep them. For more than fifty years they lay in the vaults of the treasury, and then they were transferred to the Smithsonian Institution. The individual pearls are not large, nor is the 148-pearl necklace that accompanied them, and although they still have a lovely luster, this very modest treasure was considered too showy for even a first lady to wear except on quite grand occasions.

A single pearl often adorned an engagement ring, however, and small chokers were popular, as were earrings of one or two pearls. Mrs. Lincoln had a passion for clothes and jewels—Washington whispered that it was because she was trying to make up in glitter what she lacked in charm and beauty—and even slashed her gloves to show off her rings, but by and large the United States did not really accept jewels as fit adornment for American women until after the post-Civil War boom developed into the Gay Nineties—and the new rich began vying with one another in ostentation.

This was the gilded age. Block-long houses costing literally millions to build sprang up on Fifth Avenue in New York, in Chicago, in San Francisco, in Newport, R.I. (where they were ironically called "cottages") —and to the west of Philadelphia along the new Pennsylvania Railroad's main line.

Some copied French châteaus, others imported whole Indian palaces stone by stone; Japanese and Chinese decor vied with Tudor beams and great gabled clapboards. The men—except for a few eccentrics like "Diamond Jim" Brady—did not wear jewelry, preferring to display their wealth in yachts, horses, fine liquors, shooting lodges, and great playhouses, but they did deck out their women with great lavishness.

It was not then, however, as easy for Americans to come by great jewels as it was to build houses, and for a time millionaires' wives had to be content with jet and rhinestones. The first breakthrough came in 1886 when the Hope family of England went bankrupt and Hope was forced to sell his jewels. The prize stone among them was the Hope diamond, that blazing blue stone which can be seen today in the Smithsonian gem collection, and which came to America via Jacques Cartier and Evelyn Walsh McLean at the turn of the century. But there was also a Hope pearl, con-

When the Imam of Muscat gave this string of pearls to President Van Buren, he instantly gave them to the government because of their great value. They are still in the Smithsonian, with the dresses of the First Ladies.

sidered the largest in the world, although not the most beautiful.

Like the Hope diamond, it too had once been in the treasury of Louis XIV; it was brought by the great jewel merchant, Tavernier, from India, although it probably originated in Burma. Pear-shaped and weighing three ounces, it was as magnificent in its coloring as it was in size—it was clear white at the top shading to copper green at the tip. The luster was uneven and the shape somewhat clumsy, but attractively capped with an arched crown of gold set with small diamonds, rubies, and emeralds, the pearl was stunning when worn as a pendant.

When both the Hope diamond and the Hope pearl came up at the same auction and were bought by rich Europeans, headlines resulted, and from then on American millionaires and their agents began to take an interest in great European jewels and jewelers.

The next big sale almost escaped American attention, however. This was the sale of the French crown jewels, which New York heard about only at the last moment. Fortunately for Tiffany and Company, at the time of the sale, John Young, Charles Tiffany's partner, was abroad on a buying trip. Tiffany got word of the sale before Young did and cabled him on the newly laid transatlantic cable to drop by and purchase what he saw fit. He did, and his purchases were so successful that they not only made Tiffany's an important jewelry store but started an incredible American vogue for jewel wearing.

Tiffany, however, did not get the greatest pearls that came to America —Empress Eugénie's rope of more than two hundred pearls and Catherine de Medicis' historic necklace—for William H. Vanderbilt, better known as the Commodore, bought these great strands at Jacques Cartier's. They were early gifts to his wife, and she wore them often at parties and then gave them to her daughter along with all the Commodore's presents when she finally decided to leave him and marry another millionaire.

It was her daughter who made them famous anew. Consuelo Vanderbilt was not only a reigning beauty, a frightfully rich heiress, a girl of sensibility and charm, but she became renowned for being the first of the millionaires' daughters to marry a titled European. It is quite clear from her memoirs and those of others that he was literally bought to suit her parents' vanity. With the Vanderbilt millions, the Duke of Marlborough was able to repair and refurbish the huge Blenheim Palace, keep his family line going (he called her "a link in the chain"), and live in a high style. But

One of the largest pearls in the world and known as the Hope Pearl because it was owned by the same London banker who owned the bad-luck Hope Diamond.

he did not stint Consuelo; even though there was little love between them and eventually they were divorced, he decorated her as generously as he did his other properties.

As a child, Consuelo had to wear a brace for at least an hour daily so that her carriage would be regal; now on her swanlike neck she was expected night after night to wear her pearl dog collar of nineteen rows clasped by diamonds that scratched her neck, the Medicis rope of pearls that ended in silk tassels, and on occasions when royalty was present, a pearl tiara, a four-inch-wide crescent pearl brooch, and an even larger stomacher of pearls. Once, because the bank where she kept her tiara was closed, she wore the pearl crescent in her hair to a dinner where Princess Alexandra was present, and was reproved: Edward and his duke put as much faith in ritual as did Victoria, even though it was a different sort of show they were running.

On another occasion she was more successful with her jewels. This was a state visit to Russia where she and her friend, the Duchess of Sutherland, were somewhat chagrined to discover that while the Russian ladies of the Czarist court were far from beautiful or relaxed, their jewels were more plentiful. Indeed, all of them had different sets of jewels for each dress they wore to four great functions, while the English duchesses wore, for the most part, the same pearls and diamonds. The night the Duchess of Marlborough was the Czar's dinner companion, however, she was asked to wear her prettiest dress and jewels, and fortunately she was prepared with a special diamond and turquoise parure of dog collar and earrings that matched her dress and which she could wear with her pearls "for a change."

The Duchess, later to become simply Mrs. Jacques Balsan, had a fine eye for jewels and knew their value, but even she was astonished by the Grand Duchess Marie's collection which, on that trip, she was invited to view. They were set out in glass cases in her dressing room—an "endless" number of parures of diamonds, emeralds, rubies, and pearls—a different set for every dress, and a different dress for every occasion. When Crown Prince Nicholas chose to marry Princess Alix of Hesse (later to be known as Empress Alexandra), Marie hesitated a long while before giving the awkward, shy German girl any jewels, but Nicholas was generous. As his engagement present he gave her a pink pearl ring and a necklace of large pink pearls. They were her favorite jewels throughout her strange, sad life. At her coronation, she wore the ring and the necklace alone; at her wedding, she had worn them with a magnificent rope of pearls given her by the Czar—a creation of the house of Fabergé costing 250,000 gold

The Duchess of Marlborough, born Consuelo Vanderbilt, dressed in her full pearl parure and ermine wrap. Notice the wide dog collar she made famous and the necklaces which were once worn by the Empress Eugénie.

rubles. It was Alexandra who fell under the spell of Rasputin because of his hypnotic ways with her sick, hemophiliac son; after her execution, some of her jewels became a part of the Bolshevik treasury, but some came back to her mother-in-law, the Grand Dowager Empress Marie, who escaped to the United States and lived off her jewels for decades.

The Duchess of Marlborough, for all her eye for jewels, missed another pearl of Eugénie's which was worn that night of the Czar's ball by the Princess Yussupov. It was the great pearl the French called La Regent, an oval creamy-white pearl Napoleon first gave Marie Louise for her tiara and which Eugénie had reset for the neckline of one of her favorite empire dresses. It too was sold at the great sale of French crown jewels, and Fabergé of St. Petersburg bought it along with some other pearls. Fabergé was the Czar's jeweler; it was he who made for the imperial family their delicate, bejeweled Easter eggs, many of which, like the Grand Duchess' gems, are now in the United States. The beautiful Irina, Princess Yussupov, niece of the Czar, had an immense collection of jewels herself, and they too have been scattered. It was her husband who—using his wife as a lure —killed the monk Rasputin; both his own kin and their enemies the Bolsheviks hunted him down for that political error, but he escaped to Paris with a million dollars' worth of pearls and two Rembrandts.

Because there has been no single researcher or organization tracking the great pearls of history since Kunz's work in 1908, because of the great dispersal of jewels that took place in the years between 1880 and 1920 as well as later, and because both modern jewelers and jewel owners are inclined to be secretive about their sales and their purchases, it is difficult to know in this last phase of great pearl-wearing who is wearing or banking which pearls where, or which strands are more valuable because of their history than their perfection.

It was probable that Consuelo's pearl dog collar alone was worth a million dollars, and the huge rope of more than five hundred pearls, at least half a million. Others owned great ropes worth a quarter of a million or more; George Frederick Kunz in his 1908 report on pearls spoke disdainfully of the price the Empress Eugénie's pearls brought at auction: "The total amount realized for the pearl ornaments was $252,300," he wrote. "There are several American ladies who own single strands of pearls of more value than the whole pearl parure of the Empress Eugénie." It is sad, historically speaking, that Kunz did not identify these ladies. He kept a close eye on who sold what to whom and who wore what, not only in pearls but in other jewels, but he never spoke by name of the American pearl owners, nor listed sales by the jewelers, many of whom profited hugely from royal

Alexandra, the last Czarina of Russia, was renowned for her jewels—even English royalty felt her wardrobe put theirs to shame.

auctions and the jewel-wearing mania. From social historians, memoirs, diaries, and newspaper pictures and accounts, we get only a few names both of pearls and their wearers.

Among American women, there were countless numbers who wore great pearls, some of them purchased at auctions, some, as the century waned, directly from the aristocracy of England, Germany, Spain, and Italy—although many preferred better living standards, up-to-date comfort, and new plumbing to the wearing of ancient pearls. Pearl dog collars were the rage, although few could wear them as wide as Consuelo Vanderbilt, but with them were also worn ropes, tiaras, and even breastplates. Indeed, they wore as many sets of matched pearls in as many different arrangements, loops, curlicues, and varieties as could be devised. Mrs. Jay Gould had a fine collection that included a dog collar, not of rows of pearls, but of pearls set in a delicate flower design in silver. She later gave it to her daughter-in-law.

What fortunes the jewels of these ladies represented—but then, what fortunes they had to spend! A single party might cost as much as $25,000— and more if, like one given by a Vanderbilt, the favors were single black pearls from the Empress Eugénie collection. Often one evening dress cost at least $1,000 and the pearls on them $50,000 and more. *The* Mrs. Astor (Mrs. William Backhouse Astor) favored diamonds for evening—she was once described as a "walking chandelier." But in the daytime, and at less formal occasions, she was often a cascade of pearls. Mrs. Astor ruled wealthy New York society for almost four decades, forcing scores of other women into diamonds and pearls. But she had little influence in Boston. There, for the most part, Victoria's precepts were followed; display was avoided, money was spent prudently, and parties were simple—except for Mrs. Jack Gardner, another Isabella who knew her own mind and followed it. She was the great patroness of the arts who left Boston her private collection of paintings; she was also an improper Bostonian who paid small attention to the local rules of propriety. Her tastes ranged from walking a lion cub on a leash, to wearing expensive Paris frocks, to having her portrait painted by John Singer Sargent in a dress cut so low and so suggestive of a gypsy life that after it was finished, her husband made her hide it away. It seems more demure than indecent today, and no one in his right mind would ever think that Mrs. Jack, as she was fondly known by artists and writers, would ever long for a gypsy life wearing the pearl belt she wore in that portrait—it was three inches wide, and intricately worked.

While the rich were tracking down pearls at auctions and in jewelry stores, the poor were enjoying another sort of pearl rush entirely, for sud-

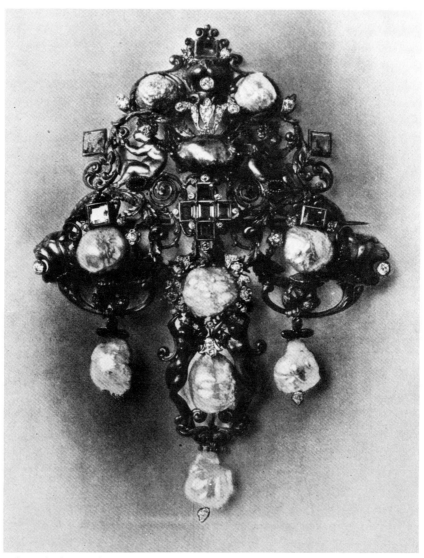

A brooch designed in Renaissance style but set with freshwater pearls from streams and rivers of the United States. Notice the cross in the center.

denly, casually, pearls were found growing in local river mussels. The first find was that of a shoemaker, a man named David Howell, who liked to gather mussels in the spring from Notch Brook, near his home in Paterson, New Jersey, and stew them in garlic and butter for his dinner. As he munched away on his mess, as he called it, that particular evening in June, 1857, his teeth struck a large hard object which, when he spat it out, turned out to be a pearl of nearly 400 grains bruised and discolored by the grease, heat, and his teeth. The next day, he took it to his shoe store and showed it, at lunchtime, to a jeweler, who said that if it had been in good shape, it would have been worth $25,000—but as it was, it was worthless. As the news got about, Howell's neighbors began crowding Notch Brook looking not just for food, but for pearls. Within a few days a fine pink pearl was found by a carpenter named Jacob Quackenbush, only a quarter the size of Howell's but harvested in flawless condition. Taking no chances on local prices, Quackenbush took his pearl to New York and sold it to Charles Tiffany, after some dickering, for $1,500. A dealer in fine goods and known for his carriage trade, Tiffany felt he had to buy it at almost any price to keep his standing status, but that $1,500 was taking a considerable risk.

The problem was, as he explained it to a magazine reporter later, that where two big pearls had been found there might be many, many more— and they'd bring the price way down. "Here this man finds a pearl within seventeen miles of our business," he said, clearly chagrined. "What if thousands were found and many perhaps finer than this one!" He took the risk, however, and passed it on immediately to the Paris branch, where it was then sold to a Parisian jeweler, who in turn sold it to someone who gave it to Empress Eugénie. It was thereafter known as the "Queen Pearl," and is still with the collection of jewels left by Empress Eugénie to the Philadelphia dentist who rescued her when she was forced to flee Paris in 1870. The Evans Collection, as it is now known, is now in the possession of the University of Pennsylvania which, lacking any display facilities, keeps it in a bank vault.

When news of the New Jersey finds spread, persons came from all directions to search the creek. "It looked like camp-meeting time," one old resident phrased it; the banks were lined with horses, wagons, people— and, as often as not, shoes. At least one schoolteacher closed his one-room schoolhouse so that his pupils could enjoy the hunt; farmers joined mechanics in the water, while on the banks merchants stood high and dry bidding on each pearl discovered. During 1857 alone the markets of New York received $15,000 worth of pearls from little Notch Brook and another

Pearl-bearing mussels were found in the Notch Brook, three miles from Paterson, N.J., in the early 1850's, a contemporary print showing whole families harvesting their catch.

Opposite, far left
Mrs. George J. Gould in her rope, or sautoir, of pearls, a tiara, a brooch, and a collar—one of the many sets owned by the fashionable in the gay and luxurious 1890's.

Opposite left
This portrait of Isabella Stewart (Mrs. Jack) Gardner by Sargent was considered so suggestive of "a gypsy life" that her husband made her hide it for years. It is now on view in the museum which bears her name in Boston.
Courtesy, Isabella Stewart Gardner Museum, Boston.

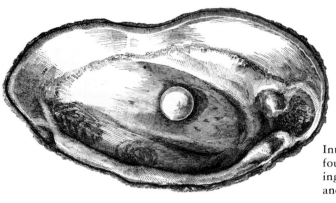

Interior of a pearl mussel found in Notch Brook showing the position of the pearl, and exterior shell.

This "fabulous $25,000 pearl" was found at Notch Brook, but unfortunately ruined by having been cooked with the mussel prior to its discovery.

$100,000 were estimated to have been kept or sold locally. But no single pearl ever again approached the size of the two original finds, and within a year, so thoroughly had the creek been plumbed that only a few thousand dollars' worth were found the next year. Within a few years, there were no longer even any mussels left and Notch Brook's moment of glory was over.

Meanwhile, in streams all over the land pearls were being sought. In Pennsylvania, Ohio, and Texas, a few finds were reported; in Colorado some 20,000 were found. All were disappointingly small, however—most were the size of peppercorns, only a few as big as rifle shot. Soon pearl hunting was just a boyish pastime; the boys would wade in when the quieter rivers were at low tide, feel for the mussels—technically called Unios—with their bare toes, and then bob under and pick them up with their hands when they found them. And so it was boys who started the next pearl rush —in the Little Miami River in southwestern Ohio, but the adults joined them swiftly as their finds grew larger. It was steadily profitable, for they could always count on a banker named Israel H. Harris in nearby Waynesville, who had turned collector and would buy anything. By 1888 he had a salable collection ranging in color through green, pink, purplish brown, cream, and white pearls. The rose-petal pinks were the finest, for rarely had any pearls anywhere been seen with just this translucent delicate color. In 1889, they were displayed in the American exhibition at the Paris World's Fair and were awarded a gold medal; by then they were famous among freshwater pearls.

Pearls were also found in small amounts from coast to coast during this period, and about $10,000 worth reached the market annually. But there was no real interest taken in the crop until pearls were discovered in the Upper Mississippi Valley. The first were found by boys the same year the Ohio pearls were on display in Paris; it was summertime, and the boys waded into the Pecatonia River in Wisconsin for the fun of wading, collected some mussels, and found pearls. Within three months the adults had taken over and were shipping about $3,000 worth a month to the market from their small stream alone, while working as well in other neighboring streams. Sugar River, Apple River, Rock River, Wisconsin River, and even the Mississippi itself (near Prairie du Chien) were all found to be breeding pearls, and pearls of considerable size and perfection. It was a little Klondike for a time; after all, pearl fishing requires no capital and no equipment, and any number can play. The Wisconsin pearls were soon as renowned for their beauty, luster, and color as the Ohio pearls but the most unusual ones were a shade of metallic green. One shipment of 93 pearls from Sugar River to London brought in more than $55,000; all told, within two years, it was estimated that more than $300,000 worth of pearls had been sold from the valley and perhaps $150,000 worth retained.

There were also brief flurries of interest in pearls in Tennessee, most of them in the Tennessee River Valley, but the next small pearl rush was in Arkansas, exactly where (it was discovered later) the Indians had had a fishery about a hundred years earlier, in the White River and its tributaries.

For years pearls had been picked up there by the fishermen and given to their children as "lucky stones"—even as the first diamonds were in South Africa—and twice pearls of some importance had been found. But these were considered flukes; not until 1895, when some surveyors collected $5,000 worth in a few months, did any real interest develop. It rose high the following year, however, and it was soon said that there was not a river in Arkansas without pearls, although the Black River fast became the favorite.

By 1898, it was estimated that some $500,000 worth of pearls had been found in the Tennessee Valley, and a thriving industry centered around Black Rock, where there were about a thousand pearl fishers. Throughout Tennessee itself another nine or ten thousand worked; men, women, and children could be seen wading in the rivers, usually along sandbars, their faces turned toward the water, their concentration absolute, and their toes busy. The cotton crops were neglected and the schools were depleted; even the cautious were persuaded that pearls would make them a living, if not a fortune. Quickly, guides appeared, boat renters sprang up, dredges and rakes were produced, and by 1891 a button factory had opened.

With the factory, the adventure became an industry. Many who had simply sold their pearls by the handful now organized to gather both pearls and shell, and the casual family pearl-fishing of Tennessee and Arkansas became professionalized. Quahog shells from the Mississippi, added to the local shell supply, turned into buttons and spread the fever; by 1900 it was estimated that for this factory alone some 35,000 clamshells were being collected annually and punched out by cutters into buttons and beads. As one area became exhausted, it was deserted for another; the gathering of shells spread to all the large tributaries of the Mississippi, into the Ohio and the Illinois and finally into the Wabash, where in 1907 baroque (irregularly shaped) pearls of a "sweet luster" (Kunz's phrase), a silvery white color, were found as well as a considerable quantity of shell. The total yield that year was said to be more than $50,000 worth of pearls alone.

Soon there was scarcely a stream in the country that had not been searched and found productive; in northeast Maine, the streams around Moosehead Lake were favorites; in Massachusetts, many were found in the ponds and small streams. Nonesuch Pond near Weston was the scene of a small pearl flurry; in Connecticut, Mystic River yielded some, Bantam Lake yielded many; in New York, pearls were found in the swift shallow northern streams in the Adirondacks, and Grass River in 1896 and 1897 became a great lure, while Pearl River in Rockland County became famous for its brown pearls, one hundred of which were exhibited in the Paris Exposition of 1900.

Even in the coal regions of Pennsylvania pearls were found; at the headwaters of the Schuylkill near Tamaqua, Quakake, and Mahanoy City, a good-sized pearl rush developed among the farmers who used the mussel shells to scrape the hair off the hides of their slaughtered pigs. These were not beautiful lustrous pearls but they were pearls: dark blue, pink, lavender,

Negroes as well as whites set up camps along the Arkansas River during the pearl rushes of the late nineteenth century.

and white. Maryland's pearls were also small but some were lustrous, and those found in the small brooks near the head of Chesapeake Bay were a delicate pink.

Near Rome, Georgia, which was believed to have been the site of the Indian town of Caofaqui where De Soto found natives well decorated with pearls, the Etowah and the Oostanaula rivers both yielded a few pearls. On the banks of the Ochlockonee River in Florida, another place De Soto reported Indians wearing pearls, other beds were found.

It must have been great fun to be the first to find pearls. The early stories carried by the newspapers were full of a sense of wonder and delight. A workman finds a pearl in the cuff of his best Sunday suit after being baptized in the river. A boy whose mother is a cripple cuts his foot on a shell and opens it to find a pearl. A mother cleaning up the children's toys realizes suddenly her family is playing games with pearls. A farmer finds a number of pearls in a posthole he is digging in a field that earlier that spring was flooded. A Negro who cares for the hogs finds a pearl in the muck he collected along the riverbank as feed. The newspapers were full of odd stories of lucky breaks, which added to the fever, but there was another side to it inevitably—many pearl hunters found their feet shriveled, their hands cut from the sharp shells, their stomachs upset by a steady diet of mussels, and in only too many cases, their hands empty of profit.

For river-pearling was at once too pleasurable, too easy, and too diffi-cult. The situation was delightful—quiet, shallow waters dappled with sun. The work was casual—a simple water telescope made at home with a tin can and a piece of glass was about as much equipment a fisher had to carry, although the hopeful also brought baskets. The company was friendly—most of the pearl rushes were family affairs—the group pitching their tents, wading most of the day, at night gathering around the campfires, frying the fish, playing the banjo or the harmonica, on Saturdays going into the nearest town to sell the pearls, to shop, perhaps to dance or drink. But while the life was pleasant, the competition made profits difficult, and greed made exhaustion inevitable. Wily shills worked up advertisements to lure the workhands from the farms, the railwaymen from their jobs, the teachers and pupils from the schools; sometimes the bait of one free picnic on a pearling river was enough to draw hundreds from a thirty-mile radius, at other times sales of rakes, scoops, drags, or flatbottom boats were coupled with exaggerated accounts of great finds and high rewards and used as lures to the romantic and the yearning. During the height of the Arkansas boom fishermen sold thousands of mussels unopened; sometimes there was havoc as the firstcomers opened their shells.

Most mussel shells were opened by knives, and the deft had a great advantage; in Mississippi Valley, where pearls were few and shell the prize, a steaming method was used. To this day no satisfactory mechanical method has been developed, however; steaming damages any pearls found, piling shells in the sun creates a stench, and promotes disease, and no machine has been devised to replace the good grip of a left hand while a right hand pries. More seed pearls might have been found among the freshwater mussels if the Americans had been willing to comb through the fleshy parts of the mussel but they were not; for most the dream was of a big pearl the size of a pebble and as beautiful as a drop of cream, and seed pearls were tossed aside.

Only for a few hundred of the lucky did such dreams come true. As Kunz put it: "In many localities the pursuit yields far less profit than pleasure, and many a man who spends the summer pearling is in a fair way to spend the winter at the expense of someone else."

It is strange that while the oriental pearl was celebrated widely in song and story, there is little in American literature about this phase of discovery. John Steinbeck wrote one story about fishermen and another about abalone-pearling in southern California, but Mark Twain's stories of life on the Mississippi ignore the pearl rush of the nineteenth century just

This seed pearl necklace was made from freshwater pearls by an American, Mrs. Florence Koehler, in the late nineteenth century. *The Metropolitan Museum of Art, gift of Emily Crane Chadburne.*

as James Fenimore Cooper, who focused on Indian lore, ignored the Indian pearls. As we noted earlier, relics show that both the Mississippi and Ohio valley pearls were often used in burial or cremation ceremonies by the Indians, as well as being extensively used as ornament and money by the living.

Some time around World War I, United States river-pearling ceased being profitable, although shell collecting continued. Increasing industrial use of the rivers changed the tranquil currents so necessary to the Unio; pollution of the waters through city building changed the nourishment; dams and bridges destroyed coves, altered streams, and in some cases actually killed off species of mussels.

In 1937, the shell expert J. P. E. Morrison was asked by the Tennessee Valley Authority to check out the shells in Mussel Shoals before the dredges moved in to make the present great power dam, and in his report, he told them that the dredging would wreck this unique mussel breeding ground, but "no one cared," he said. The chief mound he was assigned to remove and catalog turned out to be 365 feet long and about 20 feet high; about half of it was composed of unworked-shells. Eight archaeologists, each with twenty student workers, and some thousand WPA laborers were employed to speed up the task. It was believed the shells were piled up about 10,000 B.C. and were simply relics of food eaten, although they may have borne pearls, since all varieties of mussels do. It was a curious heap; about 25 varieties were represented but in no order or design. Since the river was acid and the area limestone, the shoals had developed as a natural breeding ground for the shellfish—the river bit off the chunks of limestone, the clams lived off, and bathed in, the alkaline waters. When the flow was cut off, the shoals vanished, and today below Wilson Dam only the name recalls the fact there were once mussels at Mussel Shoals.

The tough, hardy, pig toe clam, however, is not yet defunct, although it is decreasing rapidly in numbers. This shell, as we shall see in a later chapter, is highly prized for its use as nuclei for the cultured pearl. Along the West Coast, abalone shell is also still harvested in a small way.

Many of the freshwater pearls of the eighties and nineties were worn in brooches, necklaces, and earrings by American women and some were exported abroad. The Eastern millionaires' wives preferred their pearls to be round—a great many of the freshwater pearls were baroques—and to have an aristocratic history, but the Middle Western women prized the pearls of their own rivers and paid well for them. More than one jewelry store was built on America's river pearls: Evarts and Company of Dallas, for instance, began in 1897; the first Evarts carted a basket of pearls up from the Coronado River to the city and sold them. Around the turn of the century, Peacock's of Chicago set some in platinum as brooches. But most customers still preferred orients.

By 1909, Kunz was able to say that pearls were America's most popular jewel and that never in the world's history had so many owned such fine pearls.

Not all women who wore great pearls were the wives of millionaires. Entertainers both here and in France earned their pearls by other means than marriage. One of the finest collections of pearls anywhere was worn by Madame Nordica, for instance, the popular and talented opera star of the late nineteenth century. As well as a full matched parure of necklace, bodice breastplate, earrings, dog collar—hers was so artfully strung that it came to a V point in front—she also had a fine necklace of different colored pearls. There were five blue, three black, seven rose-colored, and six creamy white pearls set in gold and diamonds in this great necklace, and it ended in a magnificent pendant greenish-rose abalone pearl weighing 175 grains.

In Paris, Bohemian beauties also sported pearls in profusion. "The white pearls of Léonide Leblanc and the black pearls of Cora Pearl were famous," wrote a French jewel historian. "At the close of the century the jewel caskets of Liane de Pougy and Caroline Otero provoked astonishments from even the most hardened free livers." The girls fought with open jealousy over who had the most pearls; once upon hearing that Otero was wearing every single pearl she possessed—including an Empress Eugénie necklace—to Maxim's that night, Liane de Pougy sought to outshine her. She entered Maxim's after Otero had, wearing a simple white dress without a single ornament but followed by her maid "bending under a burden of diamonds."

The American and French vulgarities were despised by end-of-century youth, and at Oxford and the Sorbonne, poets and writers made sport of the surfeit of jewels being displayed and spoke contemptuously of the "tradesmen" and "butchers' wives" who owned masses of jewels. These young intellectuals—including Oscar Wilde, who traced some Renaissance jewels—preferred the bizarre—like cat's eyes and hyacinths—to precious stones, and praised baroque pearls over round ones. Those who curried their favor—like Sarah Bernhardt—helped to bring jewels into harmony with the *art nouveau* of Paris; snake bracelets, peacock's eyes, small medieval designs of animals and flowers made up in malformed pearls, and iridescent butterfly wings became a minor rage. Jewelers catering to the young executed some designs in fine enameled pieces and used good stones well set, delicately as

did Fabergé, but there was more amusement than grandeur in these fash-
ions. Small as they were, each piece reflected that this period, too, was a
time of ferment.

But as well as being worn as part of the equipment or curios of the
nouveau riche desiring to show status, pearls were still highly esteemed as
wedding gifts in keeping with the gentler tradition they carried as symbols
of sweetness, modesty, and chastity. They were even received at the White
House in this guise; one of the favorite presents which the witty, pretty Alice
Roosevelt, daughter of President Theodore Roosevelt, received when she
married Speaker of the House Nicholas Longworth, was a $25,000 string
of pearls, and she wore it with delight although there were those who said
it belonged in the state treasury.

By the time World War I was over, however, pearl parures worn in
great masses were finished. Royalty was deposed, the grand dukes were
living in poverty, and the American millionaires were worrying about the
servant problem, their contraband liquor supply, and their daughters, who
were chopping off both their hair and their skirts, frequenting speakeasies,
and snuggling into raccoon coats. Now it was the flappers who made fun
of the great pearls; they took the family ropes, slung them around the
necks of their tight short dresses, and set them swinging wildly from side
to side while dancing the Charleston, or, later, the Lindy Hop. The more
radical ones even took pearls a step further—they wore with their pearl
sautoir a red ribbon band *à la victime,* tight around the neck as a symbol
of aristocracy going to the guillotine in their pearls.

The mocking ropes did not last long, for there were still many who
loved pearls. In Paris, gamine couturiere Gabrielle Chanel, realizing swiftly
that a new informality had come, showed short strings of pearls with
sweaters and skirts—the new costume of youth—and with trim, well-tailored
suits. Suddenly the ropes were broken up, the brooches stripped, and graduated strings of a mere 20, 30, or 40 pearls came in to be worn night and
day by anyone with any pretensions to fashion. If the pearls were good they
could even be seen on the tennis courts; many a Philadelphian or a Bos-
tonian took hers off only to sleep. Some honored the strands of graduated
pearls; a few revealed they had pearls that once belonged to the ropes of
queens, duchesses, princesses—but most knew them only as "my pearls."
Synthetic pearls showed up often, and rising young movie stars, ignorant
of great old romantic pearls, bought the new, still somewhat rare, cultured
pearls. Men bought pearl buttons for their evening shirts and add-a-pearl
necklaces for their daughters, never realizing that buying each pearl singly
cost far more than buying the whole lot in one fell swoop, for each bride

Lillian Russell was one of the beauties of the Gay Nineties who copied the society women's opulent use of pearls.

Opera singer Geraldine Farrar's matched tiara and dog collar in diamonds and pearls were said to be equaled only by those of Mrs. Jay Gould, wife of the railroad magnate. Like other divas of importance, she wore her own jewels on stage.

wanted a necklace of pearls. Others got their pearls as gifts from their husbands or lovers—but soon many bought them out of paychecks they earned themselves. It was a fashion change in keeping with the source of pearls.

Cultured pearls were by now in use in buttons, and some round ones were being worn in necklaces and earrings—sometimes without the owner's knowledge. Mikimoto, the great Japanese pearl merchandiser, was trying hard both to legitimize cultured pearls as "real" and to publicize them as jewels, and scientists believe that many were sold unlabeled. Natural pearls came chiefly from Bombay via Bahrein in the Persian Gulf, a hot, smelly (from rotting oysters) village of ancient origins, run by desert sheiks. Oil was known to be there then but it had not been worked; the pearls alone made the sheikdoms around the Gulf the richest per capita area in the world —in some years the take reaching more than $9 million. Bahrein's pearls were both plentiful and beautiful; it was believed that this was because the Gulf contained salt water but was fed from the bottom by fresh springs. It was not a well-populated place, however; the heat was intense, the wind blistering, and disease was rampant; only 50,000 lived in the area. The discovery of oil and the industrialization of the Gulf wrecked the pearl beds in the forties but increased the income and lowered the death rate, although no one has yet been able to do anything about the weather there but build air-conditioned buildings. Divers in the twenties protected themselves from underwater pressure with leather caps and from sharks with shark charmers who cried incantations and blew on shells and horns. Most divers lived in poor hovels, staying inside at noontime when the heat was intense and sleeping on the roof at night to catch a few breezes.

Another natural pearl source during these years was Ceylon, which had produced some of the world's most beautiful pearls but which now, under the British, produced few. The most vivid account of the modern fishery is that of Leonard Woolf's in his recently published autobiography *Growing*. Woolf, later a writer and publisher, was in 1906 a British government agent in charge of the Ceylon fishery, a February to April event which attracted about 5,000 Arab and 5,000 Tamil divers, and a motley collection of some 25,000 merchants, traders, adventurers, and thieves from all over the world. Four Britishers ruled by moral authority, auctioning off the oyster shells and their precious booty without the use of force, but it was not easy. "As the fishery went on and the whole camp became full of the smell of putrid and putrescent oysters, a horrible smell hung over it and myriads of flies swarmed over everything. . . . In the day one trudged up and down the koddu [enclosure] through the sand under a blazing sky—it is like

Bahrein, once a great pearl island in the Persian Gulf, is now a center of oil production; this sketch was made in the mid-nineteenth century.

Fishing in the late nineteenth century for pearls in the Gulf of Manaar or Malabar which separates Ceylon from India; note the divers resting in the water.

walking about hour after hour in a hell. . . ." It was the custom later during the oyster-fishing season to heap all the oysters up in one pile and not open them until the fishing was completed. To shorten this task, which particularly annoyed the buyers who hung about impatiently, Ceylon for a time used a simple X-ray machine which could sort oysters with pearls from oysters without them, before they were opened. Ceylon, in recorded times, never had the great pearl crop that the Persian Gulf harvested year after year until the 1950's, and in the 1920's, shifting sand on the sea bottom made its production decline steadily.

There were also rich beds in Australia then, in the China Sea, the Sulu Sea, and off the coast of New Guinea. The big pearl market was Bombay, India, and at its low-roofed bazaar each year, hundreds of pearl buyers gathered as they had for centuries. Slowly but surely, however, the ease of cultivating and harvesting the pearl oysters of Japan and the assured perfection of the cultured pearls found within wrecked the demand for the lustrous beads of old achieved through so much trial and tribulation and at such risk of life, and today the Bombay market is a ghost market.

Other factors, meanwhile, briefly discouraged the wearing of jewels. On the heels of the roaring twenties came the stock market crash of 1929 and the Depression of the thirties. Again the diamonds and pearls of the once rich went up for auction or were secreted in bank vaults; again great parures were broken up and real value separated from display value. A few tried desperately to enliven the scene with ornament and sentiment; the Duchess of Windsor, in exile, decked herself out in pearl beanies in lieu of the crown she had dreamed of before Edward VIII chose to abdicate the throne of England in order to marry her. Like the intellectuals of the *fin de siècle,* she wore amusing jewels—roosters and peacocks with mother-of-pearl feathers, wildflowers in rubies and emeralds—on her simple black dresses. Some of her pearls were cultured and some were old.

World War II followed the Depression; it too was no time for jewel-wearing—but rather for jewel-selling. Only afterward could it be seen that this war, like so many others, had ushered in a new era in jewels; new owners, and had brought the slowly developing cultured pearls of Japan to worldwide prominence.

It was Consuelo Vanderbilt, the one-time Duchess of Marlborough, now Mrs. Balsan, who noted most succinctly what had happened to jewel lovers. Fleeing from the German occupation of France with her French husband, trying to get home to her native land, she thought of her jewels and disdained them. Once she had been tempted to fondle her pearls when nervous. Now she wrote: "Passports were now more precious than jewels,

Queen Elizabeth II of England—even her "informal" crown is wreathed with two rows of pearls—the ancient symbol of divine right.

and it almost became a nervous habit with me to explore my handbag for the reassurance mine brought me."

Other fugitives found reassurance in a diamond sewn into the hem of a jacket or wedged between the sole of a shoe and the vamp. When the Rothschilds fled Hitler, great caskets of jewels entered the market; it was said that the bank they established in England was built on a pair of earrings.

The story of what happened to pearls, however, is different from that of most jewels, for the development of the cultured pearl had more bearing on it than did the war's social upheavals. Because it is a fascinating as well as an important story, the cultured pearl deserves more than one chapter, and so the rest of this narrative will be largely devoted to its discovery, development, and present-day status.

The Duke and Duchess of Windsor in 1943; she wrote in her memoirs she did not consider herself "a pearl type" when young but her pearl-studded beanie hats began the return to pearl-embroidered fabrics.

5

The Discovery of the Oyster's Secret

Know you, perchance, how that poor formless wretch
The Oyster, gems his shallow moonlight chalice?
Where the shell irks him, or the sea sand frets,
He sheds this lovely lustre on his grief.
SIR EDWIN ARNOLD (1832–1904)
"The Oyster"

*E*ver since their discovery, it has been known that protection and care of the pearl-bearing oysters and clams increased the harvest of pearls. In the centuries which we know only through legends, sea dragons and dogs—both real and imaginary—were the pearl's guardians. But guarding is not cultivation. More than protection is needed to farm large and beautiful pearls in dependable amounts; man must actually manipulate nature. And so the cultivation of the pearl did not begin until after the taboos of the great nature religions had given way before the worship of an anthropocentric deity, the God in whose image man was believed to have been created and in whose eyes man was believed specially favored. When pearls were precious in a religious sense, they were sought after eagerly, protected, collected, and harvested with care but since their origins were considered sacred, none dared, at least openly, to scrutinize or interfere with the mysteries of their forming. It was believed then that pearls were formed from the tears of the gods, and that on certain sunny days in the spring of the year, the

139

oysters rose to the surface of the water and opened to receive this divine nourishment. That no man had ever seen oysters do this did not disturb the general belief; it was an article of faith that the gods of nature worked in wondrous ways. Pliny, who tried to be objective but was so much a part of his time that his Natural History is today often called by scientists a mine of misinformation, repeated this legend of tears-into-pearls as fact. It was an almost universal legend; even the practical Chinese believed that pearls were formed in the eyes of dragons and were wept forth into the seas and rivers. But whether it was the roundness of pearls or their liquid radiance that caused this association with tears or the plain fact that they were found only in water, we are not informed. For centuries the association held, and still echoes today in the bride's pearl-embroidered dress and pearl necklace, for the wedding day is a poignant one to all who feel it as a rite of passage wrenching a daughter away from her natural family into a new and unknown world.

How early it was guessed that in actuality pearls were formed from the internally secreted fluids of the oysters rather than external tears we do not know. Quite early the shell, created from the same hardened secretions of nacre, was prized almost as highly as the pearl itself. But not until after A.D. 200 was there any suggestion that this knowledge of the process existed and was being translated into action. It was the Arabs who began irritating the oysters of the Red Sea into producing more nacre in order that more and better pearls might be harvested.

It is annoying that we of the Western world are so dependent on secondhand accounts of Arabian science; we know of these attempts only from the writings of the Greek Philostratus, who repeated the gossip of the time while attempting to write a serious biography of a man named Apollonius. The story is preposterous and is worth mentioning only because it suggests that some sort of inquiry into cultivation had begun. As Philostratus tells it, the Arabs first poured oil on the turbulent waters of the Red Sea, then dove down, and finding an oyster, pricked it open with a sharp instrument and poured out the inner fluids into pearl-shaped molds. Since nacre doesn't pour out of an oyster, Philostratus must have got it all wrong, or what is more likely, have been deliberately misled by the merchants who told it to him—a business practice as old as business itself. We can only guess what really took place; the oil-soothed waters sound sensible, the pricking open of the oysters may also be true. But having pricked them open, did the pearl fishermen then insert the molds *into* the oysters? If they did, they did succeed in growing pearls; if they didn't, they were only a little better off than those who depended solely on nature's bounty.

The next time we hear of men growing pearls, we know that insertions were made, and we also know something of the ritual and the materials used, but little more about the technical procedure. This story is told in that marvelous collection of letters from Jesuit missionaries to the Far East which states flatly that as early as the fourteenth century the Chinese were making pearls by injecting into river mussels pulverized seed pearls moistened with the juice of a holly leaf and shaped into round pellets. How the oysters were opened and under what biological conditions are facts not reported but a lot of folderol is. The ritual began when the largest mussels available were collected and placed in a basin half full of water set in a secluded place where the dew could fall on them, but where no female would pass by and where neither the barking of dogs nor the crowing of roosters could be heard. (What significance these have we are not told.) While the dew fell and presumably the oysters opened naturally, some seed pearls *(yo tchu)* of the medicinal kind were washed and moistened with juice expressed from leaves of the *Che-ta-kong* holly and the resulting paste rolled into perfectly round pea-sized pellets. When these pellets had dried, they were then poked into the opened mussels and the mussels returned to the riverbed where, for one hundred days, they were fed with equal parts of powdered genseng, china root, peki root, and peche roots all molded together with honey and shaped into grits the size of rice grains.

Did it work? The missionary who reported seeing them claimed the pearls which resulted were vastly superior to the natural. But while we know that scientifically it might have worked, we have no testing in the West of the method, nor any precise comparisons between such pearls and natural pearls. Why did the monks receiving the letters never experiment with the process? Some of the ingredients would have been difficult to get in France—both the holly and the roots are indigenous to China—and the folderol smacks of the sort of fertility rite that was displeasing to the Jesuits.

Moreover, there was apparently very little real research into pearls in Europe at that period. They were in plentiful supply in the rivers, used in medicines, and when large and lustrous prized by kings and queens alike. But in Columbus' notes we find that he decided that American pearls were made from dew dropped into an oyster bed from the mangrove trees that abounded in the Venezuelan shoals. This theory tells us something about the simplicity of Columbus' mind and a lot about the state of marine biology in 1500. Anselmus de Boot somewhat later theorized more complexly. Pointing out that the pearl and the shell were similar in content, he suggested that the pearl was a drop of surplus fluid excreted by the oyster

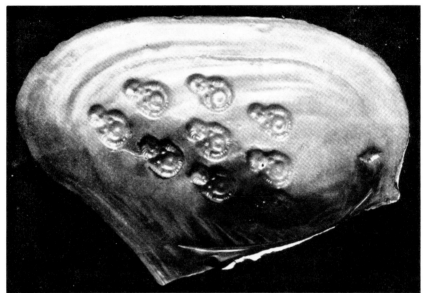

The old Chinese method of button pearl culture; above, the shell of a river mollusk, *Dipsas plicatus,* studded with metal figures of Buddha which were layered with nacre; below, the nuclei here were either small seed pearls or porcelain beads.

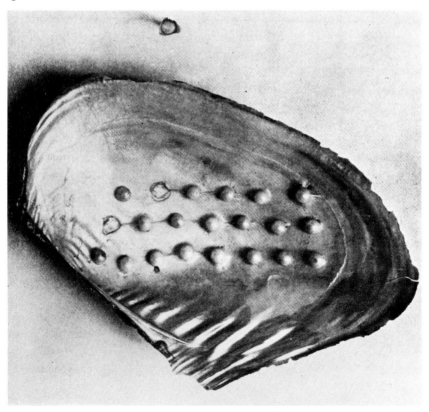

but not discharged. Another of the late medieval scientists added to this description of process the suggestion that a grain of sand got into the oyster or mussel and this formed a nucleus around which such surplus liquids collected. Sometime in this period the name "nacre" was used for the oysters' fluids, a French word suggesting both the sea and creation but pronounced by the English—and now generally—"naker." The sand-nucleus suggestion was countered by the theory of another scientist that it was undischarged eggs that caused the pearl to form, while a third entered the argument declaring that "ruptured organs" started the nacre flowing and produced both the pearl and the shell. Such controversies went on for several centuries and were repeated even in the eighteenth century when something of a pearl-study fad developed among chemists, and scores of pearls were cut in half for study. If the insides of all natural pearls were the same, the question might have been resolved, but a pearl may form around a variety of irritants, including bacteria, some of which may wither away inside the nacre.

While the scholarly debate rumbled along in the West, the Chinese artisans slowly perfected their experiments, and as early as 1600 were able to insert small, carved (from mother-of-pearl) images of Buddha into live, pearl-bearing river mussels (*Crystaria plicata*) and, after six months of care, take out tiny pearl icons of considerable religious and commercial value and some charm. In today's nomenclature they are simple button pearls, that is, they are rounded only on one side and flat on the other where they were connected to the shell. But they were forced pearls, and it is probable that it is from them that the first Western scientist to work on pearl cultivation got his ideas.

This was Carl von Linné of Sweden, or, as he preferred to be called in the Latin nomenclature he propounded to fellow scholars, Carolus Linnaeus. Late in 1748, Linnaeus wrote to a Swiss anatomist who was his friend: "At length I have ascertained the manner in which pearls originate and grow in shells; and in the course of five or six years I am able to produce in any mother-of-pearl shell the size of one's hand a pearl as large as the seed of the common vetch." (Vetch is commonly called witch grass. The pearls would be called seed pearls today because of their smallness.) He did not, however, reveal his procedure either then or, some years later, when he sent off some pearls to the Linnaean Society in London with a note saying he "possessed the art" of pearl-growing and would sell it to the Swedish government if they proffered him a suitable reward. In due course, the government offered him what amounted to about $5,000 for his secret, but although he claimed he told them the procedure, they never paid him

and so he withdrew his permission and sold the secret to a merchant named
Peter Bagge of Gothenburg for a mere $2,500. Bagge never reported har-
vesting any pearls, however, and the whole thing remained a mystery until
a German professor, going through Bagge's papers in the 1850's, found a
memorandum and reported it in part. Instead of using the clam's opening
mouth, as the Chinese and Arabians had, Linnaeus apparently pushed a
thin silver wire through the shell of the river mussel to insert a small pellet
of limestone into the living creature, which was then returned to a pond
or lake for several years while the pearl grew. If Linnaeus reached the
mussel without penetrating it too severely, some of his pearls might have
been spherical; if he injured the body of the mussel it might die; if he
missed the mussel entirely and the nucleus fell between the mantle and
the shell, the result would have been akin to the button pearls of the Chinese. Unfortunately, because of his secrecy, we do not know exactly what
sort of pearls Linnaeus harvested or how many; it is probable he cultivated
some spherical ones but that his successes were not many. The kind of
mussel he experimented with is still not known.

By now the Chinese were using large specimens of *plicatas,* which
they opened gently with bamboo spatulas, then cut away the flesh of the
creature with metal probes, and finally inserted against the shell parallel
rows of Buddhas or other molds. The results were all pearls which
sold very cheaply as talismans at shrines or were set by jewelers as hair
ornaments.

The industry thrived especially in two villages in the northern province of Chekiang, which was also renowned for its rice and its silks, through
the seasonal employment of around 5,000 people. In the nearby village of
Chung-kwan-o, a temple was erected to the thirteenth-century discoverer
of pearl-cultivating procedure, Yu Shun Yang. In the nineteenth century,
shells with the pearl Buddhas still adhering to them were brought into the
United States as curiosities; in its backroom collection of shells, the Smithsonian has some which are seven inches long and contain a dozen of the
Buddhas. Looking at them, I was struck by how startling it was that any
creature could have survived such manipulation and secreted so much nacre
in a single season of growing.

As word of the Chinese work slowly made its way around the world,
many similar experiments were made with a variety of mollusks. In Ceylon,
at the ancient beds in the Gulf of Manaar, a Dutchman named Kelaart had
some success with oysters. In the shoals of Tahiti, a Frenchman, Bouchon-
Brandely, used Linnaeus' method of drilling holes in oyster shells and inserting pellets of mother-of-pearl or glass. In southern California another

French scientist, Louis Bouton, using a similar method, worked on abalone *(Haliotis)* and reported that, like the Chinese pearls, in six months the pearl products were quite attractive. Indeed, his reports to the Paris Academy of Sciences in 1898 led the jewel expert Kunz to speculate on the possibility of a "profitable business in growing pearls on the Pacific coast of the United States." Kunz was further enheartened when in Iowa, a Cedar Rapids man named Vane Simonds figured out a way to place less stress on his mollusks during the time of insertion. Simonds allowed the river mussels (Unios) to open naturally in the sun, and then, while they were open, he pushed a small wedge of wood into the shell and returned them to the water, the wedge still in position, to let them recuperate before he inserted the nucleus of the pearl. (A chemist suggested using chloroform for the operation, but if any field worker tried it, it was not reported.) In La Paz, Mexico, a laboratory experimented with the breeding of the pearl-bearing oysters themselves, hoping in this way to increase the supply of pearls, but most scientists were leery of this, suggesting that it was not healthy conditions but stress that oysters needed in order to grow pearls.

More interest was taken in Japan, where a little-known businessman named Kokichi Mikimoto had one thousand acres of sea bottom in Ago Bay populated with almost a million oysters and was producing from 30,000 to 50,000 button pearls annually. What were his prospects, according to Kunz? "Although these culture pearls," Kunz wrote in 1908, "are somewhat attractive and superior to the culture pearls of China and other fresh waters, they by no means compare favorably with choice pearls. They are rarely, if ever, spherical, and only the upper surface is lustrous; consequently they serve only the purpose of half pearls. . . . Compared with choice pearls, they are not only deficient in luster, fragile and are beautiful only on the surface and not available for necklaces." He noted, however, that good specimens of these pearls were selling for several dollars each in America and a few individual ones for $50 or more.

Kunz's strong feeling for science and for American tenacity misled him into predicting that American attempts were more likely to succeed than the trial-and-error work of Mikimoto. He warned his reading public against being too hasty about financing companies "soliciting capital for establishing so-called 'pearl farms,'" especially when the investigator seeking funds "surrounded himself with mystery," but agreed that there was a scientific basis for the belief that it may be possible "in time" to bring about pearl growth through some sort of forcing techniques. He favored infecting mollusks with parasites over the use of inserted nuclei; versed as he was in the biological aspects of pearl-growing, he did not realize

Japanese amas, or pearl divers, circa 1800. Half-nude diving continued through the nineteenth century; women are still the chief sea divers of Japan but since 1950 dive only for edible shellfish. Prints are by Utamaro; the originals are highly colored.

that the stress of inserting anything caused quite enough nacre to flow for pearl-forming purposes—if it was inserted in the proper place and manner. One phrase in a letter written to him in the summer of 1907 revealed that the great breakthrough in pearl cultivation—the culturing of lustrous, round pearls—had already occurred, but he missed it.

That phrase was "in the tissue" and it was written in a letter from a marine biologist at the University of Tokyo, Dr. T. Nishikawa, which was included, although not analyzed, by Kunz in his great work on pearls.

Mishikawa was one of two young men of Japan who discovered the

oyster's secret almost simultaneously around 1905 but it was years before the world was to know about it, and then only through the pearl production of Mikimoto, the great pearl cultivator. Not until 1949, when the American government published its study of the pearl industry of Japan and laid bare both its origins and its complex procedures, was the full story known.

But before we tell that tale of excitement and despair, victory and defeat, cooperation and intrigue, let us take a look at the lowly creature that produces the noble pearl, and see what the real problems of pearl production are. The mollusk family is a dull-looking crowd viewed ex-

Kokichi Mikimoto, discoverer of the method for culturing pearls in mass quantities and Japan's great merchant, seen here in 1947 (when eighty-five) with a hoard of cultured pearls farmed during the war years.

ternally; it is only when you get under their skin, to use an old metaphor, that it is possible to understand what fascinating creatures they really are.

Theoretically, all mollusks are capable of producing pearls—the mussels and clams in the rivers, the oysters and conches and abalones in the seas—since all pearls are formed in the same manner as is the mollusk's shell. Of them all, however, the oyster *Pinctada* is the finest pearl-bearer.

This oyster's shell, known in the nonbiological world as mother-of-pearl, is not just a housing for the oyster, as a snail's is, but a physiological part of the living creature it grows out of, and like human skin, it cannot be shucked off without peril. In this sense shell is like our top layer of skin, but since an oyster also has a flexible, easily penetrable skin (called the mantle), its shell and skin are designated separately and distinctly. The mantle, however, instead of having epithelial cells on the inside, as most of ours have, grows outward through excretions, and thus grows the shell much as we grow fingernails or hair. It is these cells that secrete nacre, which is fine *crystalline calcium carbonate* ($CaCo_3$) in the form of aragonite crystals and which gives the shell and the pearl their luster, *conchiolin* ($C\ 32H48\ N2\ 11$), which cements the crystals together, and *mucous*. The proportions of these ingredients vary from oyster to oyster by type, by individual creature, and by seasons, different environments, and in different amounts of light. Why the lustrous crystals are found predominant in some specimens but not in others, however, or why some oysters produce finer nacre than others in the same family is still a question without a full answer. Various experiments suggest that light plays a role, so does salinity of the water, so does heat, and so does age.

In general, however, it can be said these oysters (of the not so edible type) produce finer nacre than do edible oysters or the mollusks of river and lake, and that among the many species of oysters, the finest pearl-bearers are the *Pinctada* (or *Margaritifera*) *vulgaris* of the Persian Gulf and Gulf of Manaar, and the *Pinctada martensii* of Japan and the *Pinctada maxima* of Australian fame.

Crusted on the outside, shiny on the inside, the oyster shell consists of two symmetrical halves connected by a large muscle which controls them through valves. At ease in a tranquil sea, the muscle is relaxed and the oyster gapes; attacked by an enemy or disturbed, the shell is suddenly shut and can be opened only with difficulty. After some time out of water or when overhot or deprived of oxygen, the muscle weakens in control, the shell opens, and the oyster is gasping. When dying and dead, its shell is open.

Exposed, the oyster's inner anatomy is not so mysterious as is its nacre-producing facility, except in regard to sex, but it is unusual. Fast becoming favored over frogs in high school dissecting laboratories, the oyster seems at first to be only its large muscle (the adductor) but closer examination reveals the usual equipment of mouth, liver, stomach, heart, intestine, and gill, plus a surprise—a single foot.

This foot can extend outside the shell to walk, or perhaps crawl about on the ocean floor, and can climb up rocks or coral. The movement is slow but not drifting; the foot makes it possible for the oyster to go from one place to another with purpose, especially in youth before the shell has grown too heavy under its layers and layers of nacre and conchiolin. The French scientist Hervé, working in the warm waters near Tuamotu in the South Pacific, dyed his oysters bright blue for clearer viewing and noted how it was done: First the shell gaped slightly, then the foot came out, explored (by feel—the oyster, so far as we know, has no eyes) retreated, came back out, felt around again, and then stretched itself forward purposefully, suddenly contracted and began to move, shell and all, to more attractive territory. Like people, Hervé's young oysters were more mobile than old ones, and when really aged—about seven or eight years—moved only when compelled to and then preferably at night. As well as the foot, the oyster has another protuberance, the byssus, by which it attaches itself to a surface. It is a gripping organ but only in action is it like a hand, for it is secreted by the oyster and if ripped off by storm waters or sharp rocks can be regrown apparently at will. A young oyster will explore quite extensively to find a suitable dwelling place and then, having found it, will adhere to it with his gripper like a leech. Some species like rough waters; but the pearl grows best in those oysters that seek tranquil, but flowing water.

All oysters are quiet and peaceful citizens of the sea. Their sex life, however, is by human sociological norms haphazard and chancy. Sex roles are confused; apparently oysters change sex, and if there is any rhyme or reason as to when or why, science has not yet discovered it. Nor is there any coupling. Eggs are ejected by an oyster in what we call the female stage right out into the water where they are fertilized by sperm ejected by passing oysters, who are in a male stage for the mating season at least. A single oyster may produce more than a million miscroscopic eggs; another oyster may respond with enough sperm to vitalize them all. But the infant mortality is great; the all but invisible progeny are at birth carried along on currents, lacking shells, a foot, parents. For a day, indeed, they are true creatures of the sea, drifting into life or death as the sea wills—drifting even into the unwitting mouths of the oysters that spawned them. On the second day, the foot begins to grow slowly, enlarging in spurts which seemed to Hervé to conform to the cycles of the moon, while the layers of shell grow at the rate of .003 millimeters a month. On the shell the concentric growth lines are, like the growth lines in trees, clearly evident; as the nacre and conchiolin harden to form mother-of-pearl, they form a striped ripple pattern which gradually extends wider and wider, each successive layer of crystals being marked by a new striation, lending the luster of the shell's nacre additional charm and design not found in pearls themselves.

As it grows, the oyster's needs are few. The oyster feeds himself endlessly through a fairly simple process: He lies in a gentle current with his valves open, catching food by means of the undulating hairs attached to the interior part of his mantle, and picking what he likes through his mouth. If he pulls in sand, pieces of sponge, or other inedibles, they collect around the edges of his shell. As they pile up and begin to bother him, he snaps shut his valves (with a discernible click) and jolts them back to the water. As over and over he jolts himself clean, slowly a pile of waste collects about him.

If he is caught tranquilly eating he is in danger of being eaten himself from the inside out. Among his predators, however, there are none who yearn for oyster shell, and if he senses a threat, the oyster clamps his shell shut and pulls his byssus inside, making himself almost impregnable. Storms are not as hard on him as are his fellow sea creatures; he can be dashed against rocks and ripped open, he can be smothered by sand, catapulted onto land by earthquakes but in the quiet lagoons where oysters like to live, these disturbances are rare. Fishlike skates with teeth strong enough to break the hardest shell, however, are not; neither are octopi, who play with oysters as cats do with mice, gripping them tightly enough to keep their shell closed, starving them almost to death so that their shell opens naturally. Thus do oysters on the half shell become the treat of the deep-sea night.

As well as these bigger enemies, there are small ones. Crabs can reach into the opened oyster shell and scoop out the flesh in one swift clawing motion. Tiny tritons, like newts, are trickier; they slither undetected down the inside of the shell of the oyster and ram a long tube into its mouth through which a single drop of poison is poured. Tritons work in pairs, and a pair can kill two or three oysters in a bed in a week. Starfish strangle oysters much as octopi do, but plankton smother them when they come in such great tides that they seem to color the water. Even on the farms where the oysters are protected by wire baskets, the red tide of plankton is a feared enemy of pearl cultivators.

Light, heat, age, and the amount of salt in the water in which an oyster lives affect it almost as much as does the food it eats and the food it provides for others. The oyster cannot spawn unless the water is of a certain heat, but if it lies in shallow or stagnant water and overheats, it will die. Sunlight or the lack of it affects its growth; in the open sun, the shell is thicker but not as wide as is that of an oyster of the same species who is gripped to the shady side of a rock. If it gets too cold, nacre deposits cease, but unless it is freezing cold, the oyster survives. Too much salt or high temperatures cause the shell to grow heavier and deposits of conchiolin overbalance deposits of nacre—but some of the heaviest shells of all grow in fresh water.

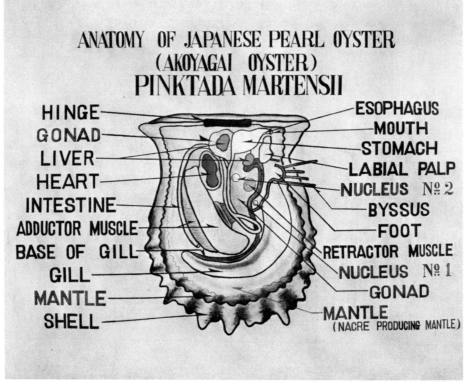

ANATOMY OF JAPANESE PEARL OYSTER
(AKOYAGAI OYSTER)
PINKTADA MARTENSII

HINGE
GONAD
LIVER
HEART
INTESTINE
ADDUCTOR MUSCLE
BASE OF GILL
GILL
MANTLE
SHELL

ESOPHAGUS
MOUTH
STOMACH
LABIAL PALP
NUCLEUS № 2
BYSSUS
FOOT
RETRACTOR MUSCLE
NUCLEUS № 1
GONAD
MANTLE
(NACRE PRODUCING MANTLE)

Nuclei for round pearls are inserted in either the gonad or retractor muscle or, frequently, both. The adductor muscle and foot are sometimes eaten as delicacies.

As for pearls, they are now known to be the result of reactions to irritants that lodge themselves on the shell or penetrate the mantle. If they fall (or are placed) upon the shell, the secretions of the oyster or clam glue them firmly and the result is a blister pearl. If they penetrate the tissue of the mantle slightly, they are covered roundly by the secretions from the epithelial cells at the point of penetration, but the other end may get partially glued to the shell and the result is a misshapen pearl, neither round nor button, which is called baroque after the work of the Fontainebleau artists who loved to paint the fantastic shapes of rocky grottoes designed for the delight of the seventeenth-century French court. (In art this nonsymmetrical form is also known as rococo or grotesque.) In short, all pearls are the result of reactions to irritants, but a round pearl develops only when the irritant penetrates the outer skin (epithelium) of the mantle and deeply fractures the secondary skin (parenchyma), carrying with it a few cells from the epithelium in the process. These cells continue to live, and form within the parenchyma a sort of pocket or sac that embraces the irritant which is then, layer by layer, bathed first in aragonite, then conchiolin, then nacre. It was this process, first investigated by two Japanese experimenters early in the century and later postulated as theory by Oda, the chief researcher for Mikimoto in the 1940's, which formed the great breakthrough in pearl cultivation and permitted the culturing of round pearls. Skill and science have further improved the conditions under which the oysters do their delightful work, but no substitute for the ways of nature and nacre has yet been discovered.

The objective scientific and legal story of the first cultured round pearls has been carefully detailed in a report made by the aquatic biologist Dr. A. R. Cahn to the United States government in October, 1949, during the early years of the American occupation of Japan. It is a fascinating book-length document that for all its technicalities reflects the fierce competition between the pearl cultivators and the scientists to discover nature's secret, and suggests tersely the tremendous difficulties involved in the whole process of pearl cultivation, even after that secret was discovered.

The story begins sometime around 1900, when a teenager named Tatsuhei Mise, who was clever with his hands, acquired a stepfather who was an inspector of oysters. Young Mise had no training in science but was a skilled carpenter, and it is probable—although this is suggested only by the facts—that it was actually the stepfather who first set him off and who guided him on his experiments in seeding oysters to make pearls. In any event, in 1904 Mise brought to the Japanese marine scientists the first round cultured pearls they had ever seen along with a tool he had developed for his procedure. The procedure was new: It consisted of transplanting a bit of mantle from a pearl-bearing living oyster into another oyster at the same time a pearl nucleus was inserted; he called his tool a grafting needle and asked for a testing of both the tool and the procedure so that he might patent them.

In 1907, he was given a patent on his grafting needle but his request for a patent on his cultivation methods was denied. Why? It is around this question that scores of debates have been held and many accusations flung. There is no question but that he was on the right track. Within five months another man, this time a scientist, had come forward with a similar procedure. He was Tokichi Nishikawa, a graduate of Tokyo University (1897) with a major in zoology, who had been working in the bureau of fisheries and who had produced his round pearls under laboratory conditions. But Nishikawa's request for a patent was also denied.

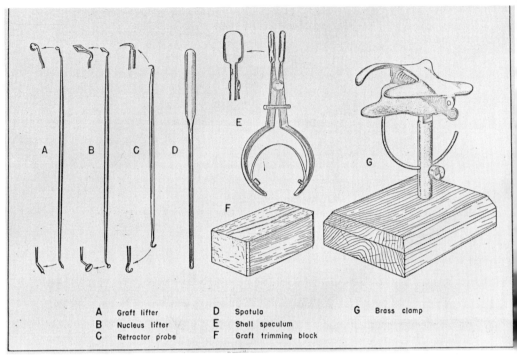

A	Graft lifter	D	Spatula	G	Brass clamp
B	Nucleus lifter	E	Shell speculum		
C	Retractor probe	F	Graft trimming block		

Tools for inserting a nucleus into a pearl oyster have changed little in the fifty-odd years of their existence. The two needles on left are modified from original transplanting needle invented by Mise in 1904. From the Government report distributed by the U.S. Department of Commerce.

Bottom left
Only X rays will reveal with certainty the differences in pearl formation. This reveals the clamshell nuclei in a strand of cultured pearls.

Bottom right
An X-ray picture of a pearl formed solely around a tissue graft—a non-nucleated freshwater pearl. Almost all such pearls are baroques.

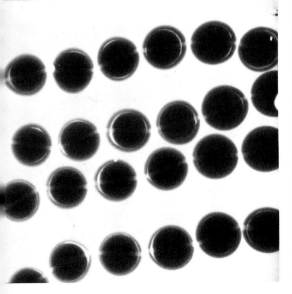

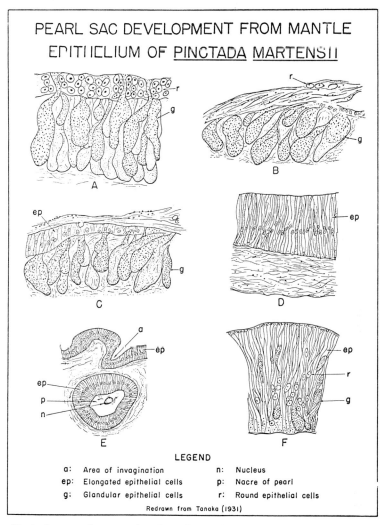

PEARL SAC DEVELOPMENT FROM MANTLE EPITHELIUM OF <u>PINCTADA</u> <u>MARTENSII</u>

LEGEND

a:	Area of invagination	n:	Nucleus
ep:	Elongated epithelial cells	p:	Nacre of pearl
g:	Glandular epithelial cells	r:	Round epithelial cells

Redrawn from Tanaka (1931)

Basic key to the round cultured pearl is a transplant of mantle tissue from another oyster along with a nucleus; these sketches show how a pearl sac then grows to protect the growing pearl. Sketch copied from Tanako for the U.S. Government report made by the Natural Resources section of the GHQ Allied Powers in Tokyo, 1947.

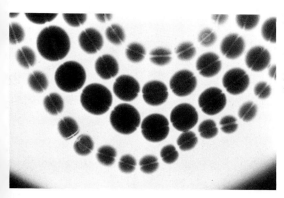

Natural pearls. Probably the original irritant—a grain of sand, a parasite—long ago dried up. Almost no natural pearls have been produced in the last ten years. *All radiographs courtesy of the Gemological Institute of America.*

155

Not until 1916 when Kokichi Mikimoto presented his claims to the title of discovery was anyone granted a patent on cultivating round pearls. It was as if they had been waiting for the "Pearl King" to crown him with glory, ignoring all others.

That was the way, at least, the American scientist Dr. Cahn saw it. When he studied the matter he came out firmly on the side of the first man to apply. He withdrew the title of discoverer from Mikimoto and declared Mise and Nishikawa the true heroes. It is a delicate point still; even today there are arguments among pearl experts about it. Although Mikimoto began using the Mise-Nishikawa techniques *after* he acquired his own patent, and although he publicly admitted that both Mise and Nishikawa retrieved the oyster's secret scientifically *before* he did, as a pearl merchant without peer he also related far and wide how he had by trial and error made round pearls long before anyone else, how he had slaved longer and harder over the task—and suggested that while laboratory procedures were important as technicalities, the real test came in the marketplace, and there his crown was indisputable.

There are further complications. It is sometimes suggested that there was a deliberate conspiracy to discredit young Mise. Personally, I doubt it. Very rarely have men been granted scientific credit for a single show of intuitive brilliance. The Mise grafting needle—which was actually a thin, pointed, metallic tube that could carry both a nucleus and a bit of mantle epithelium—was superior to anything the scientists were already working with and so Mise received recognition for it, but clearly Nishikawa had already been working along the same lines, and under scientific conditions. When Nishikawa applied for his patent five months later than Mise, Mise was charged with infringing on his methods; an obviously unfair move which does suggest conspiracy. Doubtless supporters of Nishikawa pushed through this move. But it is clear that Nishikawa himself had no part in it; after he had received his patent for transplanting tissue (not for making round pearls—that was the special glory saved for Mikimoto), he turned around and signed an agreement with Mise that henceforth the tool and the procedure should be united and the total process shared under the title of the Mise-Nishikawa method.

Other factors may have played a role in this Mise-Nishikawa transaction. Because both were dead before Dr. Cahn made his independent report, no questioning of either of these two men took place, and I can only surmise about them. But in the record of their early experiences there is one curious coincidence that may or may not have some bearing on their sudden emergence in the pearl world. This was that both had knowledge of Australian oystermen and their work with oysters: Mise through his stepfather, who, as a government inspector of oysters, helped his carpenter son to make pearls just after he returned from a trip to the Australian oyster beds; Nishikawa, in connection with his work as a zoologist, went to Australia to visit the oyster beds just before starting his pearl-making experiments. It seems possible to me that sometime around the turn of the century an unsung Australian oysterman hit accidentally upon the method Mikimoto had sought for so many years and passed his secret along unwittingly to these two brilliant young Japanese.

Another conjecture concerns the bureau of fisheries. Both Mise's stepfather and Nishikawa worked there; Mise's stepfather was a long-term employee; Nishikawa worked there for several years before he joined the marine biological staff at Tokyo. The charge against Mise of infringement suggests that possibly the stepfather carried secrets home to the boy; it is also possible that the experiments were a common task, and that skill and patience in the frustrating task of transplanting the tiny pieces of epithelium were all that separated both Mise and Nishikawa from other workers in the fisheries.

It is also possible that Luther Burbank actually deserves at least some portion of their scientific credit. His experiments with the grafting of fruit and the hybridizing of various species began a half century before. It would seem reasonable that, given the knowledge of how to make a button pearl, men of curiosity would want to experiment with whether a finer pearl could be made through tissue-grafting. Medical experiments with the grafting of human skin began about the turn of the century, after Burbank and after the discovery of that first great pain-killer, chloroform (which, you may recall, was also suggested for oysters)—so why not the grafting of oyster tissue? Experiments might even have begun in California, and been discarded because they did not work on the local pearl oyster, the abalone, then tried in Australian waters with the *Pinctada maxima,* and finally passed to the Japanese where, using *Pinctada martensii,* they succeeded so gloriously. It would appear that the name "grafting needle" used to describe Mise's tool and the word "transplanting" used in Nishikawa's patent might have been used precisely because hybridization was the category of scientific experiment the laboratory was working on—not simply pearl nucleus insertion.

These are my own thoughts. Dr. Cahn in his report clearly felt that Mise and Nishikawa had been wronged because of the mercantile interests of Mikimoto and the value of these interests to the Japanese government, which shared in his profits and leased him his island farm. As a scientist,

Cahn had little use for Mikimoto's well-publicized claims; to him, the fact that Mikimoto was a genius as a businessman meant little beside the scientific laboratory facts and the legal patent records. Cahn was right to enter Mise's and Nishikawa's names in his study.

But he did not give Mikimoto enough credit. For Mikimoto's claim that he had produced round pearls before 1907 when Mise and Nishikawa recorded theirs clearly was true although their roundness was undoubtedly accidental. Just as in nature some irritants penetrated the tissue of the oyster in such a fashion as to produce round pearls, so had some of Mikimoto's inserted bits of salt and clam shell been forced into the mantle and embraced by nacre. Information to support this cannot be found in the legal records of the time, but American newspapers reported it. The most notable account was a story in the old *New York Herald* published on October 9, 1904, which stated flatly that for several years Mikimoto had produced some round pearls of good luster which were very small but beautiful. The article, which was unsigned but written by an American correspondent for the *Herald,* included an interview with Mikimoto about his pearl beds on the shore of Taketu Island, and stressed his secrecy about his methods. (He even walled in his workshop.) It also gave credit not only to the experimental work in the Tokyo University laboratories but suggested there had been a steady exchange of ideas between Mikimoto and the laboratory for some years. It further said—quoting Mikimoto—that the late Prince Komatsu had visited Mikimoto's pearl farms and been so impressed that he had sent Mikimoto a silver cup engraved with the words, "The works of men help nature"—a phrase of sacred blessing, so to speak, for the Prince was thought to be a direct descendant of the Deity.

The fact that there were round pearls coming from the Mikimoto farms was also authenticated by a pearl importer of the time, Maurice Brower. He noted that while the "vast majority of the culture pearls"— as they were then called—were button pearls, there were some fine round ones and, in a masterpiece of understatement, predicted that the new pearls "would be a considerable factor in the market" before too long. Americans had not yet taken to them, he said, charging they were "artificial," but in London and Paris they "were gradually gaining ground."

There is little doubt, however, that the round pearls in Mikimoto's harvest were, in the main, accidents. As Mikimoto later told his biographer Robert Eunson, an American war correspondent, during these years he was terribly discouraged because even though he was growing steadily more successful with his button pearls, he was constantly risking all his profits on secret attempts to perfect a pearl that could compete with a natural pearl. He knew that he had to get the nucleus into the tissue itself, but slashing pockets in the mantle caused too many of his oysters to die, and greasing the nucleus with glycerine and pressing it into the flesh didn't work. It is probable that he began transplanting experiments about the same time the Tokyo technicians did; in 1905 he claimed to have found five beautiful round pearls in a small oyster bed he had set out a few years before, and then he knew that he was finally on the right track. Shortly thereafter, as Cahn stated in his report, he hired a dentist, one Otokichi Kuwabara, who aided him in his first grafts.

The story of Mikimoto's work deserves more than passing references to this phase. His life was a sort of Japanese Horatio Alger tale, with the Japanese government replacing the rich uncle in the American story by rewarding the hard-working, virtuous hero with a land lease at the very moment he might have been wiped out by failure. There are also humble beginnings and a highly successful ending: Starting as a peasant-artisan, Kokichi Mikimoto died at the age of ninety-six in 1954, leaving behind him fifty-four descendants, countless legends, a thriving multimillion-dollar business, and millions and millions of beautiful round pearls.

He was the son of a line of small merchants in the port village of Toba; his father had invented a flour-milling machine and become a noodle-maker. Because the father worked long hours and died early, young Mikimoto was chiefly influenced by his grandfather, and from him and one of his cronies, he learned how to sell before he was even in his teens. Noodles were his chief stock then, but since noodles were made at night, he also had time to peddle vegetables. He was thus not any ordinary peddler, he was enormously energetic, and, because he was also adventurous and religious, his clientele soon embraced a wide range of people. Near his home was the famous Shinto shrine of Ise, where the Emperor made an annual pilgrimage to report personally to his ancestors on Japanese affairs; here too, young Mikimoto made pilgrimages. (The Shintoists, like the Chinese Buddhists, do not believe in only one God but rather in a group of gods, with the Sun Goddess ruling over all.) When his father became sick, Kokichi went early each morning to a simple wooden shrine near Toba to pray for his health and, combining religion with business, took to massaging the backs of the old people worshipping there. As this developed his hands, he also learned juggling, and, ironically, through this mere pastime, he met his first foreigners and became involved in the larger world.

It was then unusual for a man of his class—the workers, or *shonins*—to meet foreigners. Until four years before Mikimoto's birth, indeed, no Japanese had spoken with men of the West. It was in 1854 that Admiral

Perry sailed into Shimoda harbor with aid and trade for the Emperor of
Japan; for the previous 250 years, trade with foreigners and Christian
missions had been banned. A military dictatorship ruled; the Emperor was
their prisoner; feudalism was the order of the day. During Mikimoto's boy-
hood, the Emperor was restored, feudalism was overthrown, and the working classes were, for the first time, encouraged to educate themselves, branch
out, become priests, schoolteachers, and capitalists—if they could. When
Mikimoto was seventeen, a British warship visited Toba, but while most
of the town stood back in awe, Mikimoto rowed out with a load of vegetables and asked to come aboard. He was first refused; only when he moved
off to a respectful distance and lay down on his back and juggled his oar
with his feet until it spun and bounced, was he applauded and welcomed
aboard. From then on he went aboard daily, saving his profits for a walking trip to Tokyo, a reverse route from that followed by the pilgrims to
Ise down the Tokaido road. The trip took ten days, and Mikimoto kept a
diary, the most important passage of which refers to his astonished delight
in the marts of the pearl dealers and seashell sellers. It was then, he said
later, that he decided he would be a pearl merchant instead of a noodle-
maker. Soon after he returned, he started a shell business but for years he
worked in it only a few hours a day; at night he worked in his father's
noodle-making factory; he also held a post on the town council and soon
married a girl of the upper (samurai) class.

The few pearls he handled in his business were from Ago Bay not far
from his home; here the finest natural pearls in Japan were found. Some
of his competitors handled small ones and misshapen ones (baroques), but
Mikimoto from the start maintained he sold only perfect, large, round ones.
Before the revolution, which had defeated the old guard and emancipated
the worker, pearls had been found only by accident; as fishermen became
established, more and more of them talked of protecting the pearl beds at
Ago Bay from enemies, and under some prodding from the bold Mikimoto,
an organization was formed and Mikimoto was elected president. His reputation for perfection plus this honor brought him his first important order
for pearls—from the Empress Dowager. He was then twenty-eight—stocky,
strong, imaginative, honest, and ambitious. He had, according to his biographer Eunson, one other distinguishing characteristic: large earlobes. A
Japanese man with large earlobes was expected to grow rich—such ears
were said to be made for the catching of gold.

When, in 1888, Mikimoto was able to persuade a single fishing village
to switch from the harvesting of oysters and abalone as food to their protection as shell and pearl producers, he was already dreaming about how

soon he could begin specializing in the one kind of oyster that produced the most beautiful pearls, the oyster the Japanese called the *akoya-gai,* and make pearls grow. In the mid-1880's he paid a visit to the marine laboratories in Tokyo, saw the marine scholar Yoshikichi Mizukiri, and made some tests. Together they split pearls, powdered them, studied them under microscopes, and dissolved them in chemicals. The problems in growing pearls, he was told, were first in inserting a nucleus the oyster would accept, then in keeping the oyster alive after the foreign body or nucleus had been inserted. The excretion of the nacre was an inevitable process, but the effort of trying to throw out the foreign body exhausted the oyster.

First Mikimoto inserted broken glass. The oyster threw it out. Then he tried clay. Again the oyster threw it out. Then he tried salted shell. He put some oysters into his farms in Ago Bay, others he bedded down in the less tranquil waters near Toba. His neighbors said he had gone mad; his wife complained that she had lost him to an oyster. He did each insertion himself, and dove himself for each oyster. Some he did not touch for two years, others for three. When, around 1888, his first batch of 1,000 was finally opened (by this time he had helpers), no pearls were found. There was gloom among the villagers dependent on the fishing beds, and sadness in his home. Now he was considered worse than mad—stupid. But he kept at it. The next batch of insertions he made was of 5,000—all of them oysters bought on borrowed money. Once heralded as a leading businessman, he was now thought of as a lazy dreamer who let his wife support him; she ran the family noodle business.

More than once the infamous red tide swept through his oyster beds and killed all his oysters, old and new. The red tide (called *akashio* in Japanese) is a gigantic population explosion in the sea of minute marine creatures called plankton. The swarm is so great that it absorbs all the oxygen in the water and all shellfish die, and the mother-of-pearl mollusks are the first to go. It is still a feared enemy; the only defense against it is to hang the oysters deep in the waters in hopes the tide will wash the tiny reddish creatures swiftly by. The day after the 1890 red tide, Mikimoto was defeated. "Go back to your fishing," he told the villagers who worked for him. "I am finished." Then he himself turned away and soon after went north to Hokkaido to study the kelp (seaweed) business. Because his creditors were haunting his house, he stayed away the full winter of 1891, leaving his wife Ume to face them. When he came home in the spring, she hid him; but as the summer wore on he decided he must look at a small batch of oysters in which he had made insertions of seed pearl ground with salt. His wife went with him. It was in July, 1893, when the long-suffering Ume was rewarded by finding the first cultured pearl Mikimoto grew—a white semicircular button of fine luster. Three years later, in 1896, he received the first patent for "pearl formation" granted in Japan.

Although Mikimoto himself was disappointed in the cultured pearl's shape, his creditors and the villagers were not. He was once again a man of substance and authority, distinguished, admired, and publicized—a hero. Mikimoto, at thirty-five with four children, had shown he was a man whom Nature couldn't bully; he had made pearls.

In 1894, he set out new oysters in a new bed, no longer at Jinmyo Muro where the red tide had defeated him, but two miles away on the shoals of an island called Tatoku, or, in translation "Good for Paddy Fields" since it had once been rice-bearing. Two of his brothers, Matsusuke and Tzuneko, and a brother-in-law, Kusutaro Kume, joined him in the new enterprise, and the government backed him, although it would be four years before there was any hope of seeing even one pearl. As he had before, he placed his oysters in baskets, but this time he prepared special beds of stone, slate, and lumber around the island before he lowered the oysters into the shallow waters. Meanwhile, on the island itself his staff sank a well, planted camphor and hemp trees, and built houses. Ume said goodbye to the noodle shop (which they sold), and the Mikimoto family moved into a house on Tatoku. They had formed a cooperative which ran both the new homesteads and the pearl farms; after they had paid for the 10,000 oysters and the labor to insert into them mother-of-pearl nuclei, there was no money left for Mikimoto to go to Tokyo to attend the annual marine products meeting. "But I want you to go," Ume said. And so she sold her best kimono and gave him the money for his ticket.

Trouble still pursued him, however. The first crop of button pearls in 1898 from Tatoku was large but it had few takers; in general, the new pearls were thought of as fakes by the outer world, and the village world was unable to afford such luxuries. His wife died that year, and he had to move his family back to Toba to the house of his mother-in-law. But each defeat propelled him outward—out of the rural world of the oysters into the great world. In 1899, he opened his first retail store to sell pearls in the Ginza area of Tokyo. By the time of the second crop—4,200 cultured button pearls—he had trained salesclerks to show off the new gems and had personally hawked his goods far and wide. Faithful and inventive worker though he was in the oyster beds, Mikimoto's real genius lay in merchandising. By the first year of the new century, his name was beginning to be mentioned around the world.

By January, 1905, he had 100,000 oysters bedded down of which

1,000 were treated by various means to bring forth round pearls. That year the Russo-Japanese War was at its peak, but it interfered very little with Mikimoto. His own disaster was a recurrence of the red tide, which once again swept through his beds killing off all but 15,000 oysters. The oysters that were saved were taken hurriedly out of cold waters, and were not as large as they should have been. Once again the pearl farms were ruined; once again Mikimoto faced despair. Almost accidentally, walking through the rotting, stinking mess, he began opening oysters himself, working on the crop of experimentals. In the group which he had pressed sacs of mantle around the nucleus he found five live oysters, and in them, five perfectly round pearls.

His greatest fear then was that someone would find out his method before he had time to recoup his capital. Late in the night he went to the grave of his wife and told her about it, swearing that it was their secret. It has long been a custom among the Japanese to report to their ancestors aloud in such a fashion; in this action Mikimoto coupled the old with the new, speaking to his wife twentieth-century style, in the tradition of speaking with dead forebears. Later that same year he was invited to have an audience with Emperor Meiji with two other modern-minded men—one a timber baron, the other an engineer. These two arrived in frock coats; Mikimoto was in his working clothes with a crest sewed on his sleeve—the single word "pearl" in Japanese characters, surrounded with a perfect circle. But although he promised the Emperor he would produce round pearls for Japan, he did not divulge the method he was using.

Returning to Tatoku, he rebuilt his organization, putting up workers' houses, clubs, and recreational facilities; raising salaries and shortening the work year, following the American pattern. His hope was to increase the number of workers from 300 to 1,000—and to bring his oyster beds up to 10,000,000. He offered bonuses for babies born on the island, gave regular rest periods to his women divers, promised two holidays a month—one celebrating the finding of the first button pearl, the other, his own birthday —three festive days a year, and a seven to five day. As well as oystermen and divers, he welcomed carpenters, plasterers, and blacksmiths. He encouraged his islanders to call him "general" *(taisho)* and rewarded them when they copied his habits of abstinence and hard work. Smoking and drinking were permitted only on festive days. His genius as a boss, however, is perhaps best understood through his handling of thieves. A worker caught once, or even twice, stealing pearls faced only small penalties and forgiveness, but if caught for the third time, not only was the thief exiled from the island but so were all the people from his village. Through this

Divers were allowed to keep a percentage of the pearls fished up in prewar years; this youngster was one of the best divers, and is seen with a four-strand necklace. Few Japanese women wear pearls.

mechanism Mikimoto at one stroke cut down his losses and gave each man a stake in protecting the business. He combined the old respect for family-village ties with the new merchandising world he was helping to bring into full bloom. He thus succeeded in doing without one of industrialization's most irksome specialists—the police.

As for his acumen for publicity, few have matched him. Soon he was a juggler on a world's stage, tossing up his pearls while princes and emperors watched, and catching a full measure of fame. Nor was he content merely with Japanese attention; soon every fair of any importance was sent pearl exhibitions—the first won a medal at the St. Louis Exposition of 1904, and it was this which attracted newsmen in the United States. By then the American freshwater pearls were almost depleted and the sea gem supply in great demand. As a *New York World* reporter put it: "the pearl-bearing mussel is rapidly passing . . . the price of pearls is increasing exorbitantly every year, until now the gem is reckoned as the most precious, elegant and chaste of all the world's natural gifts."

To get his gems into the United States, Mikimoto was first called upon to pay the high tariffs—then 60 percent—demanded on manufactured products. One of his great strokes of business shrewdness was to fight this patiently until the pearls once declared artificial were legally accepted as

Far from the laboratories and the small fishing villages, pearls were being made into elaborate pieces like this turn-of-the-century brooch of pearls and diamonds. *Courtesy, The Metropolitan Museum of Art, anonymous gift, 1941.*

merely cultured, not simulated, and taxed like natural ones at 10 percent.
Again he had caught two balls with one toss; he had reduced his export
taxes, and he had established his pearls as legally natural rather than manufactured.

During this period his insertion method for producing round pearls
is best described as a "mantle flap"—the oyster mantle was pressed inward
with a blunt instrument so as to form a constricted sac, and then a nucleus
greased with glycerine was inserted into the sac. After he was granted the
patent on this—on February, 1908—he presented the Emperor with three
dozen pearls in various stages of development plus another dozen beads
beautifully cut from mother-of-pearl.

It was by no means a really successful method, however, and he continued to search for a better one. He could, of course, have turned to the
Mise-Nishikawa procedure but obviously he did not dare; his first (1896)
patent for the production of pearls protected him against this procedure
being brought into the market but if he himself used it, the doors would
be wide open to competition. So he switched instead from *pressing* a sac
in the mantle to *transplanting* a pressed-in sac from another oyster. Since
neither he nor any of his staff divulged just when or how he did this, there
are few facts on how successful it was. But in 1916 he got the patent he
yearned for—the inventor of round pearl production patent—by this procedure. Then he switched to the Mise-Nishikawa method and made up his
difficulties with his son-in-law's family. Nishikawa had married his daughter Mine in the mid-nineties but the two families had long been estranged,
probably because Nishikawa was not encouraged to work with the Mikimoto firm as an equal. Following the purchase of the Mise-Nishikawa rights,
their grafting needle and transplanting method, the mantle-sac method was
dropped. Today the Mise-Nishikawa method is the only one in general use.

Mikimoto was then fifty years old but still as eager as a boy about
his business. Because only the French were at that time considered good
jewelry designers and workers, he decided to send Japanese craftsmen
abroad to study the mounting of pearls, and upon their return, he opened
a factory in downtown Tokyo for jewelry-making. At the same time, he
opened a huge second farm at Gokasho, with 829 acres of land and 1,540
acres of sea, and added more retail stores. By 1905 he was considered to be
both radical and forward-looking for his many innovations: his eight-hour
day, for instance, was thought radical; his one price for all that replaced the
ancient system of Oriental haggling was thought forward-looking. He increased his number of retail stores, and made quite a thing of burying inferior pearls in order to establish the perfection of what he did sell. By 1911,

he had a net profit of $175,000; in the next four decades it was to leap to $5,000,000, but even before then, his success was impressive both to other merchants and to Mikimoto himself.

Obviously it was time for another bold thrust and so Mikimoto went international, and instead of selling through other merchants, opened his own branch stores in London and appointed agents in New York and Paris. By the end of World War I, his pearls were famous enough to be a subject of education for Japanese diplomats who had long been schooled to discuss geisha girls as discreetly as they did foreign affairs.

Mikimoto was now known as "the Pearl King"—so crowned by a Japanese reporter—but for the most part he still lived humbly in a small house near his farm at Gokasho, arising at five-thirty, swimming before breakfasting on a bowl of rice and some fruit, reading the world's newspapers, and working until sundown. Not until 1926 did he attempt traveling abroad himself, and then he came to the United States because, although now close to seventy, he wanted to see three things: Mount Vernon, which he considered America's shrine, just as Ise was Japan's shrine; Thomas Edison, whom he considered the greatest man in the world, and American women wearing his necklaces. Upon seeing that the women did indeed wear his

Women divers are still seen on display at pearl farms—this is a scene at Pearl Island—and are called in after typhoons to help collect scattered oysters. Some 50,000 now dive for edible oysters and kelp in Japan and Korea.

pearls, he was delighted; the Japanese girls wear very little jewelry. He thrilled to Thomas Edison, saying candidly to him: "You are the moon in the world of inventors, while I am merely one of the countless stars." And at Mount Vernon, with Nipponese simplicity, he stood before the tomb of George Washington, and just as he had so often at Ise, reported aloud on the state of the cultured pearl industry to this Great American Ancestor.

It was a successful tour and highly publicized. To celebrate it, for instance, another great merchant, John Wanamaker, put up for sale in his Philadelphia store a string of black pearls with a price tag of $1,000,000 on it.

On his way home, after a stay of several months, Mikimoto went on around the world, stopping off in London and Paris to lend a hand in several court cases he had started there through agents to get his pearls firmly established as real, but cultured, rather than counterfeit as was still often charged. He also sought standards; many dealers were exporting imitations as cultured, and they were giving cultured pearls a bad name. Mikimoto's work on this trip was effective until the Depression but then, as prices sank and competition grew fierce, pearl imitators swamped the market with such sorry jewels that Mikimoto was forced into something far more dramatic than merely going to court. He bought up all the fake imitation pearls he could get, added a batch of inferior cultured pearls, and in the plaza of Kobe's chamber of commerce in Japan, burned 750,000 or 295 pounds in one single bonfire, shoveling them into the flames himself.

During World War II, pearl production slowed to a standstill, but Mikimoto refused to allow his factories to be shifted to war work, and the government did not press him. At the end of the war, American generals and admirals were among the notables who sought him out. In 1951 the Emperor came to visit him; in 1953 the Crown Prince sought an audience. On September 20, 1954, Mikimoto had a severe attack of gallstones and died. His last words were *"Arigatai—arigatai"* ("I'm thankful— I'm thankful") but whether he was referring to his long life or his pearls no one knows.

The present head of Mikimoto's far-flung chain of retail stores, the

Opposite

The crown of England was remade in the early twentieth century to include the Cullinan diamond found in South Africa but the ancient symbol of divinity, the two bands of pearls, was kept, and the cap of velvet was of royal purple.

wholesale business, and the several farms and factories is Old Man Pearl's grandson, Yoshitaka Mikimoto. His father was Mikimoto's only son Ryuzo, who preferred English literature to pearl work and was known for his collection of John Ruskin's manuscripts. The present Mikimoto is more merchant than farmer. To understand modern pearl-farming methods it is necessary to study more than Pearl Island. The working farms of today's cultured pearl world are varied. They deserve a whole chapter to themselves.

The actress Mrs. Patrick Campbell, famed for her wit, her letters from George Bernard Shaw, and her public smoking, is seen here in her pearl-adorned at-home costume, about 1910.

6

Cultured Pearls Today

*Rich honesty dwells like a miser, sir, in
a poor house; as your pearl in your foul
oyster.*
    SHAKESPEARE, *As You Like It*, Act
    IV, Scene II (TOUCHSTONE)

*W*orld War II, with its enormous toll of dead and injured, its vast destruction of property, and its smashing of dreams of power, had many momentous effects. It shook up Europe, made the United States the greatest force in the world, wrecked empires, emancipated colonies, and all but annihilated Japan. Many of the enormous changes that resulted are still running their course, but Japan, with the aid of the United States, has risen like a phoenix from the fires of the cataclysmic bombings it suffered, and today, a mere quarter of a century after its surrender, is one of the major economic forces of the world.

As it went with Japan, so it went with cultured pearls. In the late thirties, the pearl industry was a thriving one, still competing with natural pearls coming in from the Persian Gulf or being bought at auctions, still not quite accepted as the best in pearls but much admired and at peak production. In 1938, almost 11 million pearls were harvested. The waters of Ago Bay were the home of 65 percent of the working farms, Kobe was the office base, but explorations and branch farms were widely scattered: in Burma, in Ceylon, in Australia and the South Seas, and in the Philippines.

Even as late as that fateful day of December 7, 1941, when the Japanese loosed their air force in a surprise attack cn the Hawaiian Islands and on the United States fleet and air bases in the Philippines, pearl merchants and workers were abroad. How many were legitimate? No one has ever tracked down the mystery of one exploratory group. Were the small Japanese boats which had been oyster-fishing in Pearl Harbor for two years when war broke out only cultivating pearls—or were they spies in disguise? Did they drown—or flee? When did they leave? After the bombings of the harbor or before? Those who know have not revealed any answers; pearl merchants claim to be as much in the dark about it as anyone.

As the war progressed, all overseas production of pearls ceased, home production dwindled, and the labor force scattered. Young workers left the oyster beds to join the army, navy, or the air force; many of the merchants took their skills into government service; some of the factories were transformed into production centers for wartime necessities. Mikimoto, in his eighties, had enough political power to resist encroachments on his island and declared proudly he was a man only of pearls and peace, but he was unique. In 1943, the pearl industry as a whole was consolidated as a wartime measure and men were selected to keep its data, count its stock on hand, protect its beds where possible, and deal with the ministry of agriculture and forestry. By 1944, production was almost a fourth of what it was —a mere 1,751,054; by 1945 it was at a standstill. In the waters of Ago Bay, Mikimoto charmed enough old women and young children to help him harvest a small crop and so did some other producers but the result of a year's work was a measly 370,000 pearls most of which were fit only for powdering into medicine.

With defeat, all harvesting ceased while Japan awaited its fate as a conquered nation and the National Resources section of the United States government was sent into the area to study the pearl industry so that it could be determined whether it was worthwhile reestablishing it, and if so, how.

The immediate result of this was the eighty-page report by the marine biologist A. R. Cahn, a masterful piece of work pulling together the legal, biological, and industrial factors of cultured pearl cultivation and commerce. The long-term result was equally satisfactory; slowly the pearl growers were set up in business again; slowly, but by the thousands, the oyster beds were replanted and insertions made, and again pearls grew and were harvested in the waters of Japan.

SPECIES	DISTRIBUTION
CAHN FOUND THIS DISTRIBUTION OF MORE IMPORTANT PEARL-PRODUCING MOLLUSKS, PACIFIC AREA, IN 1947	
Pinctada martensii (Dunker)	Japan (Ise, Kii, Tosa, Hizen, Mie)
Pinctada margaritifera (Linné)	Japan (Kii, Tosa), Ryukyu Islands, Formosa, South Seas in general
Pinctada margaritifera zanzibarensis (Jameson)	Madagascar, Seychelles Islands
Pinctada margaritifera mazatlantica (Hanley)	Bay of California, Panama Bay
Pinctada margaritifera erythrensis (Jameson)	Red Sea
Pinctada margaritifera persica (Jameson)	Persian Gulf
Pinctada margaritifera cumingi (Reeve)	Eastern Polynesia, Society Islands (Tahiti), Hawaiian Islands
Pinctada maxima (Jameson)	Ryukyu Islands (rare at Amami-Oshima), New Guinea, Celebes, Arafura Sea
Pteria macroptera (Lamarck)	Ryukyu Islands (north to Amami-Oshima), Formosa, South Seas in general
Atrina japonica (Reeve)	Japan
Ostrea gigas (Thunberg)	Japan
Unio (Margaritana) margaritifera (Linné)[a]	Japan (Hokkaido, northern Honshu,) Sakhalin, Siberia, Canada, England, Europe
Cristaria plicata (Clessin)	Japan (Hokkaido, Honshu), China
Tridacna gigas (Linné)	Ryukyu Islands, Formosa, Bonin Islands, South Seas in general, Indian coasts
Haliotis gigantea (Gmelin)[b]	Japan, Korea, Ryukyu Islands

[a] Found in fresh water.
[b] A gastropod, not a bivalve.
SOURCE: Ogushi (1938).

Mikimoto was among the first to get started again. He still carried enormous weight not only with his own people but with the office of the Supreme Commander of the Allied Forces, General Douglas MacArthur—how much can be seen in the corrections made in Cahn's report. Cahn rejected the kind of publicity Mikimoto received as "the Pearl King" and "inventor of the cultured pearl" and disdained his claims to producing round pearls by the "all lapped" (or the mantle-sac) method in 1900—but Cahn was overruled from above, and Mikimoto's status as both merchant and inventor were preserved. For years the report was top secret; today it is out of print and rare, but there are still some of the originals around, and not only between the lines but in the very corrections themselves, the controversy over both the past and the future of the pearl industry's leadership can be read. Mikimoto won that fight as he had won so many; when production started up again he was still Old Man Pearl, king of the industry, and with his grandson Yoshitaka at his side, he not only saw his own private kingdom return to its former splendor, but the whole industry.

Two other pioneers were also leaders during the postwar period. They were Masayo Fujita, who, with his brother, had financed the Mise-Nishikawa method of pearl culture and built a pearl company upon it, and Hidezo Ino, whose company purchased the rights when they first went on the market. (Mise and Nishikawa themselves both died young, soon after their discoveries.) Others had entered the field before the war, and there was a recognized group known as the Big Five: Mikimoto, Yamakatsu, Murata, Mitsuta, and Horiguchi. Ten years after its renaissance, the pearl industry had passed the peak production of the prewar period and was pushing even higher at a steady 10 percent increase each year.

At least half of the pearl production during the decade of 1947–1957 took place at Ago Bay where the warm current from the Philippines known as the "black current" kept the Pacific waters at a temperature almost perfect for pearl-growing. Other important farms were developed along the opposite coast in the prefecture of Ehime and at Nagasaki and Hiroshima as these atom-bombed cities rebuilt themselves. But no matter how far-flung the beds, the merchants themselves remained in close touch. Most of them had offices in Kobe, the great pearl port of Japan, and all of them slowly became united through membership in one or another of the seven organizations that grew out of their wartime consolidation.

Basic to the exporters was their own organization: the Japanese Pearl Exporters Association chaired by Minoru Yakota, a man so highly respected by his colleagues that even in 1967 after twenty-seven years of the presidency, he was not permitted to retire as chief adviser despite his own wishes. Another organization of importance was the export cooperative, manned by both exporters and processors. The retailers, owners of retail pearl stores, had a separate organization; so did the cultivators, who formed a cooperative and set standards for interindustry auctions. As once again Japan regained control of its former beds on neighboring islands, in Burma and Ceylon (since lost again), in Australia and elsewhere in the South Seas, these producers too formed an organization—the Overseas Pearl Producers Association. Then, not content with these trade organizations, the twenty largest companies—there are more than 3,000 pearl producers in Japan but hundreds are but a single family with a small oyster raft—formed a special group called the Japanese Pearl Enterprisers' Society to uphold standards, develop new markets, and, with a fellow organization, the Pearl Promoting Society, publicize the cultured pearl.

Mikimoto's grandson, Yoshitaka Mikimoto, became president of two organizations—that of the cultivators and the Promoting Society. K. Takashima presided over the export and processors' group. K. Yamamoto, head of the old-time, well-known Yamakatsu pearl company, chaired the enterprisers' society.

Meanwhile, the Fisheries Union controlled the oyster beds, protecting them from being spoiled by the increasingly fierce competition for space, and organizing the thousands of women divers who once played such a major role in pearl-diving but who, as oyster-growing methods changed, began to serve pearl cultivators only in emergencies and did their diving chiefly for edible oysters.

Despite this network of leadership, however, the task of rebuilding the industry was a constant struggle for quality standards. Hundreds of millions of inferior pearls came to world markets from "petty pearlers" as they are called in the trade, and soon it became clear to more responsible leaders that if such practices continued, bad pearls would soon drive out the good. With the help of the government, export inspection was established· An ordinance was enacted by the Ministry of International Trade and Industry of Japan in April, 1957, prohibiting the export thereafter of any but quality pearls. Since then all pearls must bear an inspector's stamp of approval before they are exported from Japan.

With this victory for quality production, the industry took a new lease on life. Prewar Japanese products were rated very low on the American market, and the popular contempt for Japan's cheap china, dime-store gadgetry, and flimsy silks rubbed off on the early cultured pearls. The postwar move toward quality not only in pearls but in such products as radios, watches, cameras, and recently automobiles gave all Japanese exports a considerable boost not only in the United States but in western Europe, where, since it too was rebuilding after the war, important markets were growing.

Moreover, western Europe knew far more about what really good pearls should look like and be like than did the American consumer. As we have seen, Americans knew great natural pearls at secondhand; value was assumed if the necklace or brooch had belonged to someone of importance abroad or was being sold through one of the well-known, prestigious jewelers. Faced with an unpriced hank of merely threaded pearls, most American customers—and many jewelers—were totally at a loss; there were so few standards of value that one pearl bead—be it cultured, natural, or simulated—appeared much like another.

While the situation today still leaves much to be desired in the way of ethical practices, education, and grading standards, it began to get better as the allied occupation army left Japan. Haphazard pearl-purchasing and pearl-smuggling ceased, and the pearl market really improved when Japan and her customers took a hand in determining and setting standards, and, with these tools, establishing price levels.

How this is done in functional terms and why one pearl is more valuable than another are fascinating and complex subjects. Among jewels, only the diamond is judged for value by precise scientific standards; grading methods are now being worked out for pearls by the Gemological Institute of America but since they are technical they will not be in use except among gemologists for some time. Meanwhile the enormous range of price in pearls continues to baffle those jewel lovers and merchants who seek fine pearls but do not know how to judge value.

Since price is so closely tied to quality, more than mere visual or material rules must be understood; indeed, in a sense the whole story of pearl cultivation is important. So before we attempt even to face a single cultured pearl in its value context, we will trace the procedures and people who brought it into being.

The story begins, of course, on the sea farms off the Japanese coast, and to see what farmed pearls were really like at origin, I went to Ago Bay off the southern coast of Honshu close to where Mikimoto first discovered the rudiments of the oysters' secret, and where today almost half of the world's cultured pearls are still being grown.

It was a delightful experience. There in sunlit Ago Bay the rafts (which are the farms) lie, hung with branches collecting oyster spat, strung with cages of oysters, and in each oyster a pearl or two growing mysteriously, silently. It was very still at Kashikojima; the only noise was the sputter of the one-lunged police boat that wound in and out of the very still and very lovely bay.

It is different at Toba Bay where lies Pearl Island, and where there are also farms. Pearl Island is Mikimoto's old cultivating ground, and it is a tourist stop today. There are yachts there for touring the bay, an island museum of pearl curios, a shop, and a grandstand, before which the girl divers put on regular shows, for even if divers no longer serve the pearl industry they have been so long connected with pearls that most cultivators feel it would be a shame not to have a few around. Hundreds of Japanese on holiday ferry out to Pearl Island daily; all tours of foreigners include a visit there—by hydroplane south from Nagoya or by train or bus out of Osaka. Nearby is an aquarium, a lookout tower, and recently a large luxurious tourist hotel has been built high on the hill over the bay.

Japanese pearl farms are water farms distinguished by their lattice-like rafts. From these rafts hang wire or nylon baskets in which are kept the oysters growing pearls or cages in which young oysters are bred. Note the patrol boat in the background and the floating work shed near the raft at right center.

Kashikojima, the heart of the present working farms, is, on the other hand, small, and while easy to get to, seemingly isolated. There is the small fishing village—its streets lined with shops crammed with pearl and mother-of-pearl pieces—its harbor with small boats, a railroad station, and bus stop, one large Japanese hotel and one international hotel, both hidden in the trees and overlooking the bay. When the pearls are being harvested in mid-winter, the pearl experts flock in; the rest of the year it is a quiet, simple, and charming place for pearl workers and students. The National Pearl Research Laboratory is here, and as well as its workshop it houses a large display room with the tools of pearl work and stories and pictures about the men and women who have led the industry, displayed with Japanese and English captions. A small boat winds through the bay twice a day for those who wish to visit the rafts, the farms, or watch a lone girl diver in her white, shark-repellent clothes swoop down into the water like a sea-gull, bring up an oyster, and put it in a floating tub. And since there is always something doing on a pearl farm, so there are always giggling young Japanese checking the rafts, lowering branches, cleaning oysters, opening oysters, inserting nuclei in oysters—and in November and December, harvesting pearls.

There are four major jobs to be done on a pearl farm on a manual level, the first and most basic being the oyster-raising. As noted earlier (Chapter 5), a single oyster lays more than a million eggs which will float helplessly on the water a few weeks, turn into spat, and only if bedded will grow up to become oysters. To catch these, the modern pearl farm hangs from its rafts long branches of cryptomeria, a local evergreen, early each summer which, waving darkly in the water, offers a hideout during the oysters' life. Then in the fall the branches are raised, and the small young oysters are put into baskets of fine meshed wire or nylon or threaded on strings and suspended again into the bay water or placed in irrigated nurseries.

The oysters caught in this manner are offspring of the oysters suspended from the rafts and are considered the "natural increase" accruing to the

Branches of cryptomeria, or Japanese pine, are tied to the rafts in July to catch in their waving fronds the tiny eggs, or spat, of the oyster, and are taken out in November with millions of baby oysters clinging to them.

One of the Yamakatsu pearl farms: rafts hung with both pearl-growing oysters and young oysters not yet nucleated; a research building, left, an operating shed, right, and patrol boats. House to the rear serves as a dormitory for workers during busy seasons.

Pearl oysters before and after cleaning. Cages must also be cleaned.

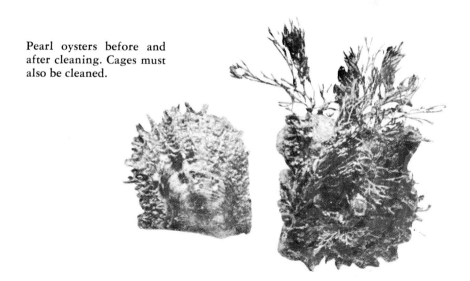

pearl farm operator who runs the baskets. But since all oysters must be handled by the Fisheries Union, it is the Fisheries Union that suspends the cryptomeria, gathers the young oysters, and auctions them off to the farmers.

Historically, pearl divers dove for pearls. With the cultivation of pearls, they began to be divers for young pearl-bearing oysters. Then, since World War II, the spat-collecting method was developed and found to be more than satisfactory; because of the care the parent oysters received, the oyster eggs gathering on the cryptomeria produced stronger, healthier oysters than did nature in the raw. And so the girl pearl divers became all but unnecessary to the pearl industry. Upwards of 7,000 still exist in Japan and Korea but today they dive only for edible oysters and work under the aegis of the Fisheries Union—which leases them when needed to the pearl industry to collect oysters scattered by typhoons or tidal waves, or for display.

During the years of their early growth, the oysters must be fed, cleaned of barnacles, and protected against both their enemies of the sea like eel,

Japanese pearl worker lifting a basket of pearl-laden oysters. This humdrum procedure has replaced the romantic pearl divers of yesteryear.

porgy, and starfish, and elemental enemies like storms and cold. Because bright white is believed to repel sharks by partially blinding them, the divers have traditionally worn white; now with the increasing use of nylon cord instead of wire, both ropes and baskets are often white, and so are the buoys that float them and often the ties that bind the raft planks. No modern methods for dealing with cold or stormy waters have been developed, however; when wind and wave threaten, the cages may be dropped into the depths, the same way they are when the red tide sweeps in, but as winter approaches, the rafts are towed to warmer water.

The oyster involved in the pearl industry—indeed, its cornerstone— is, as noted earlier, the *Pinctada martensii,* or in Japanese the *akoya-gai.* Once fed to pearl divers, it is sour in taste and no longer considered edible, except for the foot which is canned and enjoyed by pearl people as a ritu- alistic harvest treat. Its distinction from other mollusks is the loveliness of the nacre it produces: The inside of its shell and its pearl are iridescent. At three years of age it is mature: that is, the shell will grow no more than three to four inches across, but it will continue to secrete nacre for another four years if in good health.

A great merchant, Miki- moto attracted attention to cultured pearls with elab- orate curiosities like this reproduction of the Lib- erty Bell, showed them in world expositions.

Special food and medication for the growing oyster are therefore major aspects of oyster-breeding and pearl culture. More and more experiments are being made in this field; vitamins are varied and the results tested; chlorophyll is scattered on the water in the form of algae; in the laboratories rice and soybean supplements are tested and new antibiotics tried out. It has been found that not only is it important to have healthy oysters in which to grow the pearl itself, but that the health of the oyster which provides the bit of mantle for transplanting is also important.

But as yet no perfect all-around formula for feeding and medication has been found. Some years ago a parasite was discovered that no medication —including aureomycin in the water and doses of penicillin directly into the oyster itself—could eradicate. The epidemic ran its course; thousands of young and old oysters died. Overcrowding of the breeding waters was suspected to be the basic problem, so efforts are now being made to reduce the oyster population systematically; the large pearl farmers have agreed together that they will cut back the number of oysters being bred so that each oyster can have a decent living space, and this kind of stress will not be a threat either to the pearl's perfection or the oyster's health.

The cultivation of oysters is a basic task of the pearl farmer, but the cultivation of the pearls themselves is also basic.

Pearl culture begins with the insertion of a nucleus into the gonad of a healthy three-year-old pearl-bearing oyster along with a piece of living mantle tissue from another oyster. This is a delicate operation that must be performed neatly, precisely, and swiftly. If the insertion is made in the wrong spot, the pearl will suffer; if the oyster being operated upon is handled too roughly, the oyster will die.

Insertions take place many months of the year, but the chief season is late spring and summer. No oyster under two years can stand the strain of even a small nucleus; only a three-year-old oyster will live through the shock of a large nucleus, or of several nuclei. If the nuclei are small, twenty may be inserted. If 6-millimeter, two are; larger nuclei are inserted singly.

The first problem is getting the nucleus. Many experiments were made in the early years until it was discovered that mussel or oyster shell polished into beads was the most satisfactory. Then the perfect shell was sought— the one with the same hardness and the specific gravity of the pearl itself. Nishikawa himself drew up the specifications in the laboratory, but he died before the present nucleus was found in the pig-toed clamshell of the Mississippi Valley. He worked with the shell from the Yangtze Valley in China, but war with China shut off that source. Today the American supplies are dwindling, and searches have begun again for another shell; hard-

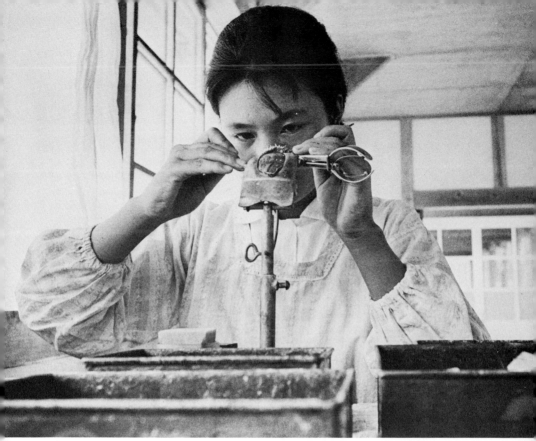

This young girl is removing a piece of mantle tissue from a live oyster for use as a transplant in pearl culturing.

The mantle is segmented and inserted with a nucleus into an oyster to stimulate nacre production for the growing pearl.

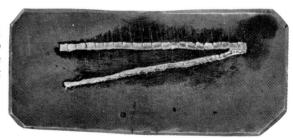

To do the insertion operation, the worker first fixes a partly open, live oyster in a desk clamp with the right valve uppermost and then exposes the main body mass. While a retractor hook holds down the foot to prevent it from moving, an incision is made into the main mass of the tissue, and first the mantle tissue, and then the nucleus—a shell pellet—are inserted into this pocket of grafted tissue and live tissue. Only three-year-old oysters are used for the operation, which takes both skill and speed. Note pegged oysters at bottom center, the sponge keeping mantle tissue moist, the cups of clamshell nuclei of varying sizes, and the completed oysters. The operation in action takes half a minute or less.

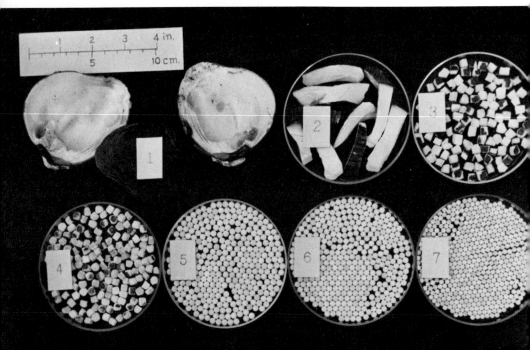

ness on the Mohr scale must be between 3.5 and 4, the specific gravity must be between 2.65 and 2.69. Like diving for oysters, the importing and making of the nuclei was once simply a part of the pearl industry; today, however, it is a separate business. The shell is collected from the Ohio, Wabash, and Tennessee rivers by dredge, brought into Kobe by boat, freighted up to Osaka, and there, in a huge factory, it is cut first into strips, then into cubes, and then lapped or sand-polished into beads of graduated sizes from 2 millimeters to 8 or 9, which are then sold to the pearl farmers. In the past few years, because the dwindling number of mussels in Mississippi waters and the expanding demand from Japan met head on, the price of shell has almost tripled, but it will doubtless rise even higher if no satisfactory substitute or more protected waters for the mussel now in use are found. As well as the Japanese, the Tennessee Valley Authority is researching future possibilities for shell beds and alternative mussels. Currently about six tons of scrubbed shell is shipped to Japan annually from the United States. Other shell is believed being imported from Red China, South America, and Mexico.

As well as a healthy stock of oysters and a supply of nuclei and transplants, the pearl farmer needs skilled inserters who can handle small tools and small oysters. For a long time this has been women's work—or rather girls'. Today, as more and more young people are seeking a city life and sophisticated education, the number of girls available for training has become fewer, and, as a result, wages have risen and training speeded up. The youngest workers are assigned to cutting transplants. They progress to small nuclei. Only workers who have two or three years' experience in insertion work are permitted to work with really large nuclei—from 6 to 8 millimeters. More and more these top-skill workers are boys or young men, working their way up in the company—perhaps on a part-time basis—to become executives. Where once the farmwork ratio of boys to girls was about 2 to 8, now it has come closer to 4 to 6. Then too, more foremen-teachers are being used, and most of them are young men.

Opposite

A picture description of the nuclei, from pig-toe clam (No. 1) found in the Tennessee rivers of the United States to the polished, round pellet (Nos. 5, 6, 7). The size and shape of the nucleus plus time and health determine the size and shape of a cultured pearl. Trays Nos. 2, 3, and 4 show the clamshell cut first into strips, then into squares; 5, 6, 7 show finished nuclei. Because of industrialization, American rivers are producing less and less clamshell while Japan needs more and more.

The process of insertion is fascinating to watch. The great secret of the Mise-Nishikawa method is the all-but-simultaneous insertion of the nucleus *and* the thin slice of mantle tissue into the living gaping oyster. Timing the workers I found that the best could perform this two-in-one operation in 18 seconds but that none took more than 30, regardless of the size or number of the nuclei. I was prepared for the double action and for the tools but the speed of the workers' hands was startling, reminding me repeatedly of the magician's adage that the hand is quicker then the eye.

All insertions take place close to the oyster beds so that the oysters will not be removed from their native waters for more than a few hours. After being pulled up in their baskets, the oysters are first placed on tables to be cleaned, and partially tranquilized—prepped for their operation. Only

Floating work sheds near rafts; at right, girls are cleaning oysters.

a few are handled at a time, the actual number depending on the number of workers. The oysters are then distributed to each workstand by twos and threes, usually by the foreman, who is responsible for seeing that those with large nuclei get the largest oysters, and that the oysters from which the transplant is cut are the healthiest specimens of all. The worker has his tools handy on his worktable—his special opening knife, his inserting needle, bits of graft, and boxes of nuclei. During the operation the oyster may be pegged open (the traditional way) or his mouth separated by the same vise that holds him in place, a sort of surgical strap and table combination called a retractor.

After the insertion, the oyster is closed, placed in a bucket, and returned to the sea baskets for further growth. There is no visual checking of inserting accuracy; by then it is too late to do it again. In some large firms, however, records are kept of just how Miss X's operations turn out compared to Mr. Y's. The loss in the few hours of opening, inserting, and returning to the water may run as high as 50 percent. Only part of this may be due to a lack of inserting skill and speed, but this is at least one factor that can be checked and changed. Other factors causing death or disease lie, of course, in the oyster's basic health, the accidents during his early years, the care or lack of it after the operation, and such freakish events as sudden typhoons, earthquakes, and parasite epidemics. Overall, of every four oysters nucleated at three years of age, only one will produce pearls; of every four pearls harvested, only one will be of export quality. The success ratio is thus about 1 in 16. Mikimoto and Yamakatsu say their standards demand an even higher ratio—1 in 20.

Harvesting takes place two to three and a half years after the inserting operation, usually in the late winter months when the cool waters cause the flow of nacre to be purer and finer. A few months before harvesting, the rafts are dragged closer inshore where the salinity is not so great; the fresher water aids the luster. Then that year's crop is hauled up and, finally, after three to seven years of skillful handling (plus lovingkindness) the results are ascertained in terms of pearls.

Some cultivators specialize exclusively in small pearls, since only the larger, richer companies can finance the long-term growth and risks of pearls 7 to 10 millimeters in diameter. But others work in the 2 to 6 range; and one company, after years of experimentation, has succeeded in growing really large oysters of the finest luster *(Pinctada martensii)* which will take really large nuclei such as 8 millimeters and nurture them through into 11½- and 12-millimeter pearls. It was a dream worth dreaming but very risky, and production is still limited. The *Pinctada maxima* of South Sea waters takes readily to large nuclei and may produce pearls up to 14 milli-meters, but is so hard to domesticate that it is rare. The *martensii* of Japa-nese waters have produced only freaks of this size; Mikimoto shows one in his Pearl Island showplace, for instance, of 13 millimeters. It was found in a white-lipped *agoya*—that is, in a *martensii* with a white edge on its shell. The white-lipped variety of *martensii* has since been the favorite for strength; it grows slightly larger than its black- or pink-lipped relatives and has been the chief producer of 9- and 10-millimeter pearls. Its size is undoubtedly part of its success, but so are the warmer waters of Kyushu where it is raised. The average rate of diameter growth is .3 millimeters a year at Ago Bay: This means that it takes three years for a pearl to grow a mere 1 millimeter of nacre. But near Nagasaki, in the southern waters, a white-lipped oyster may grow twice as fast, and the result is a larger pearl if an outsize nuclei has been accepted. Presently about 2,000 pearls of larger than 10 millimeters—the old limit—are being shipped out of Japan an-nually by the Oriental Sea Cultured Pearl Company, an offshoot of the great Yamakatsu Pearl Company, which is run by the Yamamoto family.

Izumi Yamamoto, son of the president, takes the family successes in this line calmly but it is a matter of high excitement in the trade, for few can take the great risks involved, although all are vividly aware of the po-tentially huge profits. Big pearls have always been in great demand; cur-rently a necklace of matched South Sea cultured pearls in the 11- to 12-millimeter size sells for upward of twenty to thirty times as much as a similar necklace of 8½ millimeters. Fashion plays a role in this high price but so does rareness. If and when the risks of large pearls decrease through the discoveries of new cultivation methods, the first company with its oys-ters bedded down with large nuclei will have a time advantage over would-be competitors.

Quality as well as size is also important in value. As noted, the aver-age fine cultured pearl ranges between 6 and 7 millimeters, and here total perfection in color, lack of flaws and roundness determine difference in price. The fine pearl is rarely if ever raised by chance; year after year the same producers turn out the same general quality and size, but individual pearls may vary greatly in appeal.

After the pearls are taken from the oysters, they are sorted by color, size, and perfection at the processing plants of the various companies. Color is the first standard. No one knows what makes pearls develop one color or another; some believe that different waters—even in the same bay—change the tones and gradations, others that it is a family strain within a species. The chemists recognize six major color divisions: white, cream,

This exciting sight—two large and almost perfect pearls in a single oyster—is the dreamed-of reward for six or seven years of time, trouble, and investment, but it is achieved in only about one out of twenty tries.

pink, green, gold, and black but the gradations are such that people who are color-conscious see blues and purples. There is a pervasive excitement about color sorting; it is due in part to the surprises and in part to the rarity of some colors. Blue-gray is quite rare, and when a rainbow pearl is found it is heralded as a true gift of the gods; only a few really good large rainbows are known to history—and it is impossible to duplicate them. While they are classified technically in the pink or the white class depending on their predominant undertones, every color and shade of the spectrum may occur in them. These never enter the general market; there are enough collectors of "fancy" pearls so that when a rainbow turns up,

After the harvest, which takes place during the winter months, the pearls are separated by size, shape, color, and quality of nacre and then matched—as shown here—for stringing. This task requires highly trained girls of natural skill; they assemble about six necklaces a day.

Almost half of all Japanese cultured pearls are reared in Ago Bay in Mie Prefecture, and in the harvesting months this hotel—the Shima Kanko, or Island View—is crammed with pearl experts from all over the world.

it is withdrawn to be shown to a particular buyer—and sold at a special price.

Some countries also prefer one color to another. West Germany, for instance, likes pink-white pearls; the United States market demands white-pink. The South Americas and Australians tend to like gold. A true green delights art connoisseurs; the texture of the nacre is finest in green pearls.

The final color-sorting is done by hand but the first run may be by machine. The machine used was developed for color-sorting peanuts in Texas and was imported some years ago into Japan and changed so that

Also at Kashikojima, on Ago Bay, is the National Pearl Research Laboratory where work on both oyster and pearl culturing goes on. This technician is working an electronic colorimeter, a computer that analyzes the color properties of pearls. New research with isotopes looks promising.

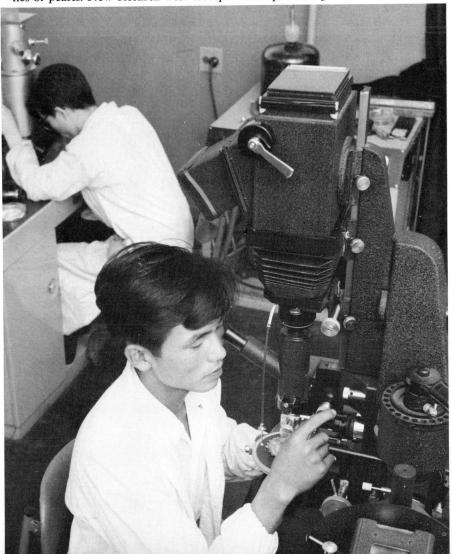

it could handle pearls. It works on an electronic eye principle and divides pearls into the six laboratory categories.

Pearls cannot be made a certain color by chemists but their color can be stained on or natural stains bleached off. Up and through the fifties the Japanese took great pride in their staining work but it boomeranged on them in western Europe, and today the fine pearl companies do very little. It is possible to tell if a pearl is stained by looking through the threading hole; if the interior nacre is not the same as the exterior, the pearl obviously has been stained, for no staining has been developed that permeates the nacre. Similarly, it is impossible to make a pearl white but surface stains can be removed through bleaches of either a chemical or a natural type. Natural pearls used to be washed and laid in the sun to bleach; now a seven-day bath of hydrogen peroxide is considered swifter and easier, and almost all cultured pearls are so treated.

After the pearls have been sorted by color and either sized up or weighed, the average cultivator is ready to take them to market.

The chief market for the growers of these average pearls is the monthly auction at Ise City, which is in Mie Prefecture not far from Ago Bay and is the center for Ise-Shima National Park where Japan's two oldest Shinto shrines are hidden in the redwoods. The auctions are not public auctions, nor are they truly auctions; they are simply streamlined versions of the old oriental bazaar where pearls are sold in lots. At one time or another all pearl companies have participated in these auctions but, in the main, only those companies go as buyers who need to augment their own stocks of sizes, colors, and values or those companies who as sellers only cultivate pearls and do not export them. No American importers go, for instance; they would not know how to function there nor would they be welcome. Instead, they are represented by Japanese exporters through whom they deal, or agents of those exporters.

Many of the sellers are independent cultivators, but others are tied in with one large company or another which prefers not to deal through the auctions but rather to purchase the extra pearls they need in advance of these sales. The Murata Pearl Company, for instance, when needing small pearls for graduated necklaces, turns first to the cultivators tied in with its own company. On the other hand the Mikimoto Company, although it has large farm-holdings, still is also a retailer of enormous size and must expand its varied stock through the auctions. For the thousands of small or beginning cultivators, the auctions are vital, for here they can sell mommes (pearls of less than 1 millimeter) and small pearls; waiting for oysters growing larger pearls to mature demands considerable financing. While all the offshore farms are leased only from the government and the government will help in pearl industry financing as will banks, an operator must still supply half of his own capital and take all the many risks.

Prices at the auctions theoretically may vary from month to month but in recent years they have simply tended to go slowly up. A committee of recognized experts sets the price per momme (a weight unit equal to ¾ of an ounce) for each lot of pearls offered. A sample bowl of each lot is then placed on a small tray, and beside it a closed box marked with the set minimum price and a lot number, and slotted at the top. Seated before tables, for all the world as if they were about to dine, the buyers then pass the trays to one another, depositing through the slots bids for the pearls they want. Highest bidder takes all, of course, but if no bid equal to the minimum is received, the pearls must be withdrawn, perhaps to be used in by-products, perhaps to be submitted at another auction. None are sold below the minimum—or "dumped"—for this would be contrary to quality policy.

Moreover, the buyers have a good look at all the pearls and are apt to recognize them if they come up for a second go-around. The auction room is carefully constructed so that no direct sunlight penetrates and no artificial light is needed—but the light is the same everywhere. (If it rains, auctions are postponed, just as the buying of diamonds is not done on such days.) The tables used, moreover, are covered with a cloth of true whiteness, and any buyer may take out any pearl from the sample bowl and expose it to various tests—check its color against the white cloth, roll it around to test symmetry, and flash test it (or twist it) to see if the nucleus blinks through. All pearl workers need a clear, even light, and most show their pearls on white, although Mikimoto has long displayed their pearls on black velvet, a tiny difference in showmanship that has often irked other pearl people.

There are other pearl auctions in Japan besides the one at Ise: at Kobe, and in the northern section of Tokyo known as Atami. But the chief one is at Ise, and will remain there so long as the waters of Ago Bay continue to produce the majority of Japan's cultured pearls.

Pearls raised by the cultivator-exporters, the big pearl people, rarely go to the auctions: Good pearls of upward of 7 millimeters are kept for the overseas trade. As well as being sorted for color and general size and weight, they must also be more elaborately processed for necklaces or set pieces.

Size-sorting can be done by machine but trained workers do it so swiftly that most companies depend on hand-sorting. A box rilled in graded sizes is used for placement, and the worker—usually a girl—uses a pair of tweezers to pick up the pearls from the heap supplied her and drops them one by one into a line-up determined not only by size, but also by flawlessness and luster. Theoretically, when her box is finished, the pearls in it are ready for the stringer; but since they must first be bored, there is one more routine check on them and that is during the boring. For while pearls are bored only by machine—a machine that looks like a sewing machine laid on its side but whose threadless needle enters both sides at once—the placing must be done by hand and eye. The stringer picks up the pearl with tweezers, twists it to see where its point of contact was with the shell, and places it in position so the boring needle cuts through this natural flaw. At this time, if there are many flaws in it, and it is deemed inferior for export, the pearl will join others put aside by various workers along the line. Eventually this group of rejects will be put into curios, sold cheaply in Japan, pounded into pearl powder for a calcium food supplement or a toothpaste, or thrown back into the bay from which it came to increase the calcium content.

A chart showing the steady increase both in the amount by weight (upper line at left) and by dollars; note that in 1963 price rises due to increased demand and higher costs moved faster than production. Japan exports somewhere between 65 and 70 million dollars' worth of cultured pearls yearly.

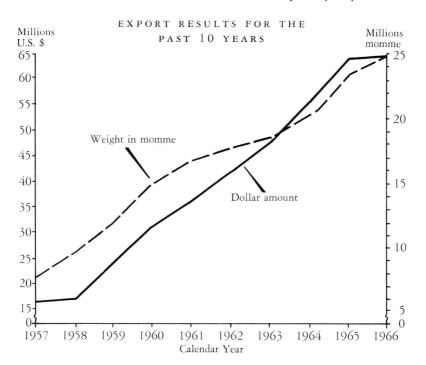

EXPORT RESULTS FOR THE PAST 10 YEARS

Millions U.S. $

Millions momme

Weight in momme

Dollar amount

1957 1958 1959 1960 1961 1962 1963 1964 1965 1966
Calendar Year

After boring comes bleaching—a seven-day bath in a mild solution of warm hydrogen peroxide. Large pearls of 7½ millimeters and up are, of course, handled more slowly and carefully than the smaller pearls. This is partly because there are fewer of them and therefore they are more valuable; and partly it is this careful handling that makes them more valuable. Many fine large pearls, for instance, never go through the boring machine at all; one pinprick at the point of the natural flaw turns them into gems for earrings, brooches, and rings. Only a few are so perfect that they are never even bleached.

Since the plastic, fake-pearl buttons replaced both natural pearl and cultured buttons in the general market, very few button pearls are seeded in Japan anymore. Half-pearls, the big mabes (pronounced mah-bees) used in fashionable earrings and rings, cannot be grown in the Japanese oyster but only in the giant South Sea oyster, which will be discussed separately.

Sometimes large cultured pearls are weighed as well as sized because of suspected inner flaws. If two pearls of equal size and symmetry differ

Amount of exports by countries: While the United States still purchases more cultured pearls than any other single country, the amount purchased by Western Europe as a whole is now greater. The pearls sail out of Kobe or fly from Tokyo in sealed lined boxes following government inspection for quality.

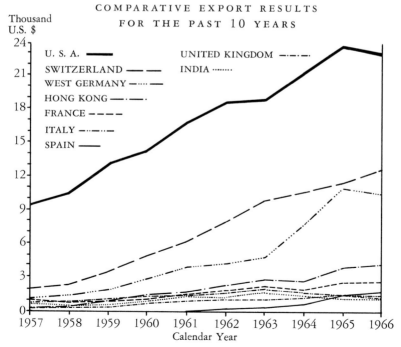

COMPARATIVE EXPORT RESULTS FOR THE PAST 10 YEARS

Japan Pearl Exporters' Association

in weight, the lighter one usually has a layer of organic material in it—sand, perhaps, or a parasite. This is rare in cultured pearls, however, which is why they are measured by caliber rather than being put on the scales as are natural pearls. Fine heavy natural pearls are considered great gems but weight plays a far less important role in cultured pearls.

Making distinctions between these fine large pearls is very difficult, expert work, and it reaches its real test when the strands of pearls are being made up for necklaces. Because the matching is so exact in the individual necklace, the differences among pearls go unnoticed by most people. A simple test of individuality is to place any two necklaces side by side; almost instantly differences—nuances of color, shape, and luster—spring into focus. But these differences are visible only as hindsight; the worker who did the original matching of each necklace had only a bowlful of pearls, all of which were in the same general category, a bowl which to the casual eye might seem to be full of identical pearls. That each necklace differs from any other as a necklace is the mark of skilled sorting: that each pearl differs individually is a part of its natural charm.

If the pearls are to be graduated—and Europe still prefers graduated pearls—the center pearl is chosen first from a bowl of larger-sized pearls, then two that match it in luster and color but are very slightly smaller are picked, then the next two—and so on. This work is done principally in the processing plants in Kobe and Tokyo, but Mikimoto does theirs at the home plants in Ago Bay and so do other big companies. Some importers, of course, prefer to make up their own necklaces. All Tiffany's finer necklaces, for instance, are brought them pearl by pearl by a merchant who may spend as long as four years collecting a single strand of large, matching gems.

Pearls of approximately the same size may seem at first thought to be easier to match than graduated ones, but they are not. The aim is to match within a tiny fraction of a millimeter by size, identical luster, and color. Again a comparison test of two necklaces reveals how each pearl differs as well as each necklace, even when all are "uniform."

In terms of value, differences in necklaces of different prices can also be studied to advantage. A 7½-millimeter pearl necklace, for instance, may be more expensive simply by reason of the size of the pearls; one of a 6½-millimeter but of better luster may be the same price. Which then is the finer necklace? Rarity and fashion raise the price of pearls of average luster; luster traditionally is the true test of a pearl's value but size is presently the determinant.

The difference in luster between the South Sea cultured pearl and the

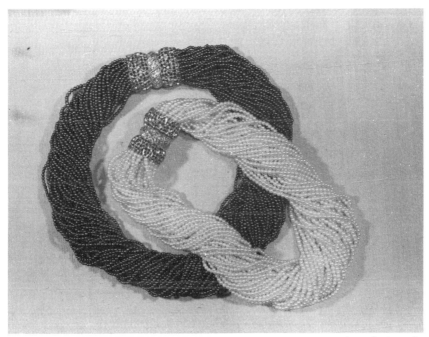

Two chokers of literally thousands of seed pearls strung on silk and clasped in gold, from Pearls of Nippon, Ltd., Tokyo.

A choker of thirty-three large South Sea cultured pearls, the center one being 14 mm. collected by the American Boris M. Tarna and his wife for Pearls of Nippon, Ltd., Tokyo, Japan.

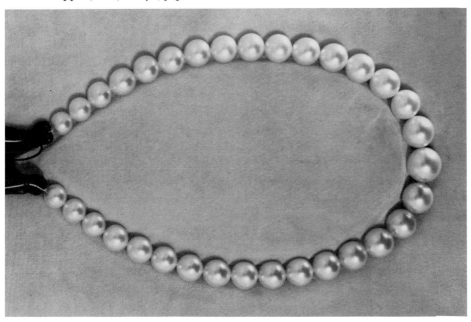

Japanese is quite marked, and here rarity is such a factor that really large flawless South Sea pearls are priced close to the price of the great old natural pearls. Most of the Australian pearls are twice as big as Japanese pearls—13 and 15 millimeters—and they have a soft, smooth whiteness, but only a fair luster. They came only recently to the scene; the beds were established in 1956 at Kuri Bay, about 1,500 miles northwest of Perth and about 250 miles north of an old pearl shell bed at Broome.

Although Australians run the farm and have some capital invested in it, control is Japanese. Even the bay's name (Kuri) is an abbreviation for the head Japanese partner in the project, T. Kuribashi, and the company is called the Nippon Pearl Company. It was Japanese methods that made the farm possible; Kuri Bay is too shallow to breed oysters but because of the location they are brought in by luggers from deep-sea beds, and the insertions of large nuclei for either round or half-pearls are made at the farm. As well as its acceptance of these huge seeds, one of the excellent features of the giant South Sea oyster (*Pinctada maxima*) is that it produces nacre about twice as fast as does the Japanese Ago Bay *martensii* oyster. This means that round pearls of 14 millimeters or the big half-pearls, the mabes (also produced in Okinawa by the *Pinctada maeropteria*), can be harvested here only two years after the insertion operation.

Because of inspection routines and Japanese marketing control, after the pearls are harvested, usually in November, they are shipped to Japan to be processed and exported from there. There are now more than 70,000 oysters under cultivation for round pearls but only from 30 to 40 percent are expected to grow pearls successfully—which means this large pearl is still very rare. Another 30,000 are seeded for half-pearls, but the loss there is also great.

Of the Australian ventures which have grown up in the area, challenging the Japanese control of techniques and marketing, the largest is the Cape York Culture Company, run by J. M. Jerwood. The Japanese control more than 99 percent of all cultured pearl production, and any and all challengers have to start from scratch on the fine points of technique not only in cultivation but in processing and marketing.

Despite admiration for Japanese skill, this control from time to time has made not only the west Australians uneasy, but has also stirred importers here and in western Europe to request some say in pearl production procedure and economics.

The focal point of this concern revolves around the question of volume versus quality. It has not been too difficult, although not easy, to meet the rising demands of western Europe and the United States for good cultured pearls, and markets continue to open up. As the American pearl merchant Ernest Reuter put it recently: "Spain has now increased her imports of cultured pearls 100 percent. If Russia and Japan come into the market, a price rise is inevitable." If this price rise is tied to quality standards and exporting is selective, that's one thing; at least merchants will be justified in passing such an increase along to the customer. If, however, the price rise is forced by volume demand, that's another—for on this point the whole market for cultured pearls could be wrecked. Other Americans beside Reuter are actively concerned: Hans Klapper, Morton Lippman, and Jay d'Elia of New York; Syd Weiss of Chicago, and Hans Bagge and Lee Sparrow of California, among others. It is of considerable help to them that the Japanese pearl industry is quality-minded, well organized, and its leaders entrusted to speak for a majority. The present Big Four of Japan (Mikimoto, Yamakatsu, Takashima, and Yakota) compete for advantage in areas of skill but are united in the conviction that what is good for fine cultured pearls is good for all of them.

In 1967 the first International Pearl Conference was held in Japan, and in the late spring, several new measures were enacted by the cultivators' and exporters' organizations in response to conference resolutions. One of these was a 30 percent cutback in the number of oysters laid down by big operators in Ago Bay waters; another was a reduction in the number of insertions. Both actions were taken to eliminate overcrowding of the waters, a very real threat to pearl quality; both actions were urged jointly by the Big Four in Japanese pearl production and American importers.

A third action was taken to double the public relations budget. There will be considerably more effort made in future years to educate the public both here and abroad as to what constitutes quality in pearls and why fine pearls are costly. The concern about bad cultured pearls driving out good is very real in Japan, the United States, and Europe but some of the Japanese differ with many of the pearl importers as to what can be done. Many of the American importers feel that the inspection system should be strengthened, and inspection should take place at the docks where the pearls are harvested, rather than in the port cities from which the pearls are exported. In some cases the Americans appear to be worried about the business secrets of processing which the Japanese hold so tightly; concern is expressed that the cultured pearl may be becoming processed almost to the point of being manufactured. The Japanese assert strongly that this is not so, except among cultivators with low ethical standards, and that the Japanese government cannot drive these manufacturers out of the pearl market without threatening free enterprise in Japan. They are seeking no government help to enforce a cutback on all pearl producers; the cutback is a voluntary action. Money for the education of the consumer also comes out of their profits. It is their hope that they can stabilize the pearl industry on a high quality level—and good pearls will drive out bad.

There is considerable sympathy for this position both here and in western Europe, where the market for cultured pearls has grown so greatly in recent years that today it is somewhat larger than that of the United States. The Cultured Pearl Association of America has been long confined to a lone office in New York (staffed by Alan MacNow, an American industrial expert who speaks and writes Japanese fluently), but it is hoping to become international and to open branches in London, Paris, and Zurich.

Not all pearl dealers go along with these efforts, of course. There are always some merchants who prefer short-run profits from volume to the long-run enjoyment of profits from fine gems. Since any and all efforts to emphasize quality will fail, however, if no one can agree on what quality is, the finest weapon on the side of the quality seekers is the new system of pearl evaluation which has been developed by the Gemological Institute of America, or, as it is frequently known, Gem Trade.

The need for a meaningful appraisal system of value has long been felt by the importers, retailers, and gemologists alike. Since 1949, GIA has been testing both natural and cultured pearls by X ray; it estimates that almost ten million pearls have passed through its hands in this period.

In the early years, many natural pearls were brought in for appraisal, and then quick distinctions of value could be made between these and cultured pearls. But slowly the value of cultured pearls became the sole question while how to appraise them grew increasingly complex as quality improved generally and market acceptance grew enormously. What Richard Liddicoat, Jr., calls "the dimensions of value" were clear-cut: the interrelated qualities of thickness of nacre, roundness, flawlessness, color, orient (luster or iridescence), and size. But how each individual pearl measured up to these and what weight of value each separate characteristic carried in relation to the others remained in need of systematic analysis.

The first appraisal grading system set up by GIA was on luster, which was separated into five grades: very bright, bright, medium, slightly dull, and dull. "The highest luster is seen in the larger Japanese cultured pearls," Liddicoat reported in the GIA's *Gems and Gemology* in the summer of 1967. "South Seas cultured pearls of the finest quality do not enter the very bright category but at best are considered bright." Pearls rated below this in luster go down speedily in value; very often those in the bottom, or dull-luster grade may also blink—that is, the brightness of the mother-of-pearl nucleus flashes through.

If luster alone determined value, however, price would descend on this scale by about one-fourth a step, but since the other qualifications are inter-related, they also had to be graded. Five grades were then set up for round-ness—at the top, perfect spheres, then so slightly off-round as to be notice-able only with measuring tools, then off-round enough to be visible to the eye. Below these two came semibaroque and baroque.

Four grades were set up for flawlessness: flawless to the observant but unaided eye, slightly spotted, spotted, and heavily spotted.

Color remained a value mark but was related to orient. Here the GIA recognized that market demand is today overwhelmingly for white pearls—although, as Mr. Liddicoat puts it: "Actually just slightly creamy pearls with a rose overtone are becoming to more women than the very white ones that one sees so frequently." Orient may lend this rose overtone to white and increase value—while if the creamy color is too dark and heavy, and thus lacks this traditional iridescence, value drops quickly. The finest creamy pearls came from Burma, where production is now disrupted by political troubles.

The paramount factor to GIA, however, was the one we have noted so frequently: size. As GIA puts it, when quality is generally alike, a 6-milli-meter strand is about three times more expensive than a 3-millimeter strand; an 8-millimeter, more than ten times more expensive than a 3-milli-meter; and a 9-millimeter strand more than 60 times more expensive! As for a 10-millimeter strand or more—well, it may run to 600 times as high as its baby sister of 3 millimeters, or up to fifty times as high as an 8-milli-meter strand. South Sea and Burma pearls run even higher.

In 1967 a course in grading pearls began in the GIA's offices in Los Angeles and New York, and master pearls graded for each quality in the appraisal system will be available for comparison. It will be the first time any gem except the diamond has been graded.

What will be the result of all this on the value of the natural pearl? Currently any good strand is far more costly than even the finest of the cultured pearls—but they and buyers for them are few and far between. Indeed, rarity has all but done them in; today the natural pearl necklace purchased at the turn of the century or earlier is worth only one-tenth the price paid for it then, even when it meets or surpasses modern standards of pearl quality. Until the early fifties, Tiffany's refused to deal in cultured pearls; now it carries no natural pearls. Harry Winston remains in the nat-ural pearl business—but buys no new ones, only historic ones. Cartier's in Paris still has natural pearls but is not buying new ones. Maurice Shire in New York has one strand that cost a million dollars in 1910, but has found no buyer at $76,000 in five years. When Parke-Bernet put a great strand that once belonged to Ambassador (to the Vatican) Myron Taylor, the steel industrialist, up for auction in New York in 1966, it brought only $42,000, although it had been appraised at $300,000. If cultured pearls drop in luster while rising in size and price, the great old pearls, still lustrous and gleaming, may yet enjoy a new vogue, although they can never be expected to bring what they once did. If cultured pearls increase in size and retain their luster, their price may be such that the natural pearls now in vaults may reenter the market on a competitive basis, either kind selling in the $50,000 to $100,000 category.

It is even possible that, because of their history, some natural pearl strands may come back as art objects. Cultured pearls have not attained museum status as gems; even the Smithsonian stubbornly refuses to display them. If some of the old natural pearls lacking a purchaser are reappraised for historic or aesthetic value, all authentically historic strands may regain at least a portion of their lost value by moving out of the "secondhand" category into the "art" or "antique" category.

There are, of course, three major grades of pearls: natural, cultured, and imitative. (Pearlness is only imitated; it cannot be synthesized or made synthetically, as A. E. Alexander, the gemologist, has so frequently pointed out.)

Obviously, the cultured pearl has succeeded not only in founding an important industry but is a gem of importance. The producer's problem is that of balancing high quality with demand; the pearl lover's problem is that of getting the quality and style at a price he—or, usually, she—can afford. We will deal with this in the next chapter, a special aside to purchasers of the pearl.

7

Purchasing the Pearl for
Style and Sentiment

*I owe my fine health and long life to the
two pearls I have swallowed every morning of my life since I was twenty.*
K. MIKIMOTO, at ninety-four

*I*n one of his lighter stories, Somerset Maugham told the tale of an English
governess who by mistake was given a pearl necklace worth a quarter of a
million dollars in place of the rather ordinary strand she had left to be restrung—and how it changed her life. Although the store discovered its error
in short order and almost literally retrieved the great pearls from off her
neck, the girl had had the experience of wearing them and was never the
same again. Within weeks she had abandoned her job, left England for
France—always a symbol of delicious sin in English literature—and become
a flirt and a cocotte, bedecked with fine jewels, the gifts of many men.

It is the storyteller's license to delineate the extremes. But even if only
a few women are stimulated by fine pearls to become hussies, it would
appear that a great many do indeed feel more beautiful, more feminine,
and more charming with a strand of pearls around their neck.

But the pity of it is how few know what to seek when they set forth
to find pearls. Diamonds are the symbol of fidelity, of brilliant, tough reality.

They are bought by men for women as lifetime pledges, and women have little voice in their purchase. But pearls are something else again. The first strand may be a gift from father, mother, or fiancé—but the first strand is rarely the last. Women go on buying pearls throughout their lives, real ones, fake ones, long strands, short strands, and only rarely do they find the pearls they seek. Pearls are the gems of romance and of bewitching moonlight; their beauty is tear-washed, it speaks of the poignancy of love as well as its joy. Not to be able to find these images in pearls is to lose something in the wearing of them. Fakes may be good enough to complement a costume or create a bright line on a dark neckline, but every woman should have at least one fine strand of pearls which is rich in meaning and sentiment.

The first question is then, *What is a fine pearl?* The grading system of the gemologists described in the preceding chapter lists the characteristics of the fine cultured pearl. They consist of size, shape, luster, flawlessness, and color. The order of this list—with size first—is based on which characteristic makes the most impact on price, a matter we will deal with in due course. When one is looking for romantic pearls, the primary qualities to be sought are luster and flawlessness.

It is hard to describe luster, the shiny inner glow of a pearl. Either you can see it or you can't. But the way to train your eye is not so difficult; to compare pearls is to learn to see luster. Look at very expensive pearls next to not-so-expensive ones, and then for good measure add a string of cheap pearls. Each strand has a different glow—and if you cannot see this difference in them perhaps you are simply comparing pearls of equal luster but different size. Discuss your dilemma with your jeweler candidly. He has learned to see luster; he can help you. If he doesn't have a wide enough collection of pearls to show you comparisons, either ask him to get some for you or go elsewhere. Luster is the charm of a natural and a cultured pearl alike.

It is also possible, however, that you are not looking at the pearls under proper lighting conditions. Great care is usually taken by jewelers in displaying diamonds; equal care should be taken to show pearls, but often is not. A clear light—preferably daylight—is best but a simulated daylight is a good substitute. The background for the pearl should be white; if there is nothing white in the store for a backdrop, use your own handkerchief or tissue. Never try to look at pearls on a glass shelf. Purple, blue, or midnight velvet backdrops are also permissible but do remember that they enhance the glowing quality of pearls. It is not educational to look at one strand against dark velvet and another against a white cloth; when comparing

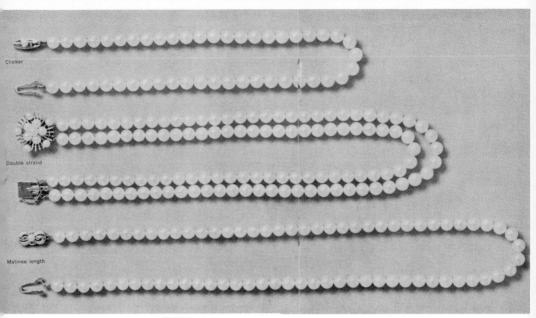

Three popular necklace lengths. Top to bottom: choker, double strand, and matinee. Fashion stylists now recommend as long a rope as possible for the "young look" but the old-fashioned necklace of graduated pearls is still favored by many girls.

The three-strand necklace is today the most popular with fashionable women. Here—at twenty-two—Princess Alexandra, now wife of the Scotsman Angus Ogilvy, wears a parure of pearls, a matching tiara, and earrings.

A pearl parure of the sixties: a long rope or sautoir of cultured baroque pearls, drop earrings, and chunky bracelet. Because the rope is baroque—although only slightly—it is not as expensive as perfectly round pearls would be.

One of the most visited mannequins in the Fashion Wing of the Philadelphia Museum of Art is this one. She wears the wedding dress of the former Grace Kelly, now Her Serene Highness of Monaco. It is buttoned with cultured pearls, and the handmade lace veil is sewn with seed pearls; in her ears the model wears bogus pearls imitating the fine pearl earrings of the Princess.

Mrs. Jacqueline Kennedy, as First Lady, matched her pearls to her costumes. These two pictures were made in 1962 when she visited India; at left, she is about to take a boat ride on the Ganges wearing white pearls with white; at right, in black and white with black pearls, she has just left the Taj Mahal.

Lynda Bird Johnson, like many young girls, disdained pearl necklaces as ornaments during the miniskirt rage, but wore half-pearls known as mabes in her ears. She and Marine Captain Charles Robb, now her husband, were attending a prewedding dinner in November, 1967, when this picture was taken.

Waving good-bye to photographers after her wedding to Patrick Nugent in August, 1966, the former Luci Johnson reveals her only wedding-day jewelry—a rosary of freshwater pearls from Japan. Her dress also was sewn with pearls.

pearls, each strand should be given the same advantages.

Any flaws in pearls are also easily seen by this approach. Don't use a magnifying glass; all pearls have a few flaws—the important question is what flaws show to the naked eye. They may be surface spots, scratches, dents, or shape flaws; that is, one pearl in one strand may be off-round: or conversely, only one may be truly round when looked at closely.

While you are looking for luster and flaws you cannot help but see two kinds of color. One is just color, the other is soft and fleeting; it seems to be somewhere inside the pearl. This is the iridescence or, as the jewelers call it, the orient. It adds to the luster immensely. It is more clearly visible in natural pearls than in cultured ones; it is nonexistent in artificial ones. The pearl's overall color is different and is a matter of individual taste. You may not be able to enjoy looking at gold pearls, for instance, even when they are of a fine luster, for they are not popular in the United States and seem more odd than beautiful to many. If, however, you are able to disengage yourself from popular standards and think only in terms of what is beautiful and becoming to you, it will help you find the romantic pearls you seek. Gold pearls are more becoming to girls with russet hair and lightly sun-kissed skins than are white pearls; they are also lovely on some brunettes with warm skin tones. On pale or silvery blondes, pink pearls bring out the rosiness of the skin better than do white, while on pale skins black pearls are stunning.

Cissy Patterson, the copper-haired publisher of the Washington *Times-Herald* during World War II, loved all pearls and was rich enough to afford quite a few. Her prize strand, however, was of lustrous black pearls. She was walking past Cartier's in New York when she saw them in the window and recognized them as having once belonged to Princess Yussupov of Russia. Going in, she demanded that they be taken from the window and sold to her. In vain Pierre Cartier attempted to tell her they were priceless—that he had intended them for display only. In that case, Mrs. Patterson said, she would give the store a blank check. So she did, and since she was a woman not easily brooked, she took the pearls home with her.

Black *cultured* pearls are likely to be less costly than white or pink pearls; black natural pearls are very rare. Mrs. Patterson's pearls were natural pearls, or, as they then were called, "orientals." In today's world of cultured pearls, largeness of size is the rarity, not blackness, and, in general, the larger the pearl the more costly it is. To my way of thinking, however, size should be related to two things: the size of the nest egg and size of the wearer. A little girl to whom price is of no concern should still look for little pearls, no matter how rich she is—for big ones look lumpy on a thin

Cecil B. DeMille's researchers into Bible stories decided Delilah must
have dressed something like this: pearl cap in an Indian style, pearl-
studded cloth-of-gold costume, wrist and ankle bracelets of pearl, and
a pearl girdle. Hedy Lamarr, who played the role, came to fame in the
movie *Ecstasy* when her passionate lover broke a string of pearls she
wore around her neck.

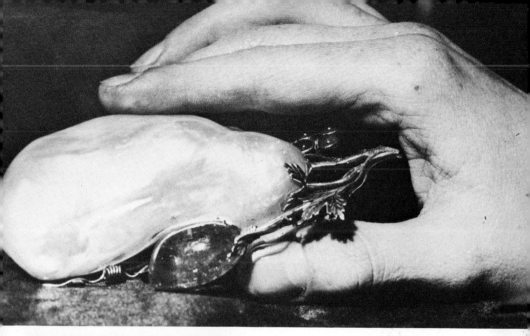

This huge natural pearl—called "the Pearl of Asia" and weighing 605 carats—was bought by the Foreign Missions of Paris in 1918 as an investment. It is of historic as well as biological interest because it belonged to the Emperor of China in the sixteenth century.

After Mrs. Cornelius Whitney was robbed of more than $700,000 worth of diamonds, emeralds, and sapphires in August, 1967, she was down to the great pearls the robber left behind: a necklace and earrings once owned by Empress Eugénie of France.

This is a double rope of cultured pearls from Cartier's valued at $9,000 a strand, worn in a modern, asymmetrical way with a coral, onyx, and diamond butterfly clip. *Photograph by Susan C. Callander.*

A knee garter for miniskirt wearers by the jewelry designer Barbara Anton; the brooch is detachable and may also be worn on a dress or in the hair.

Another chic way to wear a rope of pearls in the sixties. *Pearls by Erwin Pearl Company, dress by Charles Kleibacker.*

This biwa-ko, or lake pearl, gold, and diamond cross designed by Arthur King, seen here on a doubled rope of cultured pearls, was a prizewinner for its design in 1967.

A modified dog collar for the sixties —on a Pauline Trigère collar.

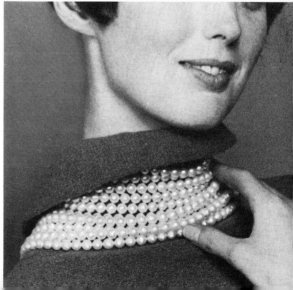

neck and clumsy on a tiny finger. On the other hand, a big girl in a thin strand of pearls does her looks—and therefore her sense of romance—no good. To judge suitable size, it is necessary to try pearls on. Trying on will pose no problems to the jeweler; in general jewelers believe that the sooner they can get a necklace on a customer, the quicker she is likely to buy it. Your problem is to find the pearls that speak to you before you try on any at all.

But cost must play a role in which size you buy, true? Yes, but first it should be remembered that it is always easier to pay for something you really care about than something you just think you probably should have. So look for luxurious charm first, then consider as a second point the fact that cost is not only dependent on size but also on several other factors. This is complex but important.

Let us take luster first. Truly beautiful, glowing, iridescent pearls can be bought quite inexpensively in the sizes of 6 millimeters and under. This is the size in which many more pearls are cultured; as we have seen, the smaller pearls take less time and are less risky to grow. If you can wear small pearls, don't be misled by price into buying large pearls of a poorer luster simply because they are more costly; get the finest small pearls and as many of them as you can.

If, on the other hand, you feel you need large pearls but want lustrous ones you cannot afford, rethink the problem again in terms of numbers. Three strands of small pearls with a fine clasp—perhaps made up from a favorite old brooch—give a size effect akin to one strand of larger pearls and often cost much less. Similarly, a clump of small pearls makes one earring as large as inch-wide pearls—and costs less. Add numbers to your list of variables and the limits of choice expand even if your pocketbook doesn't.

If you don't feel a pearl is a really good pearl unless it is big, you have still another choice: graduated pearls. Check out the varying prices of graduated pearl necklaces—you'll be surprised at how much the price varies by the millimeter range of the central pearl alone.

Is this too much trouble? Not when it means you will get pearls you will love and which will speak to you each time you put them on.

But remember, it is the pearls you love—not the way in which they are strung. The latter is a matter of fashion. Pearls can always be restrung at very little cost into any kind of necklace fashion demands and you desire. Three strands can make one rope. The small pearls from a graduated necklace can be removed and made up into earrings and the remaining string into a choker. A short string of beloved fine pearls can be put with a

Dancing with her husband at the opening of Expo 67, Princess Margaret of
England wore pearls set in diamonds—
only a small part of her great collection
of jewels. *Photograph by United Press
International.*

Arsene Calousdian designed this hair clip
using pearls of many colors for American
topknots; he also designs jewels for the
Empress of Iran.

rope of swinging artificial ones to make a sautoir. One fine pearl can make a ring—and be replaced in the necklace with a fine bead of color. And so on.

Does this mean you can have pearls made to order?

Not your pearls but your ornaments of pearls. This is where the purchasing of pearls for fashion begins. It is quite possible to love a strand of pearls and not want to wear it because it is not in style at the moment. But it is foolish not to consider restringing the pearls.

Let us review the various lengths and styles of necklaces first. They are in order of number of pearls:

THE CHOKER: This is the necklace that fits each neck so that the central pearl lies in the hollow of the throat or just below it. The pearls are usually graduated; if they are uniform they should be better than average in size. The choker is good with sweaters and bridal gowns alike; also called the Classic.

It was Jacqueline Kennedy who, in the early sixties, started a passing fad for tucking the three-strand choker of pearls, which was apparently her favorite necklace, under the neck of her sweater or dress, so that only a hint of them showed. Briefly, during the miniskirt period, pearls went out of favor for daytime wear, but they have never gone out of fashion for evening.

MATINEE NECKLACE: This measures 18 to 24 inches and is usually two strands of cultured pearls of uniform size. The pearls may be round or baroque; the clasp can be worn at the side or the back, depending on its charm. A few pearl lovers sometimes wear both a choker and a matinee necklace—Queen Sirikit of Thailand, for instance, wears a five-strand necklace of which the two shorter strands are choker-length and the others matinee-length. The matinee necklace is very good with well-cut dark dresses and is admired for its sophisticated chic.

OPERA NECKLACE: This is usually a single strand of larger pearls from 24 to 28 inches, hanging almost to the waist; it is a rather grand necklace for grand occasions and thus preferred by the older set, especially with evening gowns.

THE SAUTOIR OR ROPE: This is a really long necklace of about four feet. It can be worn swinging below the waist, caught with a brooch, or else looped around the neck. It is dashing and exciting to wear; it may be of baroque or round pearls or can be strung with colored beads or gold beads placed at regular intervals.

BIB: More than two strands of pearls strung so as to be worn together, even though all may not be in the same clasp, are called a bib. The pearls may be very small seed pearls or as large as 8 millimeters. Some bibs are so in-

Two pieces of modern jewel work created by Princess Suga of Japan from gold and baroque cultured pearls. The Princess is a daughter of the Emperor of Japan and a student of the internationally known designer Reiko Yamada at the Tokyo College of Art.

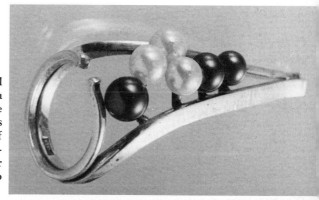

tricately threaded as to form a woven pattern but these are rare. Small baroque freshwater pearls in short-twisted strands are technically called bibs although they are usually referred to as chokers.

DOG COLLAR: Many strands of small pearls around the neck, clasped in a single clasp, were nicknamed dog collars in the Gay Nineties. They are not fashionable now but may return with beaded dresses and the opulent use of jewels and jeweled fabrics. Often they are worn with bibs.

Pearls are also worn in earrings, bracelets, rings, and are sewn on cloth, which is then made up for wedding gowns or evening dresses. The neckline of Luci Johnson's wedding dress was outlined in seed pearls; her sleeves were studded with them and so was her skirt. Her three-yard train was literally encrusted with pearls, but she wore none around her neck; her pearl rosary was worn on her wrist.

Beaded bags are made of hundreds of tiny pearls; sweaters are often embroidered with them. Most pearls used in clothing are bogus, but some of them are cultured. It is possible, if you care, to find real mother-of-pearl buttons for a good coat or costume, but most are plastic imitations.

A single strand of pearls is rarely seen today on fashionable American women. A magazine for girls declared: "A single strand of pearls separates the young from the old," and almost overnight the beloved necklace of small graduated pearls vanished from the scene.

Pearl hairpieces are varied enough to be listed separately.

THE TIARA: A crested half crown adorned with pearls, once the sole prerogative of members of the peerage and still mandatory on royal occasions in England, is now worn in most countries by women of fashion on formal occasions.

THE HAIRPIN, CLASP, OR COMB: Worn in long hair and made often of tortoiseshell, the pearl hairpiece is usually part of a parure, that is, a set of matched pieces. When a clasp, the piece can sometimes be worn in other ways than in the hair.

Price remains a separate question.

So far I have used the name "pearl" generally and only rarely qualified it with the adjective "cultured." That is because today it is almost impossible to purchase natural pearls. Very, very few are being harvested anywhere, and few are reaching the auctions. Some pearl people think this is because the price has dropped so low—it is about one-tenth of what it was in 1910. Others think that it is because there are so few customers. It would seem to me that if the price of large lustrous cultured pearls rises very much higher, natural pearls will come out of their vaults and onto the market. A deluxe necklace of fine Burmese cultured pearls of 10 or 11 millimeters now costs in the neighborhood of $80,000. There are natural pearl necklaces being held that are of great distinction which could be purchased for $100,000. This is not a great gap considering the amounts under consideration. In discussing the purchase of pearls, it seems unnecessary constantly to repeat that we are talking about cultured pearls, although of course we are; there simply are no others in most stores.

From here on, however, because of the vast price differences, we will speak precisely about the qualifications of each different kind of pearl.

The cheapest pearls are the imitations. These range from strands of a dollar or less to fine imitations, the best known of which are the Majorica pearls made in the island of Majorca off the southern coast of Spain. These consist of nineteen layers of mother-of-pearl. Other bogus pearls are made by a secret process known to resemble the historic process of coating glass

A three-strand cultured pearl bracelet with a diamond floral clasp . . .

and a platinum ring set with a huge cultured South Sea pearl perched on the crest of a wave of diamonds. *Both from The Bailey Banks & Biddle Company, Philadelphia.*

beads with a solution of powdered fish scales. Because of the skill of the fine imitations and the value of their knotted silk threads and handsome clasps, an imitation pearl necklace may cost several hundred dollars, but most are very cheap and flimsy indeed.

Cultured pearls range in price, as we have noted, not only by size, shape, luster, cleanliness, and color but also by number of pearls, origin, cost of setting or clasp, and the inevitable costs of handling and merchandising. The size jump, as we have suggested previously, is between 8 millimeters and 9 millimeters or as appraisers at the Gemological Institute of America put it: In a top-quality uniform necklace, a 3-millimeter, 14-inch strand may bring $45; a 6-millimeter, $125, an 8-millimeter, $500 plus, a 9-millimeter, over $3,000, and a 10-plus-millimeter, near $25,000, or more.

By shape, the drop in price is steadier: A perfectly round pearl worth $100 would cost $80 if slightly off round, $60 for off round, $40 for semibaroque and $20 or $25 for baroque. Luster or lack of it brings the price down on a similar staircase scale: Blemishes reduce the price in steps equal to the number found.

The number of pearls and their relation to price depend first on whether they are uniform in size or graduated. Two perfectly matched pearls of the same size are not just double the price of one, but by an old rule are double the price of each. Thus the price of a graduated necklace with one large pearl in it is reckoned by counting each set of pearls separately, plus, finally, the cost of the single largest one, but the result is far less in cost than a necklace in which all the pearls are uniform with its central pearl. Any degree of off-roundness also rapidly reduces the price of the long necklaces because then the pearls cannot be said to be uniform in size, or matching, and the cost is simply the number of beads times the value of the average bead.

Origin makes its impact on pearl prices indirectly. For instance, freshwater pearls, that is, pearls from rivers and lakes, are rarely as lustrous, round, or large as sea pearls, but even if they should be, they would not have the value of a comparable sea pearl because of their fragility. Nonnucleated Biwa pearls—that is, cultured pearls from Lake Biwa oysters which are irritated but not nucleated into production—are of a quiet luster and have an oval shape; cultured, they make charming bibs for women and small strands for young girls, and their price is exceedingly low. On the other hand, South Sea pearls bring higher prices in part because of their size —they are the round, opaque pearls of 11 millimeters and up—and partly because of their rarity. Burmese cultured pearls are prized chiefly for their warm, creamy luster but now since they are also rare (none are being ex-

This family of streetvendors of London are part of a group known as "pearlies" because of their fondness for wearing hundreds of pearl buttons sewn in elaborate designs. Note the trim on the christening robe. *United Press International Photo.*

Styles change but pearls are always in: here, in 1957, Mrs. William S. Paley, one of New York's best dressed and wife of the chairman of the Columbia Broadcasting System, wears a two-strand choker with a sequined sweater.

ported because of political reasons), they have increased even more in price.

The cost of handling and merchandising varies from establishment to establishment but every merchant has some costs. The highest costs are incurred by those who do not purchase their finest pearls from wholesale Japanese exporters but rely on pearl experts who secure each cultured pearl for a matching necklace a bead or two at a time. A necklace may thus take two to four years to collect but when collected each pearl is the match of the others and all are paragons in their size group. This sort of overhead runs up the price of a necklace, but justifiably so.

Skill, judgment, taste, and prestigious surroundings always add to the cost of any product but only the reckless think they can be avoided without peril. In general pearls have a 50 percent markup. A fine pearl, like any other gem, can, of course, be bought cheaper wholesale than retail, but even then there is bound to be some markup over basic costs because of the overhead of importing and taxes, for a fine pearl bought wholesale is in the nature of a gift: someone has to be behind that pearl who has the knowledge to discern its worth, the financing to get it into this country, and the friendliness to sell it at a small profit. There are other bargains in pearls in annual sales, for many stores do not like to carry over from one year to the next any gems that are dependent on fashion rather than sentiment. I cannot recommend that the purchaser seeking a sentimental strand of pearls with lifetime value rush into an annual sale and expect the kind of time and attention needed for such a purchase even though she may get a bargain. If you are interested in getting the finest pearls for your price, the wisest thing to do is to make that fact known to the most reliable jeweler you know and enlist his help.

What about the really cheap pearls tagged "cultured"? All cultured pearls must bear the notation "cultured," and no imitation pearls may call themselves cultured. But there are inferior cultured pearls on the market: pearls with flaws, pearls of such thin nacre that the clamshell nucleus flashes through when you roll them around, pearls strung and clasped so badly that they will scatter at a touch. If you are driven to these, I think you are better off with imitations. Inferior cultured pearls are not only a joke, they are a tragedy; for they mock the good name of fine cultured pearls.

Can a bargain in pearls be had in Japan? Going to Japan and not bringing home at least one pearl is like going to Atlantic City and not tasting saltwater taffy. Yes, you may pay a slightly lower price for pearls in Japan if you seek out reputable jewelers and honor their advice. But you must remember that pearls for sale in Japan have not had to pass govern-

And here, in 1967, Tiffany recommends a draped cultured pearl rope with a ruffled black velvet "smoking" by Ellen Brooke. *Photograph by Frederick Eberstadt.*

ment inspection standards; that here is where the inferior pearls are passed along for curios, and if by a bargain you mean you want a cheap pearl—well, that is exactly what you will get. Quality always has a price, and merchandise some markup. However, there are pearl retailers in Japan of fine reputation who handle only fine pearls.

Are pearls an investment? The value of cultured pearls has risen year after year as the demand for them has grown, but they cannot be said to be an investment in the way blue-chip stocks are, for the dividends they yield are in the form of pleasure rather than cash. In this sense, no jewels are an investment.

Compared to a car, say, or some other article that wears out with time and use, pearls are a better investment, for despite their fragility they rarely wear out. Some of the great natural pearls are centuries old and are still beautiful and lustrous; there is no reason whatsoever why cultured pearls will not last equally as long and in an equally fine state of health. They will dry up in vaults, burn in fires, can be smashed if trampled on, get stained from perfumes, and are easily lost if not restrung at intervals—for the silk threads do wear out—but when properly cared for, all good pearls are ageless.

Proper care includes wiping them off after a few wearings, a little polishing (with vegetable oil) now and again, a soft velvety bag or box for them, and a soap and warm-water wash when the thread gets grubby-looking—plus the attentions of a jeweler at regular intervals.

The jeweler will handle the restringing which is necessary at different times for different necklaces. Women who play with their pearls tend to loosen the threads sooner than do those who leave them alone; women who wear their pearls to the seashore on humid days should take extra precautions to see that perspiration is not wearing away the string. The silk string is inclined to stretch with time, and the knots may loosen. The knots are important to keep the pearls from slipping to and fro and wearing away. They are also helpful in preventing the pearls from scattering if the string breaks. Women with valuable pearls see that their pearls are restrung every year by a good jeweler who will count them before taking them in and who will handle them with care while working with them. One of the most charming stories in modern literature about pearls is told by Isak Dinesen about a bride who took her pearls deliberately to a cheerful but unknown peasant jeweler for restringing in order to teach her husband a lesson in trusting people. He was convinced she would never get all her pearls back, but she did—and something more. It is a charming story, but her advice is not the soundest.

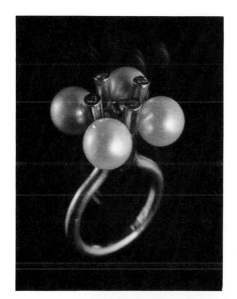

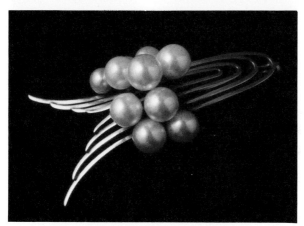

Two rings and a brooch designed by prize-winning Reiko Yamada of the Tokyo College of Art. Miss Yamada, a director of Japan Jewelry Designers' Association, has exhibited both here and abroad.

When you take your pearls (to a good jeweler) for restringing, ask at the same time about new styles. Although most people take for granted that each restringing will be the same as the last, there is no real reason why this should be so. To inspire your imagination about this I give you two slogans from a nameless advertising writer in the pearl industry: *Think big with small sizes!* (Adding a second necklace to your own will cost less than purchasing huge pearls.) *Go baroque, not broke!* (If you are yearning for a rope but the price is too high, get it in baroque pearls and let it swing below your round ones.)

If price is no problem or if you are seriously interested in pearls as art objects, do try to find out where you can look at fine natural pearls. As well as historic charm—what queen clasped them around her throat? what diver risked his life for them?—these pearls have a special sort of natural beauty that only the very finest of cultured pearls have achieved. It is a shame none are in American art museums, but there are in any event many still in our vaults, many in royal treasuries, and many in the art galleries of Europe.

It is hard to tell a strand of natural pearls from a strand of cultured pearls when it is around someone's neck but on velvet, the orients can be seen to be somewhat more uneven in shape than cultured pearls and somewhat more iridescent in luster. Are cultured pearls as fine as natural pearls? George Switzer, of the Gemology Department of the Smithsonian Institution in Washington, declares they are not. He has refused to place any on display in the gem collection. Some European scientists and merchants agree with him but some do not. David Starr Jordan, the noted zoologist and former president of Stanford University, has said: "Both natural and cultured pearls have the same luster and sheen. As the cultured pearls are of exactly the same substance and color as the natural or uncultured pearls there is no real reason why they should not have the same value."

No strand of cultured pearls has yet brought the incredible prices— many old pearls sold for $1,000,000 a strand around 1900—that natural pearls have brought in the past, but prices of the new large beauties bring close to what the natural pearls now bring. Certainly cultured pearls are accepted on the market as "the real thing"—the problem of the industry is not authenticating them as jewels but maintaining quality standards. "All we have to do is make quality pearls," one exporter summed it up. "If we do, women will continue to be just as fascinated by them as they have for five thousand years."

In short, cultured or natural, all pearls are gifts from the sea, speaking of tranquillity and moonlight, of loving and being loved.

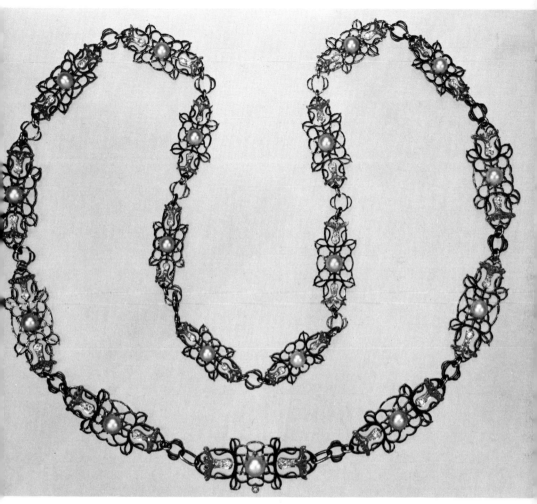

A museum piece of priceless art—seventeen superb natural pearls set in a gold and diamond chain by René Jules Lalique in 1900 and now on display at The Metropolitan Museum of Art. *Courtesy, The Metropolitan Museum of Art, bequest from Mary Kellogg Hopkins, 1945.*

Bibliography

CHAPTER 1

Shells as Evidence of the Migration of Early Culture by J. Wilfrid Jackson (University of Manchester Press and Longmans Green & Co., Inc., London and New York, 1917) provides the basic key to the ancient cult of the shells. Jackson is supported by Sir Elliot Smith, the Manchester archaeologist, in the preface, and by the scholar Vincent A. Smith, in his major work *The Oxford History of India* (The Clarendon Press, Oxford, England, 1923). This definitive history of India provided me with the description of Korkai and the poem from Tamil land's classic period. Not much has been written about this area but there are also references to it and to pearls in Will Durant, "The Story of Civilization," Vol. I, *Our Oriental Heritage.*

Another useful work on pearls from Manchester, England, concerning early symbolism of the pearl was that of Maurice A. Canney: "The Life-giving Pearl." It was published in the journal of the Manchester Egyptian and Oriental Society, 1930, No. 13, pp. 43–62. The two great scholars of mythology, Robert Graves and Sir James George Frazer, also support the main thesis that in ancient times the pearl symbolized the moon as earth-mother and was thought born of rain or dew.

As suggested by the text, I have accepted the description and the chronology of King Solomon's meeting with the Queen of Sheba from Immanuel Velikovsky, *Ages in Chaos,* Vol. I, Sidgwick & Jackson, London, 1953. I am quite aware that Velikovsky's works have aroused controversy among scientists but too many of his findings have been proven right for me to disdain them. The references to the Bible and the Odyssey are included in the text. The interpretation of the famous Persian necklace of Susa is my own, as is that of Egyptian cosmetics, but the facts about them (and of many of the other pearl pieces) are thoroughly reported in that great volume on pearls, *The Book of the Pearl,* by George Frederick Kunz and Charles Hugh Stevenson, The Century Company, New York, 1908. As for data on the meaning of various numbers in the early cultures, the most readable source book is *Mathematics for the Millions,* by Lancelot Hogben (W. W. Norton & Co., Inc., New York, 1951). A new translation of Pliny on

228

gems was edited by Sidney Ball, *A Roman Book on Precious Stones,* Gemological Institute of America, Los Angeles, 1950.

CHAPTER 2

The social history of the rise and fall of Constantinople and the early beginnings of Western European civilization are colorfully portrayed in many histories as well as in such staples as Gibbon and Durant. E. F. (Lord) Twining's lengthy work, *A History of the Crown Jewels of Europe,* B. T. Botsford, London, 1961, provides precise details of royal display from pre-Christian times to the present. There are several notable researchers into the medieval role of gems: George Frederick Kunz, *The Curious Lore of Precious Stones,* J. B. Lippincott, Philadelphia and London, 1913; Joan Evans, *Magical Jewels,* Oxford, England, 1922; William Jones, *History and Mystery of Precious Stones,* London, 1880. Kunz rambles through various legends and tales; Evans is interested in jewels in magic and medicine; Jones, who dedicated his book to the art critic John Ruskin, concentrates on literary attitudes toward jewels—his book is studded with snippets of verse and quotation marks. Many of the connections made between religious and philosophic attitudes and pearls are my own; the data inspiring them are to be found in biographies and histories of the persons and places involved and in the stories about pearls in *The Book of the Pearl* by George Frederick Kunz and Charles Hugh Stevenson, The Century Company, New York, 1908. Countless dissertations on the fourteenth-century English poem "The Pearl" also bear out the vagaries pearl symbolism took after its religious connection with the moon earth-mother was broken.

CHAPTER 3

The most complete work on pearls among the North American Indians was done by George Frederick Kunz, who made the pearl of this continent his specialty. As well as his (and Stevenson's) great work on pearls in general previously mentioned, Kunz produced a variety of other papers on the subject which vary in approach from technical ones written for the American Association for the Advancement of Science and the U. S. Fish Commission to popularizations for *Harper's Weekly.* For those who wish to use primary materials, a visit to the Indian relics in the Field Museum in Chicago or the pearl collection in the American Natural History Museum in New York is rewarding.

The recent book, *Travels of Marco Polo,* by Manuel Komroff (Julian Messner, Inc., Publishers, New York, 1952), gives a background for America's discovery. The finest history of Columbus is Samuel Eliot Morison's (Little, Brown & Co., Boston, 1955), but the discovery of pearls interests him very little. Kunz, in *The Curious Lore of Precious Stones,* has done a better job of collecting the pertinent references.

Jones, in *History and Mystery of Precious Stones,* collated the later stories of the great American pearls. Travel magazines such as *Holiday* helped me bring these stories up to date: I personally interviewed Mexican pearl experts and workers on the present-day status of pearl and mother-of-pearl.

The Jean Baptiste Tavernier references are from his great memoir, *Travels in India,* as translated by Valentine Ball (Oxford University Press, London, 1925).

CHAPTER 4

Queen Isabella's will was reproduced often; I liked the W. T. Walsh biography, *Isabella of Spain* (McBride & Co., New York, 1930), but her jewels were more completely recorded in Twining's *A History of the Crown Jewels of Europe.* Napoleon's purchases are also mentioned by Twining; the story of Marie Louise's escape is well told in Jones's *History and Mystery of Precious Stones* and in Kunz's *The Curious Lore of Precious Stones,* but only Kunz separates Eugénie's pearl parure from the total inventory of the sale of French crown jewels in 1887. Victoria and Alexandra's pearls are covered in detail by Claude Fregnac in his short but excellent work *Jewelry* (G. P. Putnam's Sons, New York, 1965); Lytton Strachey, the renowned biographer of Victoria, mentions her pearls only in passing, although it is he who tells the story of her attitudes toward keepsakes, includiug the bedside portrait of Albert (Harcourt Brace & Co., Inc., New York, 1921). Consuelo Vanderbilt Balsan's book, *The Gold and the Glitter* (Harper & Brothers, New York, 1952), records the effect Alexandra's jewels had on her; Mrs. Balsan was then the Duchess of Marlborough, and from her book also were drawn the stories of her own jewels and her changed attitude toward them after World War II.

George Washington's pearl ring was noted by Kunz as was Van Buren's necklace. American social history, however, is better told in Esther Singleton's *Social Life in New York Under the Georges* (The Bobbs-Merrill Company, Inc., New York, 1942), Bess Furman's *White House Profile* (also Bobbs-Merrill, 1951), and Dixon Wechter's *Saga of American Society* (Charles Scribner's Sons, New York, 1937). The delightful story of Mrs. Jack Gardner is culled from Cleveland Amory's *Proper Bostonians* (Harper & Brothers, New York, 1947). Amory's *The Last Resorts* (Harper & Brothers, New York, 1952) and *Who Killed Society?* (Harper & Brothers, New York, 1960) also give vivid pictures of the way in which the American rich of the late-nineteenth and early-twentieth centuries lived. The biography of *Nicholas and Alexandra* by R. K. Massie (Atheneum Publishers, New York, 1967) is an excellent chronicle of the last days of the Czars.

Only Kunz has collected the stories of the nineteenth-century American pearl rushes in detail. Other books on the subject are, in general, rewrites of his or recountings of special instances. Since the Kunz-Stevenson volume is enormous and hard to get, however, two may be worth mentioning: W. R. Catelle, *The Pearl; Its Story; Its Charm and Its Value* (J. B. Lippincott Co., Philadelphia, 1907) and Howard E. Washburn, *American Pearls* (University of Michigan Press, Ann Arbor, 1908). Among periodicals, *Harper's Weekly* and the *Scientific American* showed considerable interest in the subject between 1900 and 1908; the only recent work I have found was published by the *Pacific Historical Review,* Berkeley, August, 1956 (Vol. 25, No. 3), "Pearl Diving in Lower California, 1533–1850."

The story of the Ceylon Fishery in 1906 is in *Growing* by Leonard Woolf (The Hogarth Press, London, 1961).

CHAPTER 5

The title of the government's special report on pearl culture—without which this chapter could not have been written—is titled: "Pearl Culture in Japan" and is report number 122, Natural Resources Section, General Hq., Supreme Commander for the Allied Powers, Tokyo, 1949. Since it is now out of print, however, it must be copied individually and is expensive. Another useful book, although one far more colored by the persuasive powers of Mikimoto's personality and the author's admiration, is *The Pearl King* by Robert Eunson (Greenberg, Publisher, New York, 1955). The particular material on oysters was collected from various sources, the most delightful of which was Hervé's "L'huître et la perle dans les lagons de l'archipel des Taumets," a report to the Oceanographic Institute of Indochina at its Fifth Scientific Congress on The Pacific Ocean, 30 September, 1936.

The background data for the great Japanese discovery was gathered from sources previously cited, notably Kunz and Stevenson.

CHAPTER 6

There are a few studies of today's cultured pearls worth reading, the most notable book being *The Cultured Pearl,* by Norine C. Reece (Charles E. Tuttle and Company, Rutland, Vermont, and Tokyo, Japan, 1958). Among modern article writers on pearls two stand out: A. E. Alexander, the chemist who was formerly a vice-president of Tiffany & Company and who now serves as a consultant on quality, and Frederick Pough, whose series of articles for *Jeweler's Circular Keystone* (Chilton Publishing, Philadelphia) took him on lengthy explorations of the Japanese pearl farms. More technical but also excellent is the article on grading pearls by Richard Liddicoat, Jr., for the Gemological Institute of America's magazine, *Gems and Gemology,* Summer, 1967.

What really made this material come alive to me, however, were my own interviews with such pearl merchants as Ernest Reuter of Leys and Christie, Hans Klapper of Imperial Pearl Syndicate, New York, and Izumi Yamamoto of Yamakatsu Pearl Company, Kobe and Ago Bay. Technical experts like Bert Krashes and Eunice Miles of GIA's New York office, and Alan MacNow of the Cultured Pearl Association were particularly helpful; so were such worldly retailers as Boris Tarna of the Nippon Pearl Company, Tokyo, and Douglas and Elaine Cooper of F. H. Cooper and Sons, Philadelphia and Jamaica. A stay near the Japanese pearl farms of Mie Prefecture in Japan permitted time and study in the National Pearl Research Laboratory as well as several visits to farms in Ago Bay and in Toba Bay; countless visits with workers, salesmen, chemists, and designers were both enjoyable and illuminating.

On natural pearls of the period, A. E. Alexander, Maurice Shire, and Harry Winston were helpful although none could assist me in the awesome task of tracing the old, great pearls to their present whereabouts. For a story of how natural pearl merchants operated as recently as the 1920's, there is nothing more engaging than the book by Louis Kornitzer, *Pearls and Men* (Bles Publishing, London, 1935).

CHAPTER 7

The opening story can be read in its entirety in *The Complete Short Stories of Somerset Maugham* (Doubleday & Company, Inc., New York, 1953) under the title "The String of Beads." Most of the information in this chapter came from jewelers and gemologists previously mentioned in connection with Chapter 6. Two social chronicles were also helpful for contemporary material: *Eleanor Medill Patterson,* by Alice Albright Hoge (Random House, New York, 1966) gives a vivid picture of the rich and powerful publisher and her circle in the forties; *The Beautiful People* by Marilyn Bender (Coward-McCann, Inc., New York, 1967) focuses on the New York world of fashion in the sixties. The Isak Dinesen story "The Pearls" is most easily obtained in the Modern Library edition of *Winter's Tales.*

Dr. George Switzer's views on cultured and natural pearls were communicated to me in an interview with him in the Smithsonian; the quotation from Dr. Jordan was from a published statement in the Los Angeles *Times.*

Actual sizes of natural
pearls from ⅛ grain to
160 grains by size.

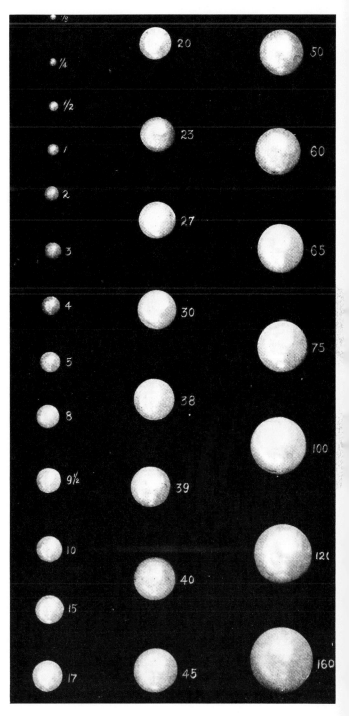

Glossary of Pearl Terms:
English, French, and Japanese

pearl . . . a dense concretion that is formed in various mollusks by deposition of thin concentric layers of nacre about a foreign particle within or beneath the mantle and free from or attached to the shell, that occurs in various forms but is typically more or less round, that exhibits various colors but is usually white or light-colored and that has various degrees of luster. . . .

> *Webster's Third International Dictionary*

A

abalone. A univalve mollusk found along the coasts of Japan, California, and New Zealand and which secretes irregular pearly concretions of unusual colors; often called the ear shell. Edible.

akoya. Japanese name for the white-lipped *Pinctada martensii,* the pearl-bearing oysters found along the Japanese coast.

ama. Japanese word for the diving girls who at one time dove for the pearl-bearing oyster, seeking pearls, and later sought young oysters to be cultivated. The *ama* now dive for edible shellfish and kelp and are still on display near pearl farms for visitors, but scientific methods of oyster-breeding and pearl-harvesting have replaced them in pearling itself except in emergencies; when typhoons scatter the pearl-bearing oysters they may be called upon to help retrieve them.

234

aqua perlata. A medicinal solution of powdered pearls, vinegar or lemon juice, sugar, and herbs used throughout the Middle Ages by Europeans as a drink to relieve melancholia, heart palpitations, and insanity. Still in use in India and Japan.

B

baroque. French adjective used to describe art objects and pearls that are not symmetrical or "classical" in shape; commonly used today to describe any pearl that is not round.

black pearl. Highly prized when lustrous and round but most often found in abalones and somewhat dull; a fine black pearl has shades of green in it, and the most famous historically was that of Count Batthyány, revolutionary premier of old Hungary. The state museum in Dresden, Germany, has a collection of fine black natural pearls.

blister pearl. Technically, a pearl found inside a coating of mud, water, and mother-of-pearl, and removed from this "blister"; often used inaccurately today to describe any pearl formed on the shell.

Buddha pearl. Cultured pearl button in the shape of an image of Buddha produced in the northern province of China from the thirteenth century.

button pearl. If the pearl is domed on top and has a flat back it is called a button pearl; the early cultured pearls of Japan were referred to as button pearls because of this shape. Not the same as flat pearl buttons, which are cut out of mother-of-pearl.

byssus. The small fibrous part of a pearl-producing oyster which it uses to attach itself to sea bottoms or rocks and to move.

C

carat. Unit of weight once generally used for the pearl and roughly equal to 200 milligrams. Grains are a subdivision; there are four in a pearl carat. It was replaced by millimeters as a size standard following the development of the Kunz gage around 1900, but is still in use as a diamond measurement. The Kunz gage reveals that a natural pearl of 5 grains is approximately similar in size to a cultured pearl of 5½ millimeters.

chank. Sacred shell of India, a member of the turbos species, and a producer of pink or pale red pearls.

chicot. Blister pearls are also called chicots.

clam pearl. Pearl once found in the common clam of the Atlantic coast, usually black, dark purple, or purple; undoubtedly well known to the Indians who sought and protected the larger ones for the purple spot that held the muscle and which they used as wampum.

Columbus, Christopher. Discoverer of pearls in South America, off the coast of Venezuela, 1498.

conchiolin. A glutinous albuminoid secreted by a pearl-bearing oyster in warm weather along with nacre.

cultured pearl. A pearl developed through the deliberate irritation and manipulation of an oyster; possibly first accomplished in the second century in the Red Sea; certainly used in the thirteenth century in northern China; experimented with in Europe and America during the nineteenth century and developed by K. Mikimoto for the production of button pearls; perfected for round pearls early in the twentieth century by Japanese marine scientists and German theorists.

Because of the comparative ease of production and the generally fine results, the cultured pearl of the Japanese has now replaced the natural pearl as the pearl gem. It is not, however, identical to the natural gem inasmuch as its nacre is not as pure in depth nor as variable, and its size and shape are due in considerable part to the presence of a shell nucleus. The differences between natural and cultured pearls are clearly visible under X ray but generally unnoticeable to the naked eye.

D

diver. Natural pearls were throughout history largely harvested by men and women divers of great skill and stamina, but with the breeding of oysters and the culturing of pearls, divers became superfluous. Some pearl-diving still takes place in the South Seas, the Persian Gulf, and the Red Sea, and Japanese divers continue to display their talents at pearl beds. With the development of the cultured pearl, divers were used to collect young oysters. Today most pearls are cultivated in beds.

dog-tooth pearl. An elongated, narrow pearl that comes to a point.

double pearls. Two or more pearls united together in a single nacreous coating, but still obviously separate pearls.

drop pearl. Pearl in the shape of a pear, but heavier at the bottom end like a drop of cream; baroque, but valued when symmetrical.

dust pearl. When seed pearls are very small and thus have little value, they are known as dust pearls; each one, no matter how small, is distinctly a pearl.

dyeing pearls. The impregnation of the nacre of natural pearls with a solution of nitrate of silver, generally employed to turn yellowish pearls black. Cultured pearls are also dyed or stained to heighten pinkness, and bleached to increase whiteness.

E

Eugénie pearls. In 1887, a large collection of the French crown jewels, diamonds, and pearls, was auctioned off at the Palace of the Tuileries, and the pearl ornaments sold then were subsequently referred to as Eugénie pearls in an allusion to the most recent Empress. Many, however, were purchased by Napoleon Bonaparte for his wives Josephine and Marie Louise, and some were Bourbon purchases. Another collection of Eugénie's personal jewels was bequeathed to a Philadelphia dentist and is now the property of the University of Pennsylvania.

F

freshwater pearl. A pearl found in a lake or river clam is called a freshwater pearl. Many are natural and accidental; in Bavaria, Russia, and Japan some are cultured but nonnucleated (notably at Lake Biwa in Japan).

G

gai. Japanese word for oyster.

Gogibus pearl. Pearl purchased from a merchant named Gogibus by Philip IV of Spain in 1620 and said then to be the largest pearl in Europe: 126 carats, or 504 grains. It was pear-shaped and came from the West Indies, and Philip wore it as a button on his cap.

grading. A systematic method of appraising the value of jewels, assessing characteristics by categories or grades. Formerly used only for diamonds, it is now being applied to pearls.

grain. Diamonds and pearls were formerly sold by weight in terms of carats, a measure stabilized internationally in 1893 (by Kunz) at 200 milligrams, and a grain (four grains to a carat) at 50 milligrams. Size by millimeter (also promulgated by Kunz) has now replaced sizing by weight in pearls.

H

half-pearl. Pearl that is round-domed on one side and flat on the other—half a pearl. It is formed when the pearl irritant or nucleus adheres to the shell, as in a button pearl. The first cultured pearls were half-pearls; the best known today are cultured in Australia and are known as mabes. At one time they were literally half-pearls in that they were the best halves of good pearls.

Hope pearl. A huge (450-carat) irregularly shaped pearl owned by the London banker Henry Philip Hope, sold at auction in 1886.

I

imitation pearl. Bead—usually of glass, plastic, wax, and dipped in a liquid solution of fish scales and adhesive, or layered in mother-of-pearl. First used in modern times for rosary beads in Paris. Imitation pearls are ranked as costume jewelry, not gems.

iridescence. The shining play of color in a pearl resulting from its crystalline composition; the orient of a pearl.

irregular pearl. Any nonspherical pearl. *See* baroque.

J

jima. Japanese word for island; also *shima.*

K

ko. Japanese word for lake.

kohl. A dark eyeshadow made of pearl dust and worn by Egyptians and others in ancient times in the religious hope of securing immortality; probably the original cosmetic.

Kunz gage. A cardboard gage cut with holes sized by millimeter in which round pearls can be fitted and measured for both diameter size and weight. It came into such wide use in the early part of the twentieth century that the millimeter-sizing (then projected) replaced the weighing (now projected).

L

La Pellegrina. See Zozima pearl.

La Peregrina. Pear-shaped pearl probably found in Panama and sold to Philip II of Spain (1527–1598).

La Regente. A big (337-grain) oval pearl bought in 1811 by Napoleon for Marie Louise's tiara. Most recently worn by Princess Yussupov of Russia.

M

mabe. Sometimes called mobe. Australian half-pearl (often mistakenly thought of as a blister) which is cultured by inserting a dome-shaped nucleus flat against the shell; when harvested, the nucleus often separates and must be cemented to it again for strength. Because of their size—sometimes they are almost an inch across—mabes are prized for rings and pins.

Margaritifera. Old Latin name for the pearl-bearing oyster of the sea, now largely replaced by the (new Latin) classification of *Pinctada.* The greatest pearl-bearer of natural pearls was the *Margaritifera vulgaris (Pinctada vulgaris)* or common pearl oyster, which occurred in the Gulf of Manaar (Ceylon), the Persian Gulf, and the Red Sea; also a good producer was the *Margaritifera margaritifera (Pinctada margaritifera)* found in the Pacific and Indian oceans.

Mary Queen of Scots pearls. One of the great early collections of pearls, the best known part of which was a six-strand necklace strung as a rosary and consisting of more than 600 large, lustrous pearls. Many of these pearls were purchased by Queen Elizabeth I of England; some returned to France; the famous necklace of Empress Eugénie of 362 pearls was thought to have been made from these ancient pearls from India.

mollusk, or mollusc. Any soft-bodied water animal living between two shells; a shellfish.

momme. Pronounced mommie; a weight measure equaling three-quarters of an ounce and used by the Japanese pearl industry to group cultured pearls of less than 6 millimeters in diameter.

mommes. Pronounced mommies; pearls sold in lots by the momme; small pearls.

moonlight pearls. Whales' eyes used by the ancient Chinese as ornaments.

Morgan-Tiffany collection. The most interesting assortment of North American pearls on display, held by the American Museum of Natural History in New York; 557 freshwater pearls of various colors.

mother-of-pearl. Oyster or clam shell with characteristics of the pearl such as luster, iridescence, and color; formed like the pearl by secreted nacre in *Pinctada* mollusks; widely used to make sacred objects, money, and ornaments since earliest times.

N

nacre. A French word pronounced either *nāker* or *nakra* and referring to the iridescent outer layers of the pearl; largely calcium carbonate crystalline (aragonite) when natural; a solution of powdered fish scales when manufactured (sometimes called *essence d'Orient*).

nada. Japanese word for sea.

nucleus (singular), nuclei (plural). Word taken from Latin, used in the pearl industry to describe the central irritant or bead around which the oyster secretes nacre to form a pearl. A nucleated pearl is one in which a nucleus has been deliberately inserted; a nonnucleated pearl refers to a pearl which has either formed naturally or accidentally or around a type of nucleus that has dried up.

O

orient. The traditional word, both noun and adjective, used to describe bright varicolored luster. A pearl of fine *orient* was a fine pearl. Still used to refer to iridescence by pearl experts.

oriental pearl. Originally used to refer to a sea pearl, when all sea pearls came from the Orient; now used commonly but carelessly to refer to natural pearls.

oyster. A bivalved sea mollusk of the genus *ostera*. A pearl-bearing oyster is not a true oyster.

P

paragon. A pearl that possesses fine quality of color and orient, is perfectly spherical, and of better than average size. Often replaced today by the word "master"; a paragon pearl is a master pearl, an ideal pearl.

pearl. A concretion formed inside mollusks from the same excreted substance that makes their shells; known as ornaments both sacred and secular since antiquity; formed in a variety of shapes, but most honored as a sphere; colored in many hues but most beloved when white.

Chemically: Calcium carbonate with the hardness of 3 to 4, held together by aragonite (the crystalline form of calcium carbonate) and deposited inside a mollusk in thin overlapping layers with a small amount of conchiolin, a watery albuminoid.

R

regalia. Symbols worn ritualistically by royalty to communicate their rank; historians believe that bands of pearls were the first regalia and led to crowns.

S

shima. Japanese word for island; also *jima.*
shinju. Japanese word for pearl.
sumptuary laws. Laws passed (generally in the Middle Ages) forbidding the use of certain objects by lower classes in order that rank would bring privilege and distinction.

T

Thiers necklace. Famous necklace of Madame Thiers, wife of the first president of France, now in the Louvre; constantly said to be "dying" because it was not worn, it has been checked regularly and pronounced "in good health." Three strands of 145 large, almost perfectly spherical, graduated natural pearls.
Tiffany Queen pearl. First pearl found in the United States since Indian times; pink, of 93 grains, found in Notch Brook, New Jersey, in 1857; discovered, sold to Tiffany and Company, New York, and given to Empress Eugénie of France. Now with others of her pearls in a University of Pennsylvania collection.

V

Van Buren pearls. A necklace given to President Van Buren but turned over by him to the government; now in the Smithsonian Institution in Washington with the First Lady costumes.

W

wampum. Pieces of reddish shell cut from clam and used in strings by the Indians as money.

Z

Zozima pearl. Later called La Pellegrina; considered one of the loveliest pearls in the world, this was a 111-grain, perfectly round, unpierced pearl of a silvery transparent sheen brought from India to Russia in the eighteenth century. A book of 48 pages devoted to it alone was published in 1818 by a German in praise of it; whenever La Pellegrina was displayed it was said to be so stunning that it met with astonished silence. Zozima himself was a Greek dealer in gems who served as the Czar's jeweler in Moscow until 1827. It is one of the "lost" pearls of history.

Index

241

The Book of
PEARLS

THEIR HISTORY AND ROMANCE
FROM ANTIQUITY TO MODERN TIMES

by JOAN YOUNGER DICKINSON

author of *The Book of Diamonds*

with more than 100 illustrations

Ever since pearls were cherished as the most precious of the gifts of the gods some 3,500 years before the birth of Christ, they have possessed an aura of mystery and mystique. In ancient and medieval history, pearls were religious symbols of purity, harmony, humility, and the gift of life, and were endowed with great magical and medicinal properties. As gems of rare beauty, they have been the favorites of royalty in courts all over the world. Today pearls are not only the gems of romance and the poignancy of love, rich in meaning and sentiment, but are still used in medicine.

As in her previous book on diamonds, Joan Younger Dickinson now relates the whole story of pearls, from their role in the shell cult of antiquity and the early pearl fisheries of the Persian Gulf to the development in Japan of the cultured pearl of today. She tells how pearls were beloved in the East, as in the ninth century when the bride of the Caliph Almunum of Bagdad wore to her wedding a headdress of 1,000 magnificent pearls; how Henry VIII of England had robes, mantles, coats, hats, and even shoes adorned with pearls; how Mary Queen of Scots, upon her betrothal to the French dauphin Francois II in 1559, received six ropes each of twenty-five purplish Oriental pearls—the finest ever seen, which are still worn today.

The Indians of both North and South America knew pearls well, as Christopher Columbus discovered on his third voyage when he reached the island of Margarita off Venezuela, which he dubbed the "Isle of Pearls." Through the

(continued on back flap)   BJH